Praise for J.M. Kearns's writing

Why Mr. Right Can't Find You

"If you've been on the lookout for ages but still haven't found The One, this is for you . . . you'll be in the arms of your true love in no time!"

—*OK!*

"I review self-help books for a living and this is the best self-help book I've ever read. . . ."

—Julia McKinnell, contributing editor, *Maclean's*

"Practical, encouraging . . . and optimistic."

—*Publishers Weekly*

Better Love Next Time

"Read it, people. . . . The book's main premise is that people often repeat the same mistakes in successive relationships, but if you can diagnose what *really* went wrong with your exes, you can have better relationships in the future."

—Erin Meanley, Glamour.com

"Aimed at getting you back in the game and emerging a winner . . . Working from the principle that past relationships contain the coded map that will lead to successful love, Kearns offers advice on how to unlock the code and stop making the same mistakes."

—*The National Post*

"Self-help books often make me skittish—but not this one. Kearns's advice is sound and good: he tells us to look inward, to be honest with ourselves, to stay the course. A chapter called 'How Good Matches Go Bad' is, alone, worth the book's price."

—Susan Schwartz, *Montreal Gazette*

Praise for Sara Dimerman's writing

Am I a Normal Parent?

"Like therapy for the mind and soul . . . The whole concept of what 'normal' is, is so beautifully contemplated in this book. . . .Thank you for this invaluable insight."

—Kim Galway from Richmond Hill, Ontario

"As a mother who reads a lot of parenting books, I found *Am I a Normal Parent?* to be incredibly helpful. . . . Sara gives concrete advice and suggestions that truly helped me with my three kids. . . . I found out that I *am* a normal parent!!"

—Karen Horsman, broadcaster

"Should be deeply comforting to anyone who has ever suffered the guilt and anxiety that is woven into the parenting experience. Sara Dimerman makes it clear that you're not alone as she shares the honest input of hundreds of parents, along with her own hard-won nuggets of wisdom."

—Adele Faber, co-author of *How to Talk So Kids Will Listen & Listen So Kids Will Talk*

Character Is the Key

"Sara Dimerman makes a convincing case that developing character in our children is one of a parent's most important tasks. In *Character Is the Key*, she provides an innovative, step-by-step template for families who want to explore the values they cherish and deepen their commitment to living by those values."

—Caroline Connell, former editor in chief,
Today's Parent magazine

"Dimerman provides strategies for unlocking the best in our children—and in ourselves—and then gets specific with techniques for acquiring the attributes of empathy, fairness, courage, honesty, initiative, integrity, optimism, perseverance, respect, and responsibility. *Character Is the Key* gives parents hope and the tools they need to raise kids with good character and bright futures."

—Susan M. Heim, author of Susan Heim on Parenting blog

How Can I Be Your *Lover* When I'm Too Busy Being Your *Mother*?

The Answer to Becoming Partners Again

Sara Dimerman and J.M. Kearns

A Touchstone Book
Published by Simon & Schuster
New York London Toronto Sydney New Delhi

Stories, vignettes and anecdotes were made up by the authors to illustrate points. They are based on observed behaviors but do not reflect specific real people.

Touchstone
A Division of Simon & Schuster, Inc.
1230 Avenue of the Americas
New York, NY 10020

This Touchstone export edition August 2012

TOUCHSTONE and colophon are registered trademarks of Simon & Schuster, Inc.

For information about special discounts for bulk purchases, please contact Simon & Schuster Special Sales at 1-800-268-3216 or CustomerService@simonandschuster.ca.

Designed by Ruth Lee-Mui

Manufactured in the United States of America

10 9 8 7 6 5 4 3 2 1

ISBN 978-1-4767-5363-8
ISBN 978-1-4516-7381-4 (ebook)

This book is dedicated
in loving memory
to Sara's mother,
Sue Freeman
(1939–2011)

Contents

Part Three:
Getting Your Partner Back

Preface by Sara Dimerman

Writing this book has been a labor of love. It's nice to know that we may be saving marriages that might otherwise have ended in divorce or continued with a couple caught in a bad place where they can no longer enjoy each other.

The idea for this book came to me after more than twenty years in private practice while counseling, among other clients, couples in trouble.

Over the years I have noticed the same pattern arising repeatedly. A wife comes to me, sometimes accompanied by her husband, to talk about problems in their marriage. These range from anger and hostility to loss of intimacy, but the end result is a chasm between her and her spouse: she's not even sure she "likes" him anymore. As we dig into the situation, she complains about having to do everything for him, about his being irresponsible and lazy, about always having to be the "responsible one." She sometimes feels as if she is parenting on her own and has to pick up the pieces after he has been around the children. Often he accuses her of nagging and bossing him around. He complains that nothing he does is ever good enough and that she isn't affectionate the way she used to be.

At some point I turn to her and say, "You're not his wife anymore, you're his mother." This is typically met with a brief silence, followed by a major lightbulb response. It turns out that the various troubles that threaten their marriage all spring from this single predicament.

When I reflected on how often this theme emerged in my sessions, I realized it was time to write a book that attacked the problem from all angles. It was clear to me I needed a male coauthor, someone I could bounce ideas off and who would balance my thoughts. I'd met J.M. Kearns when he was part of the editorial team for my 2009 book, *Character Is the Key,* and we hit it off right away. I knew J.M. had written two excellent relationship books (he's written another since) and was good at debunking myths. When I invited him to co-write this project, sparks flew from the start as we had edgy, honest, and sometimes hilarious conversations on the subject of women mothering men. And though we each brought juicy angles on our own gender, in the end we both worked on all sides of the story.

What started out as an epiphany in my office has proven to be an even bigger topic than J.M. and I had thought. The feeling of being a mother instead of a lover to one's husband is, I believe, at the crux of why so many women are angry and resentful and why so many couples are dissatisfied in their marriages. I suspect that we may hit so close to home that you'll wonder if we've been spying on you! At the same time, you'll likely feel relieved that we've validated what you've been living. Once you are able to identify and deal with this problem at the heart of your marriage, you will be able to change the dynamic between you so that you can go back to living the life you had envisioned when you first fell in love.

Preface by J.M. Kearns

When Sara Dimerman first told me the title of this book, a chill of guilt passed through me at the thought of the ways in which that title had sometimes been true in my life—and could have been said by some women I've lived with. I thought about the many times I've watched a woman doing something that benefited me—preparing a complicated meal or scrubbing gunk out of the sink—and I've thought, "I should be doing that. Why aren't I doing that? I should take over, right now . . . No, maybe not."

I also thought about the strange way that I seemed to become less able to do ordinary household tasks when I was living with certain women, and how inept that made me feel.

I thought about how my whole sense of me-and-her could be altered, until it didn't seem so natural to approach her as a romantic partner.

I even concocted a few defenses, saying that hey, if I *was* mothered, I didn't choose it, it was against my will . . . and I knew they were flimsy.

But I'm a writer, and in the end it's fun to write the truth, no matter how embarrassing it is, especially when the topic is important. What we call the Mother Syndrome lies at the heart of what is wrong with many couples, and it needs to be scrutinized in all its twisted glory.

More than a few times during the co-writing of this book, we have put thoughts on the page, wondered if they were a little too extreme, and then had them uncannily confirmed by wives or husbands.

Sara's background as a therapist and author gives her a deep knowledge of the real ground-level facts about couples and families, and I've found there's nowhere she won't go, no feeling she's afraid to look at, to get to the bottom of what men and women go through. I'm excited that between the two of us, we've been able to expose the factors that keep a couple in this sorry place, and to show a way to break free.

Introduction

A strange thing happens when you live with a man for a while. A transformation.

Back in the dating phase, before you lived together, your man was hot stuff in your eyes—intrepid, dashing, sexy. And he had his act together. He dressed nicely for your dates. He surprised you with champagne and flowers when he booked a weekend getaway. When you visited his apartment, it was clean. Okay, it wasn't *perfect,* but he had made an effort. He even cooked some linguini for you, and it was al dente!

You got married and moved in together, and things were still good. He made meals, he worked on the house, he helped coordinate your joint social life. You were starting a life together, hand in hand. You had no trouble saying you were in love with him, admired him, *wanted* him . . . and he felt the same way.

But that was then. Some months and years go by (maybe some kids arrive), and gradually things change. He seems to do less and less, and you do more and more. The balance has tilted. After a while you find you're picking up after him. Organizing his life. Doing more than your share of housework. Way more. Worst of all, you have somehow turned into a nag—a thing you'd vowed never to be! You even find yourself trying to stop him from doing jobs he might mess up. Where you used to want him to take care of the kids, now you hardly trust him to take them on an outing. Because he behaves too much like one of them.

And one day you come home from grocery shopping to find him on the couch—his socks on the floor, last night's dishes still piled in the sink, and those almost-due health insurance forms untouched on the table. After you graciously mention these facts to him and hear him respond, "Not now, I'm watching the game," it hits you: *I might as well be his mother.*

Later that night you climb into bed after making lunches, prioritizing the bills, and checking on the kids, and he looks at you with that boyish grin and that glint in his eye that used to turn you on, and all you can think is, *In your dreams.*

This isn't the way it's supposed to be. It's a terrible turnaround, an awful thing to happen to a perfectly viable couple. Once upon a time you were partners, excited about your journey together. Once you were equals, with mutual respect and admiration. Not to mention warmth and . . . sizzle. Now you're like a mother to him. Your good relationship has been twisted and distorted.

Can you get it back?

How did this happen? Who's to blame? What keeps the new situation in place?

Is there a way out? Can you be partners again? Can you stop being his mother?

That's what this book is about.

The first step in solving a problem is to understand exactly what it consists of—what is transpiring and how it feels. So we'll begin, in part 1, by documenting the signs and symptoms of becoming your husband's mother—and the damage it does.

Chapter 1 deals with five "hats" women wear as mothers of their men:

1. cleaning lady
2. cook
3. manager (and "responsible one")
4. appearance and etiquette coach
5. child rearer

We'll examine each of these and give you a chance to take stock of the actual jobs you do, the *work* that makes you a mother to him. This is partly a book about unfair division of labor. Many women are overworked and overstressed because, in addition to having a money-earning job, they are doing most of the heavy lifting at home, including housework and child care. That isn't fair, and it isn't acceptable. It can make you feel that you've been sucked into a world where you are spread too thin—while your so-called partner isn't. Because you're in charge of the home, you often feel like his boss; because you're doing so many physical chores, at times you feel like his servant. It's a twisted combination.

Which leads to the next point: Being your husband's mother isn't only about the work you do. It's also about how you *feel* toward him. Being his mother feels different from being his partner. You've been mommyfied. The mother-child template presses the wrong buttons, changing how you behave and how he behaves. You don't want to treat him like a child, but you do. He doesn't like it, and he reacts. So in chapter 2 we relate the telltale ways that the *emotional dynamic* between wife and husband is undermined, right down to your nagging and his tuning you out or rebelling or, even worse, obeying out of fear of punishment.

There's one more, very primal consequence of becoming his mother, and it's all too predictable. The intimacy you used to share begins to falter. Chapter 3 explores the sexual fallout, which is the final proof that something has gone badly wrong. You and your husband used to be lovers; now you're his *mother*. We'll explore the anti-erotic signals that take hold and the ways that the sexual magic is quashed for both partners.

If you find yourself in the Mother Syndrome, you aren't alone. How big is the problem? It's huge. You may have noticed news stories proclaiming that men have caught up and are now pulling their weight at home. Are they true? Unfortunately not. We'll take a hard look at those stories in chapter 4, when we scope out current research on how big our problem is. What we'll find is that in many important ways, women are still carrying an undue load at home. We'll also find that the problem this book tackles—her becoming his mother—is at the heart of what ails marriage today. (It's also overlooked in the enormous scholarly literature about "paid and unpaid labor" by men and women.)

Our portrait of the Mother Syndrome has one more part. We've noticed an interesting thing about it: it sneaks up on many couples, who slip into dangerous patterns without having the remotest idea of the consequences. In chapter 5 we'll show how this story goes, and why love that begins in the "wild" has such a hard time dealing with domesticity.

Having seen exactly what the Mother Syndrome is, it's time to find out where it comes from and what keeps it in place. We've found that both members of the couple cling to this unhappy way of relating to each other. They really think they have no choice but to live this way. And as long as they think that, it isn't going to change.

So in part 2 we tackle the ways in which women and men try

to explain, justify, and excuse this situation that is making them miserable and draining the joy out of their marriage. In six colorful chapters, we haul these reasons into the light and deconstruct them.

Sometimes women and men share the same defense ("my mother did it this way"), but in other cases they play the blame game ("men are incompetent" versus "women are control freaks"). Nowhere is this conflict more heated than on the subject of the children: women say they can't trust men with the kids, and men say that women overparent and shut men out. On the sexual front, both spouses tend to be in denial about causes and effects—and to misunderstand each other. Sex is the elephant in the room, but we'll climb on and take it for a ride.

When spouses explain why she does the heavy lifting at home, their reasons reflect some very deep social forces and attitudes. Women feel pressured to perform as mothers and as homemakers, lest they suffer the snide judgments of society—or especially of other women. "If my child's outfit is ill-matched, people will think I'm a bad mother (but they won't criticize my husband). If my home is a mess, they'll say I'm a bad wife." Men feel constrained by employers' expectations to work longer hours and avoid the suspicion of being distracted by their families. Women feel like they're already assumed to be guilty of that charge. Both sexes still tie themselves up in old ideas of what it is to be a man, what it is to be a woman, and which kinds of work are suited to each. Scholars have a catchphrase to account for the strange inequities of housework: they say the spouses are "doing gender."

But we say if it isn't fair, if it isn't true, you don't have to live by it. Not if it leads to a situation where you feel like his mother instead of his partner. Society is making progress; gender stereotypes about housework and child care are gradually changing.

But this is a bit like turning a huge ocean liner: it's too slow. So, in a sense, our book is revolutionary, on the couple level. We're asking individual wives and husbands to step up and defy obsolete societal values and do things in a fairer way.

This isn't easy to do, so in part 3 we give you a clear, practical road map to get you there. Before any negotiating can start, you have to get ready. We'll show you how to start changing the emotional atmosphere so that communication is possible. The next step is hard: figuring out if you yourself are really ready for change, and if so, what you want that change to look like. (Hint: Change means giving up some control! Change means opening the gate so your partner can participate more.) We'll go on to explain how to find out whether your husband is ready and, if he is, how to bring him to the table and elicit *his* wish list. Then the real horse trading begins, and we provide a recipe for good two-way sessions—which end up being more fun than you might think. The end result is to move you and your man to a better place.

When does the Mother Syndrome strike? Well, it can happen when you're married (or living together) with no children: you may easily find yourself playing a mother role for your spouse (and his buddies!). It can arise during the years when children are being raised, when the real biology of motherhood can add its mighty power to the problem, and your new identity toward your children may spill over onto your husband and help put a damper on your old way of relating. And it can invade the empty nest. Your children have had their dependent years and now it's your turn to live, to experience a little adventure and maybe some romance, but you look around and find you still have a dependent to take care of: your spouse. In other words, if you're living with a man, look out. (There are also other scenarios, like never having children or divorcing and remarrying, where the mother-lover problem can easily find a home.)

The cold fact is that way too many wives are caught in this trap, along with their husbands. And once the Mother Syndrome takes root in a marriage, it hangs on like a weed—unless it's stopped with the kind of intervention we recommend in this book.

It's a little uncomfortable, this idea that you've become your husband's mother. We've seen it greeted with a shock of recognition, followed by laughter. Maybe it captures a truth you already know. Something you admit to inwardly but don't really deal with, because it seems too overwhelming to tackle. You joke with your friends about how much of a slob your husband is, or how irresponsible and lazy—but then you have a laugh about it, shrug it off, and move on to the next topic. After all, boys will be boys. The insidious effects—that becoming your man's mother puts the kibosh on passion and robs you of the love you both wanted—are even less acknowledged.

So it's time to face the Mother Syndrome—to learn what it is, what keeps it in place, and how to escape from its grasp and get back to the couple you were meant to be.

Part One

Owning the Problem

In part 1 we'll define exactly what we mean by the Mother Syndrome and draw a detailed portrait of the problem. We'll discuss the jobs you do that make you a mother to your husband, and the way this affects the emotional dynamics between you and damages your sexual relationship. We'll go on to look at current data on how widespread the problem is; you'll find that you are anything but alone in living it. Finally, we'll look at how the problem typically develops: the insidious way it sneaks up on a couple, so they never realize that the patterns they're falling into are going to put their marriage in jeopardy.

Chapter 1

The Five Jobs That Make You His Mother

You didn't set out to be his mother. You just wanted to be his wife. That included making a home together, which was supposed to be a good thing, even a wonderful thing. Domestic bliss, they call it! Furnishing a place together, decorating it, snuggling on a couch with the TV on. Sharing meals, thinking them up, eating the foods you both love. Sharing a bed, making love, waking up together. Waking in the middle of the night and watching the other one sleep. Not too shabby a dream!

Sure, you knew there would be work involved—there always is. You would both have jobs; that was a given. And they would take you away from each other. But you'd return, because now home meant the two of you. It was a place you'd carved out of the world. An all-access pass to each other. A place to vent and laugh and recharge. A place to play: sometimes you would even be like teenagers whose parents are away, naughty and carefree. (At least until your own kids came.)

And there would be housework too, of course. Tasks aplenty. Things you loved to do, things you liked to do, things that just *needed* doing. Same for him. Some you were good at, some he was. That was the plan, if there even was one.

But now a few years have passed, and if you look at what all this "domestic bliss" hath wrought, it isn't so pretty. The pieces of the homemaking puzzle have fallen into an unexpected pattern. You're not sure when it started, or when it started to *matter*. Did you take over too many tasks, or did he back out of them? How did you come to think of him as a shirker of responsibility? Whatever the answers—and we'll get into them more deeply in chapter 5—it's clear that the relationship has taken a wrong turn, and the happy homemaking that was supposed to be shared has turned out to be some kind of trap.

You are playing a part you never auditioned for. Somehow, the functions you perform have coalesced into one big role called *being your husband's mother*. So we're going to start by breaking down this role into its component parts. They all involve your shouldering too much of the work and too much of the responsibility, and soon that pattern veers into your being his boss, his supervisor, his manager. As if in some reverse fairy tale, the prince you fell in love with now seems like . . . a frog? No, something worse in a partner: a child. And it's all because of what you're doing and what he's not.

So without further ado, here are five hats a woman may wear as the mother of her mate. How many do you wear in your husband's life? (The first four roles increase exponentially if children are in the picture; the fifth is *about* children.)

Hat 1: Cleaning Lady

When women complain about their mothering roles, cleaning lady is usually at the top of the list—aka laundress, duster, vacuumer, clutter remover, and bottle washer. It's what used to be called "housekeeping," and most of it is tedious, menial work. A whole lot of it. Sure, some people actually enjoy certain tasks. Ironing is a turn-on for some. Scrubbing gunk off the seams of a sink with an old toothbrush can be a delight. But overall, not so much. Cleaning just isn't much fun for anyone.

Some cleaning is directly for your man, like picking up his magazines, laundering his undies, and vacuuming crumbs off the couch he spends so much time on. He's the direct beneficiary of these efforts—the lucky winner of a world he messed up that is magically made whole again. And some of the cleaning is for the whole household, including you. Everyone uses the kitchen, the bathroom, the stairs. Not everyone uses the litter box, but everyone can smell it.

The motive for cleaning is very simple and would seem to be universal: fear of dirt. Cleaning sucks, but it's better than the alternative. If you don't hold messiness at bay, it grows and it builds. As a woman living with a man and maybe some munchkins, you likely see that threat every day. You see what your home could turn into, so easily. And you wonder why you are the only one who really appreciates the menace, who really *gets it,* in all its grubby detail.

So you stand bravely against the tide, looking for a little help. If you have children, with a little luck you may have turned them into allies, at least partially. They at least know how to clean up their rooms, when reminded. And they know how to clean *themselves,* or they're learning. But still, kids tend to be so caught up in a whirlwind of purpose and passion that you can't expect them to stop everything and notice that a mess is being created.

That leaves the guy who was supposed to be your main ally. And it's bad news when he is MIA. The one who was supposed to be a grown-up—that was one of his charms, wasn't it? He was clean, too, remember? He dressed nice, he smelled good. He seemed to come from a hygienic world. What happened to him?

Somehow he's been replaced by a guy who sees nothing out of order and doesn't know what needs doing, who is either making the mess or is part of it. And who seems like one of the kids. How did your shining knight turn into this guy who doesn't notice he spilled raspberry juice in the fridge? Who invites over the new couple from down the street and then directs them to the bathroom without realizing that the toilet is scuzzy? Why do you have to *tell* this man when there's housework to be done?

Men have some very creative explanations for why they don't, or can't, do much in the way of cleaning. (They are especially eloquent about dusting and laundry.) Sometimes they lay the blame on women; sometimes they don't. We'll savor these flights of imagination in part 2, when we look at excuses and accusations.

We'll also look at a woman's dilemma: to nag or not to nag. Many women don't want to be a nag. They've seen it done, and it isn't who they want to be. But some are willing to give it a try.

Lindsay's story

> I don't even *mind* nagging my husband, if he would hear me. I have asked him a million times not to leave his underwear lying on the floor. He looks at me with a glazed expression, as if I've slipped into Swahili.

He doesn't "take off" his underwear; he *sheds* it onto the floor in a smooth, animal motion. The bathroom floor, to be exact. He does this so he can get into the shower, and I approve of that goal. But when the undies drop, they are lying twenty-two inches from the hamper next to the sink. That's right: the same hamper where I will later deposit them.

I've really tried to reach him on this topic. I asked him why he never mastered the maneuver of gripping one's briefs while stepping out of them. That way you're still holding them when they're off! It only requires one hand, and he has two. Failing that, he could pick them up. But he doesn't.

Finally I said, "What is the problem? Are they so awful that you would need *tongs* to lift them off the floor?"

This got a huge laugh, and he gave me a naked hug. "Tongs," he said. "That's *funny*."

I'm worse than a nag. I'm, like, a hilarious nag.

Laugh-inducing or not, the cleaning area rankles. It's a big part of what turns a woman into her guy's mother.

Hat 2: Cook

This one is way up on the list too. Though women know it's a problem area, they're a bit conflicted about it. Unlike cleaning toilets or dusting knickknacks, many women take pleasure in making great meals for their families, and this feat is more likely to be appreciated by their husbands than their kids. On the other hand, it takes energy to be constantly creative, and you're just as tired on a Tuesday night as your hungry man.

If it was *just* the creative part, that would be cool, but there is so much else behind that lovely moment when steaming plates get served. It feels like a full-time job—and for many professionals, *it is.* Planning meals, food shopping (which can be done right or can go badly off track, in price and in choice of ingredients). Organization and prep—chopping and slicing and dicing and parboiling and marinating and grinding and mixing and *whisking into a perfect froth.* You can't do this stuff in your sleep, unless your blades are duller than most. You would love to off-load a reasonable share of it, but that would require someone who was concerned and knowledgeable, or at least ready to learn. In a fair world, that person would be your spouse, and in some households the man does carry a lot of this load. But does he in yours?

Mary used to be a professional private chef for a rich family. She's an expert on efficiency and quality: she knows how to crank out gourmet dinners for very fussy palates. So her words carry real weight when she describes the downside of making a holiday meal for her husband and six close friends.

Mary's story

> Thanksgiving was coming. I did the shopping on Tuesday. Tim came with me to the supermarket, but his questions about my ingredients just slowed me down. He wasn't up to speed, and I didn't have time to explain everything. So in the end I just sent him off with his own shopping cart to get the simple stuff. The next day—all day!—I did the prep and some precooking and shopped for some things we'd missed in the confusion.
>
> Then came the big day and I was on my feet in the kitchen from dawn till dinner—and I served the most fabulous four-course turkey dinner with my own oyster stuffing. Tim got drinks for people and everyone seemed to have the best time. I know they had a lot of great conversations around the table,

because I could hear them laughing from my post in front of the stove—one door over.

And so one woman takes on so much of the load that she ends up missing out on the good time she creates. This story contains a husband who wanted to help, but somehow that didn't work out. Instead, she ended up treating him like a kid, and then, while he partied with the adults, she felt like "the help." What is missing from this story is any real sense of partnership.

Hat 3: Manager (and "Responsible One")

Do you find yourself increasingly acting as the manager in your home? This can include being your husband's administrator, scheduler, and social coordinator—or his boss. Even having to keep track of events that *he* set up. Having to schedule medical appointments and remind him about them. Being the only one to make lists—what to take on vacation, what to tell the babysitter, what supplies need restocking . . . And maybe you're the one who handles the logistics for the whole household: hundreds of major and minor decisions, including difficult financial ones.

Administration can be exhausting work. It means having to keep on top of other people's schedules and commitments as well as your own (as if your own weren't enough). It means remembering that Caleb's piano lesson (which he usually walks to) is canceled on Wednesday, so you have to tell your neighbor not to pick him up after it, and you'll have to leave work early to get him from school, and on Thursday you'll have to get your mother-in-law to pick up your daughter from ballet because her lesson ends at the same time as your son's makeup piano lesson. Unfortunately, those who manage are often accused of being bossy or controlling, but most women say that they would be only too happy to relinquish some control, if only their spouses would step up.

This management problem feeds on itself. When you handle all logistics, your husband may get in the car and not know where he's supposed to drive. The habit of relying on someone else morphs into a sort of helplessness. So a grown man loses the confidence to play his part in running the household and feels he has to defer to you even when he's perfectly capable of making the decision himself.

The topmost peak of the administration mountain is the feeling that you always have to be the responsible one, that you are accountable if anything goes wrong or fails to meet expectations. The buck stops with you. That can feel true even if you're not the one who took on the task in question. Your husband may have agreed to get the kids to school, but somehow you feel responsible when the school calls to ask why they are late.

We believe that spouses should share this burden of ultimate responsibility. Your husband isn't really your partner if you are stuck with the watchfulness that never gets to rest, the worry center that can't take a break. In a home where each spouse has the other's back, you can sometimes relax, knowing the other one will take up the slack. Which wasn't true of the following wife.

Selena's story

I was an independent contractor doing PR for various clients, working out of our home. I had one big corporate client, a bank, that generated most of my income. Things were going great until the economy tanked and that bank failed. Suddenly, it was as if I'd lost my job, but being self-employed, I couldn't get unemployment insurance to help us make it through.

I got a part-time waitressing job to bring in some income, but I began to really worry about how we were going to crack our monthly nut. I remember one day at home when I was close to a nervous breakdown; I'd been avoiding looking at our bills but had finally forced myself to eyeball them. The news wasn't good. It looked to me like we were going to have to cut out more frills and even cut back on some necessities. I was thinking, "We gave up HBO and Showtime. Now what? Basic cable? Do we really need a land line at home?" The cell phone bill was even worse: we'd gone way over our plan. I opened another envelope and my health insurance premium had gone up $200. It already had a $5,000 deductible and no co-pays. I seriously thought I might have to stop it for a while. But what if I got seriously ill? And our credit card payments were inching up as the banks raised the interest rates. We really needed to pay them down—but how? I was in a cold sweat, thinking, "What do we do if I can't find a real job?"

Then the door opened and I heard my husband come in. He called my name and sounded excited.

"You're not going to believe it," he said as he burst into the room. "I got us two weeks in Florida at my boss's time-share. It's only going to cost us two grand!"

"How did you pay for it?" I asked.

"I got a cash advance from our Visa. There was just enough left!"

I crumpled onto the desk. He came over and said, "What's wrong? I thought you'd be excited!"

> I felt utterly alone, like I had the weight of the world on my shoulders.

Selena's dejection wasn't so much about this one case of reckless spending, though her husband may have thought so. It was about his not being on the same page as she was in her constant concern for their financial well-being. Life is hard enough without having to be the only one who really grapples with the threats—large and small—that a family faces. If anything can make tough times seem not quite as tough, it's knowing that your partner cares just as much as you do and is trying just as hard to get the boat past the shoals. That's part of what partnership means, and it's a crying shame if it isn't happening.

Hat 4: Appearance and Etiquette Coach

Women put in time and effort to maintain a (rather fabulous) level of style and appearance. This pleases men, but not always enough to make them reciprocate. There's already a double standard: men don't have to worry about makeup; their wardrobe choices are much simpler than women's; and what he calls shaving hardly scratches the surface of what she does with a razor. . . . But still, a little effort would be nice. Does he have to take such a liking to a green polar fleece that he wears it every day for a month? Can he not see those verdant nasal hairs in the mirror?

And manners can be an issue too. You know he's a man, and you don't want him to achieve your own delicacy of touch, but the right balance between effete dandy and rank beast wouldn't hurt. Otherwise you feel as though you have to complete his upbringing and be his finishing school. Like Kendall did.

Kendall's story

We're getting ready to head out to a dinner party. My husband doesn't really know the hosts, who are well-off and have a lot of connections in town.

When I finish my makeup, I look around and Ron is standing there in jeans, with the unbuttoned-shirt-over-a-T-shirt thing happening.

"Not so much," I say, trying to keep it light.

"What? This is a great shirt."

"I loved it in 2007. It's okay, but it's creased and it isn't meant to hang out."

"I always wear it this way. What's the big deal?"

"The big deal is the Caruthers are a bit swank."

"So I'm not their kind of people?"

"Come on, Ron. Can you at least tuck it in and do it up? We're running late."

"I'm ready. If you want me to go, let's go."

We get in the car. On the way there, I try to make some light banter, but he doesn't speak to me. So now *he*'s the one who's mad? Fine, let him be.

When we arrive, Bill Caruthers greets me with a big hug. He's gleaming in chinos and a fabulous cream-colored jacket. He shakes my husband's hand but Ron doesn't engage, drifts over to the bar, examines a corkscrew as if he's wondering what it's for. Not finding the answer, he settles for a big gin and tonic and wanders into the crowd in the backyard.

Later I see him in the dining room, a little drunk but a lot more sociable, charming the hell out of Sue Caruthers. He looks over at me and sticks out his tongue. I laugh, because his shirt is buttoned and tucked in.

Things are going better until I see him tasting the meat loaf, right off the buffet.

It would be nice if you could take a more cavalier attitude about the ways your man presents himself. Unfortunately, there's a kind of guilt by association with couples. People tend to score the duo by the worst slipups of either member. But you aren't just trying to save your own image. (Who would even think such a thing?) You're also trying to protect your spouse from himself, prevent people from thinking bad things about him.

But what really twists the knife is when you catch an element of *choice* in your man's lapses. Like a kid, he knows how to be on his best behavior or how to take a looser approach. When it matters, a guy can elevate his game. He does it at work when he needs to; he did it when he was trying to win your love. So what irks you is that, now that he's comfortably hitched, he doesn't make the effort, doesn't put a little thought into his leisure wardrobe, doesn't take pains to be gracious and mannerly in social situations when you'd like him to. That's when you feel like you're forced to be his mom.

Hat 5: Child Rearer

If you have kids, you know that the work of caring for them and raising them into adults of good character is infinite and often invisible. Answering their questions, listening to their stories, entertaining them, giving praise, providing discipline and boundaries, suggesting activities, leading, feeding, protecting . . . the list does not end. If there was ever an effort that needs to be shared, this is it.

But what if the other adult in the house doesn't seem to take it as seriously? Or complains that you're making him "babysit" his own kids? What if, when he is "minding" the children, he doesn't pay close enough attention, misses the point of what's going on, or takes reckless chances? Or, absurdly, you have to break up fights between him and the "other" kids? That isn't what you need in a co-parent: it just adds to *your* parental burden. Bottom line: If he isn't helping you parent the kids, he becomes one of them.

This is a huge, make-or-break issue that raises the ante on the other things a woman does for her man. (Cleaning, cooking, and managing all become much bigger, and more critical, jobs with kids involved.) Because parenting situations are so fraught and so urgent, they can force you into a kind of ruthless takeover of power. When a child's safety and well-being are at stake, you can't be casual about misfires and lapses. The consequences matter too much. So your real assessment of your spouse emerges; there isn't time to sugarcoat it. And it can sting.

The Sum of Five Hats

Okay, we've taken a look at five hats you wear around the house. When do they add up to being a mother to your man? The short answer is, when you're doing more than your share, and he's doing less. Let's see how this shakes out in the five areas, by considering what an equal world would be like.

It's probably good to think of the first two hats, cleaning and cooking, as one big category: call it homemaking. Spouses can make trade-offs in these areas: extra work in one can earn a waiver in another. You might do everything around meal providing, and that would be okay if he spent a lot of time vacuuming, scrubbing, and doing laundry. Or you could share within each area: he might do the grocery shopping and you do the sautéing. Heck, why be consistent? Share the chef's hat, if you will; pass it back and forth in exchange for the broom. It's all good, as long as the housekeeping is fairly divided. But if you're doing most of it, you're his mother.

It's too bad all housework isn't fun. In an ideal world, you would each do the jobs you love doing, and that would leave nothing undone. But in the real world there are probably many tasks you consider a chore, and he does too. If you're doing them all, you're his mother. Saintliness won't cut it either: if you "love" so many jobs that he gets to do none, you're his mother. It won't do to say you care more about these things than he does (though we will look at that excuse in chapter 9). After all, eating well matters to an adult, and being clean matters to an adult; so if he doesn't care about these things, he won't remain an adult in your eyes. So there again, you're his mother.

When it comes to hat 3, managing the home and family, both people need to be involved, making the important decisions together. There are supposed to be two CEOs in this corporation, and if you're the only one, you're his mother. You can divide the logistical stuff according to your talents (maybe one does the taxes and the other does the scheduling), but both people need to be engaged. That's true of hat 5 too: if he isn't making it as a parent, he is going to be out of the most important loop of all, and he'll be seen as less than grown-up. You're his mother.

Least but not last, there's hat 4, the one where you are the finishing school and he is the work in progress. This is oh so parental, your telling him what to wear and how to behave. It is the very definition of being his mom, unless he gives similar advice to you, in some happy trade-off that no one resents. But if you are consistently the one doing the coaching, it means that in your eyes he is not fully formed, not sufficiently schooled. You're his mother.

So the five hats add up to one big one that says "Mother," and that isn't okay when the child is your husband. You may be so used to this way of life that you can't see it, but that doesn't make it any less crazy. It starts with work, unfairly distributed. That's bad enough, but it doesn't end there—not even close. The net effect of toiling in all these ways is frustration, anger, fatigue, resentment, loneliness, and an awful sense of loss—the realization that you don't see your mate the way you used to.

So you treat each other, and feel toward each other, in ways that you never wanted. And not only do you not like who he's become, you don't like who *you've* become. The next chapter is about that.

Chapter 2

Broken Dynamics

When a woman becomes a mother to her husband, it isn't just about wearing the five hats we looked at in chapter 1. Yes, she ends up doing too many tasks, but that isn't all that goes wrong. There are repercussions. As more and more work and responsibility shifts onto her shoulders, she and her husband gradually fall into new ways of treating each other—bad ways. People get hostile, they get hurt, they get mean. The dynamics of the relationship change.

For the moment, we won't get into the blame game. That will come in part 2, when both sexes vent their complaints. For now, let's stay neutral, and just look at *behaviors*: how spouses act toward each other. What we'll see is that the unwanted mother-child alignment turns an equal, loving relationship into something very different, a twisted parody of what it used to be. That's because a wife isn't *meant* to be her husband's mother. It's a role that rings false, rankles, and makes both people feel cheated.

A real mother is happy to take care of her child and wear the mother hats for him, but when you're forced to be a mom to a grown man who is supposed to be your spouse, that twists everything into a different shape.

The behaviors we're about to catalog are not how a good mother treats a good child; they are how a wife-turned-into-a-mother treats a husband-turned-into-a-child.

The Invention of Nagging

Let's start with nagging, and the typical responses it evokes. It's often the first breach in spousal relations, and it can open the door to all the rest. Strangely, it begins in the most harmless ways.

The most innocent request of all is a request for help with something the wife is doing herself.

- Can you open this jar?
- Would you mind lifting this water bottle?
- Can you help me move this couch?

"Sure, let me get that." A guy likes to lend a hand. So far, no trouble . . .

Only slightly less innocent is this kind of question:

- Honey, can you move those paint cans into the storage room?

Or, running into the house laden with supermarket bags, this one:

- Baby, I'm running late for that conference. Would you stow these groceries and empty the dishwasher?

These are reasonable suggestions, launched in a friendly manner. But the reception is another matter, for several reasons:

- She is not so much asking him to help *her* with what she's up to as asking him to do something himself.
- These tasks will take longer, so they're invading his personal timetable. They may conflict with something else he was about to do, or they may be things he was planning to do at another time.

So a husband may say, "I'm just heading out to run some errands. I don't have time to do those things right now." Or, "I was *gonna* move those paint cans. But right now the fourth quarter is starting."

Or he may just think these things. But a subtle shift has occurred: he feels as if there's an accusation in the air, to the effect that he is neglectful of things he should be doing. It has even more sting if he believes he would have gotten around to the task anyway, in his own good time. The request implies that he wouldn't have. He isn't getting credit for a thing that he *was* going to do. Which feels unjust.

Let's look in on Nancy and her husband, Mac, on a Saturday early in their marriage.

Nancy was feeling stressed by the to-do list that was rapidly growing in her head. She half wished that she hadn't invited the Wilkersons over that evening—especially after such a long and difficult workweek. She contemplated hiring someone to clean the house before the guests arrived, but she knew they couldn't afford it. As she looked around, she couldn't fathom how she was going to get everything done. So she stood in the living room doorway and said, "Sweetie, Jennifer and Josh are coming over in a few hours. How's about vacuuming the living room?"

At first Mac didn't respond. His eyes were glued to his laptop, a spreadsheet he was doing for his boss. Nancy called his name again and repeated her request. He looked around quickly and incredulously. Then he spoke. "I just vacuumed the living room last week. It doesn't need it." And that was supposed to be that. But Nancy saw lint from her own black socks on the cream-colored carpet, along with a few bits of rye toast from his late-night snack. She didn't want her very observant friend Jennifer to view these things. Mac's response seemed definite and non-negotiable. But she just couldn't let it go.

"Fine," she said, and stood there looking at him.

He finally let his work be interrupted. As he looked back at her, for the first time there was annoyance on his face. Suddenly this felt like a mini power struggle, and a chilly feeling went through him. If put into words, it might have gone like this: *Even if I thought this vacuuming needed to be done—which I don't—and even if I wasn't in the middle of something, the fact is I'm being told what to do. So now if I do it, I'm obeying orders.*

He gazed at her as if it was still her move.

"Honey," she said, and gave him a playful pout.

He relented and said, "I'll be done with this in a bit, and I'll vacuum."

We aren't at nagging yet. But we're almost there. Nagging implies repetition of the same request over time. Why repeated? Because it wasn't heeded the first (or second or third) time. Nagging also carries some hostility. And it reeks of plunging expectations: *I'm asking you to do this but I don't really think you will and besides, I shouldn't have to ask, but here I go anyway.* Nagging feels like an indictment disguised as a request. It may or may not result in the task's getting done; but it puts it out there, so the naggee can't be quite so unscathed.

Again, we're not laying any fault here. But it's amazing how a simple desire to have something done can morph into a disturbance of the peace between two people.

Can nagging be stopped before it starts? There are two ways a man might react to these early, non-hostile requests. He might do the tasks in good grace, possibly with a note to himself, to the effect of *I'd better adjust my timing here and do stuff before I get asked to.* Or he might fall back on an old reliable: the token show of compliance. "No problem, I'm on it, babe." Only he isn't. And he won't be. The show of consent is really a form of foot-dragging or procrastination or, eventually, refusal. These gambits are likely to provoke outright nagging.

So you *really* nag him. And what does he do?

Well, he may still pull the fat out of the fire and step up and do the job, realizing that things are in danger of taking a nasty turn. That would be a thoroughly adult response. But more likely (if you're reading this book), he reacts to the nagging instead of the work that needs doing. He tunes you out, and if you corner him, he acts like a rebellious boy and refuses the assignment. There, we said it. He acts like a boy. That's a step in the regression that leads to the Mother Syndrome, the moment when he begins to see you as a mom, not a partner. Or he may take another tack: he shoulders the job but grudgingly, passive-aggressively does the bare minimum. So you don't like how he did it. So you decide you have to redo it. Either way, a Rubicon has been crossed. In your eyes he's becoming one of two things: a boy who is ducking his responsibilities, or a boy who bungles them. A shirker or a bumbler. Or both. In his eyes, you've become a critic, a boss, a nag. You've become the prosecution.

Toxic Behaviors

That leads to a whole bunch of other toxic behaviors, on both sides of the impasse. See how many you recognize.

- You snipe at him a lot and harp on things he did wrong. He arrives home from work and before he's even taken his coat off, you say something like, "Don't forget to hang your coat on the plastic hanger. Every time you use the wire one, your coat ends up as a heap on the floor and I end up having to hang it up properly."

- He expects a lot of things to be taken care of, and if they aren't, he acts put out. You've spent all day running around. Picking up his shirts from the dry cleaners, taking your toddler to and from day care. He walks in after you've cooked dinner and bathed your son, and before he even asks about your day, he demands to know why the kitchen is in such a mess.

- You seldom give him the benefit of the doubt that he is capable of doing a good job. Your shadow looms over him like a dire prophecy as he attempts to assemble the cabinet and you wait with bated breath for vindication. Even though he's actually read the instructions and has sweated for many hours over the many parts and pieces, you comment on how misaligned the doors are when it's finally done and put one of his discarded nails in the coffin by saying something like, "I wonder how long that'll stay together."

- Even when he does try to help, you often redo his work, making him feel that his efforts were worthless. He doesn't really believe in making a bed, because you just have to mess it up again to get into it, but on some days, in a giving mood, he makes a good-faith attempt to make it up real nice when you didn't have a chance to. So you enter the room in the late afternoon and he's lounging on the bed smiling at you.

"Can you get off?" you say, and you circle the bed, tucking in the covers in the finest hotel manner until they're tight and firm. It doesn't matter to you that he hates the covers tucked in at the bottom, because it crushes his toes, and every night he has to forcibly yank them out of their locked position. All that matters is that the bed conforms to your code.

This and the previous item are ways of discouraging men from participating in housework, which are known in sociology as examples of women "gatekeeping." We'll explore gatekeeping more in chapter 9.

- He seems to have lost the confidence to handle things he used to deal with easily. He stares at the menu in the restaurant for what seems like an eternity. You're beginning to feel embarrassed that he's taking so long while your friends are waiting to order. He flips the plastic-coated pages frantically back and forth, waiting for something to catch his eye. Eventually he asks you to order for him.

- Somehow he has a lot more leisure time than you do. You're always busy and he isn't. He always has time for TV. He picks up his magazine and cell phone after dinner and heads for the couch. On the way, he snags the remote control and then settles down for the evening. You've noticed several things. One, he seems testy when you try to join him in front of the TV. It's like his viewing habits can't include another spectator; channel surfing and watching several shows at once just don't leave room for extra opinions. So he actually prefers that you be busy most of the evening in other rooms.

Speaking of being busy, you know for a fact that he has a huge backlog of promotional work to do on the web-design business he's supposed to be starting to bring in more income. And when you ask how it's going, he always says he just hasn't had time to get into it. Not to mention the (growing) list of his untouched household tasks. So why is he able to veg in TV-land, when you can't? Apparently his tube time is just too essential. It trumps everything that other mortals might deem important.

You can hear his laughter from the other room as he switches back from ultimate fighting to *Two and a Half Men* reruns.

- There's never a time when you don't think he should be more productive—not even on a Sunday afternoon. You can't bear to see him idle. Even after he's helped prepare lunch and do homework with the kids, you're incensed when he takes time out to play a game on the computer, chat with a friend on the phone, or read the newspaper.

- He skulks around like a guilty dog when you're doing demanding chores. On a gloomy weekend you decide that the kitchen needs deep cleaning. He hired a one-time maid service to spiff it up when you were away for two weeks, but they seem to have missed all the nasty stuff. So you pull the racks out of the oven and attack it with volatile chemicals, you take apart the cleaning fan to get the gunk out, you work in the tile crevices with a toothbrush, you scrub the floor on your knees.

  The place is out of kilter for several hours, and he seems totally disoriented by that, tiptoeing around the scene like there might be concealed mines. He can't acknowledge what is going on, because that would mean he'd need a reason for not participating. Then, desperately wanting a beer, he sneaks to the fridge with all the dignity of a scared burglar.

  With diabolical intention you bang the mop against the bucket and he jumps out of his skin.

- He complains that you're nagging him even when you're not. You ask him if he's going to take care of the broken lock on the back door and he says he can't do it right now.

  In a friendly way you say, "I didn't mean right this minute, just when you have a chance."

  He says, "You don't have to keep reminding me. I know it needs doing and I had a plan of when I was going to get to it. I have to buy a part and it means going to the lock store." His tone implies that you're unjustly prosecuting him without knowing all the facts.

  "It's okay," you say, "no pressure here."

  He says, "I'm not a child and I'll do it when I'm damn well ready."

- Your tone and words are often condescending. His are bitter. You tell him that if it wasn't for the GPS, he'd never find his way anywhere. He tells you that you'd follow the GPS down the wrong street even when the building you wanted was right in front of you.

- When he does something "bad," he tries to avoid getting caught by Angry Mom. Sometimes men rebel against adulthood's rigid harness and do things they shouldn't. (Women are not immune to this failing either.) Most of the time these are minor peccadilloes, but they can easily turn into something worse when a guy has begun to see his wife as a disciplinarian instead of an equal. You ask him where he was all afternoon when you couldn't reach him at work. He's evasive, but later you find racetrack receipts in his pants. You confront him and accuse him of lying (and wasting household money). But it's the cover-up that rankles most. He says he had to lie because you would have come down on him too hard. You say he's a child. You remember a time when you were open with each other and quick to confess your little sins and to get past them.

Relationship Repercussions

At first, a few of these things happen; they sometimes lead to little tiffs and you make up and things are all right for a while. But unless the underlying problem is dealt with, the trend snowballs, and more and more of the above-mentioned behaviors get a check mark. Unfortunately, behaviors are habit-forming. The more you treat each other a certain way, the harder it is to stop doing it.

There are several strands in this unhappy fabric. We have you guilt-tripping him about not contributing enough, and we have his negative reactions. We have the parent putting down the child and making him feel incompetent. We have the child losing his nerve and actually becoming helpless at things he is perfectly capable of doing. Or acting like a spoiled brat who expects everything to be done for him. When he tries to hide his infractions, that eats away at your trust and you start to be suspicious when he gives you ordinary reports about what he's been up to.

As things devolve into more hostility, we get counter-attacks, on the principle that the best defense is an offense. A husband critiques his overworked wife's smallest mistakes, trying to transfer the blame. A wife yanks any meaningful contribution out of her husband's hands, leaving him with nothing to offer.

All of this antagonism spills over into other areas. You stop listening to each other; you stop turning to each other for legitimate needs because you're afraid of losing ground in the ongoing battle. Your obsessive goal becomes proving that the other person is wrong or bad. Winning at all costs.

So, the conflict leaks into your most personal moments as a couple. Even the most innocent occasions can be infected.

- After a good day, you go to some trouble and surprise him with a special meal that he really likes–spicy tacos al pastor with lots of toppings. You wanted to mend fences and give him a treat, but he acts guilty, then says he can't digest that kind of food, and a fight breaks out.

- You're in the car together, doing some errands on a weekend, and he suggests going for a ride in the country. But you squelch him with a comment about how much he has to do at home.

Instead of asking him for emotional things (like a sympathetic ear or a shoulder to cry on during a difficult time), you smolder with resentment that he didn't pick up on what you were feeling and what you needed. And he stops being open with you, because he doesn't want to make himself vulnerable. Both people are afraid of losing points in what has now become a battle of bruised egos. You've lost some of your respect for him. He hasn't turned out to be the giving, reliable, can-do guy that you expected. You're starting to see him as selfish and lazy and not to be counted on. Your view of his character is slipping—and be assured, so is his opinion of you.

If you look through the examples of broken dynamics that we've presented in this chapter, you'll likely notice that there is blame on both sides. Sometimes the source or instigator of the animosity is the husband, sometimes the wife. Both are contributing.

In our earlier discussion of the five mothering hats, and in most of this chapter, it may have seemed as if we've been portraying the husband as the villain of the piece. It's true, we've mostly described each role as experienced by the wife; we haven't given much of the husband's side of the story yet. But we will. In part 2 we'll look at all the justifications that couples use to explain why they're in this predicament, including the charges and countercharges that they lay on each other. And we won't neglect the husband's point of view. Interestingly, couples also place the blame on outside causes, like societal pressures, upbringing, and employment policies; and they make some very good points. We'll break 'em all down and see what they add up to.

But for now, let's return to the struggling couple with the broken dynamics. These hostile flailings add up to a relationship gone badly wrong. As coping mechanisms, they're just not making it. Hostility, hurt, resentment, and guilt lie in wait, ready to erupt at any time. The way you used to feel about each other hardly has room to breathe. Those affectionate, romantic lovers are hard to find.

That's why it's time to talk about one of the most important casualties of becoming a mother to your man. It's a dynamic that you certainly don't want to have lost, but it has taken a fall because of the messed-up ways you now relate to each other. We're talking about your sex life and the intimacy you used to share. In the next chapter we'll explore this sexual fallout, how your relationship went from hot to not, and the devastating impact that this change too can have on your marriage.

Chapter 3

The Sexual Fallout

Can the effects of becoming your husband's mother reach all the way to your intimate life together? Oh yes, they can and they do. In fact, the crowning proof that you and your spouse have gone astray—the final piece in the screwed-up puzzle—is that your sex life goes south. From hot to not.

There are two sides to this coin we've been looking at. On one side, you've become something you *didn't* want to be: his mother. On the other side, you've stopped being something you *did* want to be: his lover. That's because the two roles are incompatible. You can't be both. You take on one role, you lose the other. As they used to say in Western movies, there ain't room in this town for both of us. There just isn't room in one relationship for both these ways of being. The mother stance is inherently antisexual. It kills the romance like a cold wind.

In this chapter we'll look at the ways that being his mother divests you of the chance to be his lover. We'll be answering a question that many women ask: "Why are he and I not lovers anymore?"

The first reason is rage.

How Anger Cools the Sexual Jets

You get into bed with him—*if* you're still sleeping in the same bed—and you find that you don't want to give him any more of yourself today. He's already had too much. All the thankless effort that we enumerated in the first chapter has exhausted your tolerance. And the hostile dynamics that we inventoried in chapter 2 have left the two of you far apart. So you're chronically "not in the mood." It would take too long to get from that angry, resentful place to becoming aroused.

In the next passage, Lisa describes an ordinary moment on a weekend morning, a moment that could have been so much better. Her story captures the conflict within a woman in living detail.

Lisa's story

> Things always seem better in the morning. It's as if the memories of yesterday's frustrations have been partially erased and I awake resolute with the intention to start fresh. I look over at my sleeping partner and he seems almost angelic. His hair is tousled like a little boy's and even the crease lines on his face are endearing. I tiptoe out of bed, past my dead-to-the-world teenagers' rooms, and downstairs to make a pot of coffee. But my plan to make eggs and toast is kiboshed as my attention is suddenly diverted to the sinkful of dishes from the night before. The dishes my Beloved had promised to take care of before he hit the hay. I

reach for my pink waterproof gloves, and sudsy water envelops the dishes as I wipe crumbs off the kitchen counters, cursing under my breath. Then I notice that the living room light was on all night. I think about the many times I have reminded him to turn off that damned light before coming to bed. I wonder if he forgot to turn the alarm on too.

I plow through the dishes, consumed with rage, thinking sadly back to how I felt ten minutes before. In spite of my best intentions, my plan to launch the day on a positive note has been thwarted. It's no surprise that this incident hits me like a ton of bricks. . . . I don't see it as an isolated occurrence, but as part of an ongoing (and endless) series of shirked tasks and ducked responsibilities.

Lost in thought, I don't hear Jim amble downstairs. His hands encircle my waist. "Hi, sexy," he says. "Love those pink gloves." He doesn't have a clue that he's done anything wrong. I consider saying nothing about the dishes in the sink and the light left on all night. I even consider offering to make him toast and eggs, maybe even bacon too, but I can't get the words out. Instead I bark, "Why is it always me that has to start my day off cleaning up after everyone else? It's bad enough having to supervise the kids all the time. I'd just like to have you on my team once in a while."

"There you go. I never do anything right," he responds. "You always find something to complain about." He storms out of the kitchen.

The dialog continues in my head. Only it's a monolog now. "I would like to come downstairs just once to find the kitchen the way that I left it. You're the one who came home late having forgotten to eat anything, and then insisted on messing up the place by making a whole new meal. You're the one who said you'd clean up. If you had, then maybe I'd have time to make coffee and something special for us to eat."

After the dishes are washed and drying on the rack, after I've turned off the light and swept the floor, I have a change of heart. I think about my original plan for the day. I wish I could begin again so there would be a new tone. I go in search of my partner.

I see him on the computer, playing poker. My inner voice goes back into prosecutorial mode: "Nine o'clock on a Sunday morning and you're playing poker. Don't you have anything better to do? Like make your bed or help me with the shopping list?" I resist those thoughts. Struggle to replace them with others, like the way he looked as he lay sleeping. I'm half-successful. I have a fleeting moment of seeing him as downtrodden, henpecked, and always being told what to do and how to do it.

So I summon all my capacity for forgiveness and force my legs to carry me over to where Jim is sitting. He hears me approaching but chooses not to let on. My hands massage his shoulders as I bend down to kiss the top of his head. "I'm sorry," I say, almost meaning it. "I got off on the wrong foot today."

"That's okay," he mumbles, still seemingly immersed in his game. "I'm used to it."

"Let's start over," I say. I rotate his chair in my direction. He reaches for me, forgetting the game all of a sudden. I straddle his lap, cradling his head against my breast. I gently rock back and forth, reminiscent of rocking my children to sleep. Strange how I'm thinking of them right now. He reaches under my nightgown. I have a fleeting, unwelcome sense of the way I used to feel at moments like this. I look into his eyes, trying to generate the sense of flirtation that was once so easy. But when we lock gazes, it's vaguely embarrassing. We don't strike sparks;

instead, I see him as a dreamer who still thinks he can get some, a pathetic parolee who thinks a pardon is coming his way. And he sees . . . well, he looks away too soon to see much of anything. I allow him to indulge in my softness for a moment, but when he begins to fumble with his jeans, I think better of this whole plan and jump off his lap, giving him a quick peck on the head.

I'm still mad, and I'm sad, and disappointed. But it's time to make breakfast, create a grocery list, and dive into the week's laundry.

We suspect that the conflict within Lisa is all too familiar to you. Your head wants a romantic mate, but your heart just can't go there. Anger is always just below the surface, mostly simmering but also appearing as an occasional volcanic eruption. There's no chance for makeup sex, because you never really make up. Makeup sex may be highly prized, but "I hate your guts" sex has never been much in demand.

The idea that anger is always there may have some of you scratching your heads. Maybe you find that you've gone beyond anger to indifference. We think that indifference is not a pleasant thing to be feeling: it's a sort of numbness. And it often masks discontent. We also think that if you had a glimmer of hope for your relationship, you might gladly leave indifference behind, even if renewed anger was the first step toward progress. You may think you're feeling indifference, at least some of the time, but stop and consider that for a moment. If you really didn't care, would you be reading this book?

How Your Image of Your Lover Changes

Anger and resentment are obviously big factors, but there's another interesting element in Lisa's story. She says, "I see him as a dreamer who still thinks he can get some, a pathetic parolee who thinks a pardon is coming his way." What that means is that her perception of *who Jim is* has changed. The character he has now become is no longer worthy of her lust.

That's what happens when a man is reduced in your eyes from a partner to an unreliable supervisee. Just maybe, he doesn't even appear sexy to you anymore. He isn't the hot dude you once desired. That dashing man has been replaced by a stranger, someone you don't recognize. As your view of him went downhill, as you came to see him in a less admirable light, his appearance seemed to change. His smile seems a little crooked, his eyes less clear. Because *what* you think of someone affects *how* you see him. Once, you thought he was awesome; you felt lucky to have him. Sure, he was cute as hell, but more than that, he was energetic and giving and responsible and resourceful. That's a long distance from a passive, incompetent schlub who doesn't pull his own weight and needs you to be his mom.

As one client told Sara, "Every time I pick up one of his dirty socks, my libido goes further down."[1]

Anti-erotic Signals and Rituals

So, in all sorts of ways you send that negative message to him. You "tell" him that you don't think of him as lover material. Anti-erotic signals and rituals. Sometimes they're conscious. But much of the time they aren't, because the idea that he could be sexual material doesn't even occur to you. You take your clothes off in a functional way, as if you had no idea that such an act could be arousing. When you *are* wearing something hot, you discard it as soon as you get home, not thinking to let it work a little magic on him. It's almost as if you're saying, "There's no one here I need to look good for." Later on, you get into bed wearing your tatty nightshirt and become absorbed in your crossword puzzle. You've become the Uninterruptible One.

When it comes to anti-erotic rituals, human creativity knows no limits. Here are some seemingly benign examples that when added up can equal a big fat turnoff. Maybe they're even more effective when not consciously calculated to douse the erotic flames, because they indicate that a sexual option hasn't even gotten onto the radar screen.

- sitting on the toilet for an especially long time with the door open. While this may facilitate verbal communication, it also adds one more dubious image to the portfolio that each spouse is responsible for lodging in the other's brain. A long-married friend once shared that she always closed the door when she went to the washroom and her husband was around. She called it simple modesty, but she also admitted that the "on the throne" perspective was not her most flattering angle.

- picking your nose or any other part of your body. Let's face it, both genders pick and scratch at various parts of their bodies, and sometimes it can be downright enjoyable. But doing so in front of a spouse may not bring out one's Venus or Adonis.

- belching, farting, or snorting. It is not a sin to be human, and humans are animals whose bodies make strange noises as part of normal survival mechanisms. Sometimes these events occur unbidden and cannot be prevented by even the most vigilant tightening of an orifice. Nor should they always be! We heard of one woman who admitted, after a ten-year marriage and a divorce, that she and her ex had never, in all the time they'd known each other, heard each other fart. We worry that way too much gas may have been stopped at the door and forced to make another circuit through already stressed intestines. So it's fine to let 'er rip, when health and comfort require it and one isn't at a posh dinner party. But that doesn't mean that doing so at a moment that might otherwise be erotic is not a way of sending an effective (and sometimes noxious) signal.

- filing or clipping your nails in bed. But wait, done the right way and in the right garb, this could be quite an arousing tease.

- bringing your bills to bed. A surefire way to get your man to turn in the opposite direction is to slide over to his part of the mattress and ask him to look at invoices with you and discuss ways in which they are going to be paid in time.

- agreeing to take a bath with your man and then pushing your hair into a plastic shower cap just before climbing in. Sometimes the practical just has to be ignored, and if it isn't, the bathwater may suddenly feel cold.

- climbing into bed and making a phone call to your best friend or your mother. Delay and distraction can be provocative when the right kind of sexual focus is maintained, but otherwise it can be a sure path to permanent postponement. Not to mention the fact that giving your attention to those who are not present in disregard of those who are is one of the cell phone era's most egregious forms of bad manners and is therefore a really unkind way to tell your bedmate that he doesn't rate in your eyes.

- taking every opportunity to invite the children into your bed. If they are young, do you find one (or more) is sleeping between you? Perhaps you look forward to snuggling up to your child more than you do to your husband. You may even find that despite the conflict that this creates between you and him—he wants to "train" them to sleep in their own beds and you want to encourage the family bed—you ignore his concerns.

Yes, there are many chilly breezes that can blow across a bed, and though they can be amusing to write about, it isn't much fun to be on the receiving end. If, in spite of this, a husband still wants to get it on with his spouse, she may sometimes give him a tumble, maybe on a day when he has atypically done something useful or she is feeling generous, but it comes off as a reward or a treat, like you'd give a kid who was "extra good." For the man, this isn't the same as being desired as an equal: it's charity sex. And when the door of sex is closed to him, that reads as a sort of punishment or reproach, once again signaling his fall in status.

From His Side: How Being Mothered Kills the Sexual Magic

So far we've been talking about the wife who no longer wants to get it on with the husband who still does, but the loss of desire can easily go in the male direction too. Confidence is a big part of sexual performance, and it isn't so easy for a guy to be confident when he feels like a child. If his wife has become too managerial—has morphed into his supervisor—a man may feel like he'd be sleeping with a critical boss. This can be exacerbated even further if his wife makes his poor sexual performance another item in her list of his domestic failings. Many of the destructive dynamics we explored in the previous chapter can be emasculating to a guy, and emasculation doesn't tend to send blood to the right places.

We talked about how a wife's perception of her husband can go downhill, so that he no longer seems to her to be the desirable male he once was. He literally seems to change in her eyes, into a less physically attractive person, because of the irresponsibility and incompetence she charges him with. A similar thing can happen to the woman *he* sees across the kitchen table. Someone who comes off as bossy, critical, angry, and demeaning can seem to change her appearance; the same face that once seemed beautiful and inviting can take on a sharp, forbidding look. Time and familiarity make a good enough stab at diminishing the attractiveness of spouses to each other without being aided and abetted by toxic interaction.

Even if this hasn't happened to the man—even if he still thinks his wife is hot stuff and hungers for her—he may just not feel invited to the sexual party, for the reasons we looked at above: because she is no longer seeing him as a sexual partner, and because she has become lost in a job title (his mother) that conflicts with that part of herself. So a man may see a fabulous woman on the couch or across the bed but not know how to scale that mountain anymore. He may know in his head that she is desirable but not be able to communicate that idea to his more primitive parts. Or he may still throb with desire for her but not know how to make his play, no longer know the way in to that inner sanctum.

The Effects of Passion's Loss

When you think about it, there could hardly be a worse place to pitch your sexual tent than a mother-child relationship. In fact, trying to takes you into one of society's deepest taboos. So it's hardly surprising that when a woman and a man have slipped into this alignment, sexuality ends up quashed.

Not having physical passion anymore is bad enough in itself, but it also has serious consequences. It has a ripple effect that spreads into other aspects of your relationship, especially when it continues over time. When you lose this dimension, when intimacy is rare or nonexistent for months or even years, you lose other good things too.

When couples are loving and intimate, the glow spreads into surrounding hours and days and makes life's major and minor hassles easier to handle. Intimacy can take many forms, from rubbing a person's foot to cuddling to sex in its many guises. Sometimes it means intercourse, sometimes orgasm, and sometimes it means reaching under the covers on a cold night and finding a warm hand to hold. Genuine intimacy is like a password two spies exchange in a foreign land; it's two flames joining together against the abyss. It's fundamental and it's irreplaceable. Not being intimate with one another puts a couple out of tune. Both husband and wife are likely to be more easily irritated, to nitpick at the little things, and to erupt at one another more quickly. They will hit false notes, mistake each other for the enemy, forget what they would feel if this person were taken away.

Both are less likely to feel loved, cared for, and attractive. Over time, each person's self-esteem and self-image can be affected. They may look elsewhere for positive feedback. The ultimate and most potentially devastating consequence of allowing your sexual bond to die is that your marriage may not survive or you'll continue living together in a discontented, lonely way.

Barb shared how her life with Gerry had become a horrible, empty parody of togetherness. Over the twelve years that they'd been married and had two children, their relationship had fallen off track. It had been rocky for a while but had deteriorated to the point that the only time they communicated was when they had something nasty to say to one another. The rest of the time they stuck to their own routines. After dinner, Gerry retreated to his home office (cave) and Barb continued doing homework with the kids and often watched TV with them. When it was time for bed, she ushered the kids upstairs. They followed their mother's lead and often didn't even say good night to Dad. Once the kids were in bed and asleep, Barb experienced the loneliest part of her day. "It's so much emptier to feel the distance between you and your spouse when you're knocking around the same house," she said. "It's even lonelier than living alone."

Intimacy and sex are a mortar that helps hold the bricks of a relationship together. Making love promotes love. And it also promotes itself. Have you ever noticed that the less sex you have, the less you want? It's like fasting. After a while you don't even notice being hungry anymore. The reverse is true too. If you continue building on intimacy and making love, you crave it more. It's like people who exercise. Many people who really get on track with exercise say that they get to a point where they can't live without it. It releases endorphins, feel-good hormones that leave you wanting more.

Unfortunately, a superficial, "quick fix" approach to waning sex isn't going to work when there's a powerful underlying mechanism that has drained it of its oomph. The only way to genuinely restore the connection is to deal with the thing that is impeding it.

* * *

We've seen what the Mother Syndrome consists of and how it affects emotional dynamics and sex. The question arises now, how big is the problem? How many couples have it, and how does it stack up against the troubles commonly recognized in marriage? Some reports say men are catching up in housework and everything is hunky-dory. Is this really true? Are wives who mother their husbands a rarity, or are they in good company? In chapter 4 we'll take a look at the current data and find some answers.

Chapter 4

How Big a Problem Is the Mother Syndrome?

So far, we've drawn a pretty detailed picture of the Mother Syndrome, including the household jobs that come under its umbrella, and its emotional and sexual dimensions.

Now the question arises, how big is the problem?

This is actually two questions in one:

1. How many actual marriages have the problem?
2. How *serious* is it? In other words, how many troubles commonly attributed to marriage (causes of divorce) are actually *this* problem?

How Many Marriages Have the Problem?

Let's take the first question first. How widespread is the situation we've been talking about, where the wife feels like she's become a mother to her husband?

Given that you're reading this book, you probably know it applies to you. But that still may leave you wondering, "Am I unusual, or is this happening to a lot of women?" You may have seen news stories, trumpeting the latest data, that seem to indicate a contrary trend. *Surprise! Men are catching up, doing their share at home!* Does that mean you should feel isolated, or is this information somehow bogus?

We checked in with the research on this topic, the reams of articles that a whole industry of scholars cranks out year after year. And what we found is fascinating.

The first point to emphasize is that nothing the researchers say can invalidate your own assessment of your situation. If you recognize yourself in what you've read so far, no statistician can pooh-pooh that.

The second point is that the sociologists don't study our problem *directly*. But boy, do they study it. We didn't find hundreds of articles about the problem of a wife feeling like her husband's mother—at least not in those terms. What we did find, though, is a mountain of research about the hours worked by women and men, in paid jobs and at home. And about the division of labor between the sexes, and the burning question: Has parity been achieved?

The basic story line goes like this. Since the 1960s, women have been entering the employment market in a big way. Today, most wives work full-time or part-time at paid jobs. That was supposed to be progress, but what women found was that they were facing two shifts: one at the day job and then another at home. The women's movement had hailed a revolution, but it wouldn't be complete (or fair) unless husbands stepped up and shouldered more of the housework and child care. So what happened? Did men come through? Or is the revolution stalled, as

Arlie Hochschild's influential book *The Second Shift* argued in 1989?[1] That question is what an army of academics continues to probe, in all its complexities.

Now, clearly this relates closely to the issue of our book. We looked in chapter 1 at the different hats you wear that make you his mom, and they have everything to do with certain jobs you do at home—jobs that he doesn't participate in enough. The cooking, the cleaning, the child rearing, the management—and the overall role of being the responsible one. You wouldn't be in this pickle if he were sharing this work equally with you.

Let's get back to those news stories. A typical one appeared in *Time* magazine in 2011.[2] Like any cover story, it was designed to raise eyebrows. The title was "Chore Wars," and the subheading read, "Men are now pulling their weight—at work and at home. So why do women still think they're slacking off?" That seemed to imply that men have caught up on the home front and are now doing half the work. If you glanced at it in the supermarket, you'd think, "Gee, *my* husband must be way below par. Apparently the other guys are making the grade."

But when you look closer, the story is different. The article *isn't* saying that men do as much housework as women. In fact, its own stats, derived from Bureau of Labor Statistics (BLS) reports, show quite the opposite.[3] Take married couples with kids. What the data tells us is that women are still doing two-thirds of the homemaking, and if you look at the "core tasks," which are unrelenting and non-glamorous, the amount is three-quarters or more. They're also doing two-thirds of the child care. In other words, women are still doing the heavy lifting at home. But there's a consolation prize. *Time* says that guys are doing a lot more housework than they *used* to, back in the day.

So what about men's great leap forward since the 1960s?

Well, it turns out that the bar was set so low, back in those misty times when the male was the breadwinner and the female was the homemaker, that even a minimal performance now looks good by comparison. What happened is that undetectable levels of male housework became detectable. *Time* boasts that a typical married dad tripled his food prep and cleanup hours since 1965. But what were they back then? A tidy .9 hours per week. That's an impressive eight minutes a day with that lime slicer and that dish towel. No wonder dads had time to read the paper and sip a gin and tonic. Today, that .9 weekly hours has turned into 2.7, according to *Time*. Yes, it has tripled, but it is still only about a third of what a woman does in food prep and cleanup. That means her share of the total is three-quarters.* When you look at the rest of the housework (e.g., laundry, cleaning, vacuuming), you see the man quadrupling 1965's half hour per week to a big two hours today. The trouble is, his wife is doing 8.1 hours per week, which is over 80 percent of the total. When you add in child care, the wife's total is 28 hours per week, and the husband's is 11.

In any case, the research clearly shows that men don't pull their weight at home. But *Time* still insists that men and women work the same hours. How can that be?

Simple. What it's saying is that men work more hours at their *day jobs* than women do, and that *makes up* for the extra work women do at home. The result: If you add up the *total hours* worked in both areas (paid and unpaid), the two genders come out about the same. Your husband's total daily toil isn't any less than yours, lady. So what do you have to complain about?

---

*When she does three times his hours, that's three-quarters of their combined hours. For example, if he does 3 and she does 9, the total is 12, and her 9 is three-quarters of that.

It's a powerful-sounding argument, but it turns out to have quite a few holes in it. Things are not so simple, and the research backs this up. You are *not* alone: the circumstances that make you feel like your husband's mother are the rule, not the exception.

Here's why.

First, all the numbers we've been looking at are only averages, from large samples of people who were studied. But an average means lots of actual numbers are higher and lots are lower. So there are many homes in which the wife's total hours are greater. Yours may be one of them. Second, some scholars think men exaggerate their housework hours in their time diaries (on which the BLS stats are based) because they want to live up to changing cultural ideals.[4] That would skew the numbers too.

But even if a man and his wife have the same overall total, there's a serious problem. Day job hours are not the same as homemaking/child care hours. Comparing them is like comparing apples and oranges. In many ways, the unpaid work that you do at home has its own unique price tag. Explaining why is the most important thing we'll do in this chapter.

In the first place, the home is a separate realm, complete unto itself, where a whole lot of important stuff gets determined. Why? Because home is *the main place where a husband and wife spend time together.* That together time is where the relationship between them is mostly forged, where the tone is set. The unpaid work they each do at home is either in balance or it isn't. If it isn't, they can't meet as equals in the one place that matters most. That changes who they *are* to each other. If she is doing most of the housework and child care, she is liable to feel like his mother. Once that happens, a happy marriage is out the window, regardless of any extra paid hours that he may work (usually in some other location, off on his own where love doesn't grow).

It wasn't always like this. Back when Dad was the only breadwinner and Mom was home all day, Dad brought home that merit badge and carried it through the evening. He wasn't measured by his contribution to housework. But that was then, boys.

Here's an ironic thought. Maybe the very advances men have made on the home front have worked against them, in a way. Could doing a third of the household work actually be worse than not doing any? Maybe. When men stayed out of the homemaking game, they couldn't be judged on their performance. They were in the bleachers, being honored for their manly earning power. But when they stepped onto the playing field, they suddenly became exposed. A guy's wife could score him on how much he was doing at home and how well he was doing it. He was subject to a whole new evaluation. If he wasn't pulling his weight, he suddenly looked like a second-stringer.

Gone is the day when he could hold his own by being the sole earner. In today's world, home is where equality must either flourish or wilt. We saw in chapter 1 that one of the hats that make you his mom is the management hat. In particular this means that if you have the *authority* at home, if you're basically his boss in the main place where you both spend time, then you're *really* his mother. A 2008 Pew survey found that women are dominant in 62 percent of couples where decision making is not split equally. (In case you were wondering, only three in ten couples have equality in decision making.) So, are a lot of women turning into their husbands' bosses? That's what the data says.[5]

Summing up this point: The reason household work hours are oranges and not apples is that they have the power to affect the *quality* of the relationship between two people. If they're out of balance, they can create a tilt that makes love slide right out of the picture.

But still, we can hear some statistician say, quantity counts for something. If enough apples are piled up, don't they balance the oranges? What if the husband's working hours are *much* greater than the wife's: wouldn't that cancel out the extra homemaking she does? Suppose her job is very part-time, and his is very full-time. Can't she then do a whole lot more housework and child care than he does without that being unfair? It's kind of like he's partway back to the old breadwinner status, so when he gets home, she won't *expect* so much from him.

Our answer is yes, of course that can be true, but couples like that are not the ones we're talking about in this book. Such wives are less likely to feel like their husbands' moms. In fact, they are the exception that proves the rule. We assume that a lot of you reading this are working either

1. a full-time job
2. a part-time job with appreciable hours, often with kids at home

The first case obviously provides excellent soil in which the Mother Syndrome can grow. But let's be clear: so does the second. Even if the wife works part-time and the husband full-time, there *can* be a problem, especially if his total hours (paid and unpaid) are less than hers. But even if they're about equal, trouble can brew. For the reasons we just looked at, her greater load on the home front can infect their relationship. We also have to ask, *why* is she working fewer hours, and why is he working more? Does she want to have a full-time career, but his lack of engagement at home makes that difficult? Is he stretching his job time to avoid facing domestic tasks? (Does he go to work early so he won't have to get the kids out of bed and off to school, or come home late to avoid meal challenges?) Every situation is different, but there's no doubt that a woman who works part-time can find herself in the grip of the Mother Syndrome. (It also bears saying that we have heard from wives who work few paid hours or none at all and yet are thrown into the Mother Syndrome by their husbands' lack of engagement in household work/child rearing.)

There's another aspect of how women work that can skew the numbers: what if you're doing two things at once? Wives multi-task more than husbands and are working a lot of the time when they modestly say they are not. The stats we've been looking at mostly come from time diaries made by real people for academic researchers. In some of these diaries people record what they were doing at a given time, and also what *else* they were doing (secondary activities). If the first thing is watching TV, most of these studies count that as leisure, but what if a wife was folding laundry while she was watching TV? Taking this into account increases the gender gap at home.[6]

So there's a difference between a woman's "free time" and a man's. Research studies show not only that men have more leisure hours than women, but also that men's relaxation is less often corrupted by any hint of work or disrupted by the demands of other family members.[7] Men, in fact, place more stock in the distinction between work and play, as we'll see in chapter 8.

Then there is the "invisible" part of a woman's work. As you might expect, a lot of what a wife does is not captured in the time studies. It takes a huge amount of effort and concern to coordinate a family. It takes energy to be responsible. The typical wife is always vigilant, always on the alert for what needs to be done. The husband who needs mothering may not notice that the rug needs vacuuming or the child's nose is running or the doctor's office left a message or no one has heard from his mother about the planned dinner on Sunday. Women spend a lot of time on the phone maintaining connections with family and friends, often when they're supposedly not working. They write cards, arrange gifts, remember occasions, keep on keeping up.

All this may help explain why wives feel rushed so much of the time. A 2006 Pew study of working moms and dads found that 40 percent of working moms always feel rushed, as opposed to 25 percent of working dads.[8] We aren't saying that men don't feel enormous pressure from the conflict between job and home. What we are saying is that women are still bearing the brunt of the problem. Nor are we trying in this chapter to say who's to blame or what *causes* the unequal division of labor at home. We'll get to those questions in part 2, in a big way. What we're doing here is documenting how widespread the phenomenon is.

And the clincher is that when a wife is employed full-time, it doesn't mean we find her husband doing more housework. Perhaps the most shocking observation in the studies we've seen is how completely unaffected men's home performance is by women's working more paid hours. When a woman works as many day job hours as her husband, he still works the same number of household hours as the guy down the street whose wife works part-time. It's as if men will only go so far into "women's work," regardless of how far women go into the once-male sphere of day jobs. As one article put it, "Men adjust little to their wives' employment, neither reducing their employment hours, nor increasing their household work."[9]

The overall point here is clear: the scales are not balanced as far as who is bearing the brunt on the home front. Contrary to some news reports, sociological research shows that the division of labor in the average home is not equal and not fair—and to generate such averages, it must be even worse in a great many marriages. What we have is a situation where too many men no longer have the luster of being the sole breadwinner, but neither have they earned the cachet of being an equal partner at home. Instead, they find themselves in a realm where the wife is the more competent, harder-working, controlling force, and they are found wanting. Thus the conditions are rife for an insidious mutation to rear its ugly head: her seeing herself as his mother.

How Significant Is the Problem as a Threat to a Marriage?

All right, we've answered the first part of this chapter's question. We've shown that the problem is widespread. The data confirms that lots of marriages have a precarious imbalance of labor, which can lead directly to the Mother Syndrome. That leaves the second part: what does the research say about how significant the problem is as a threat to the survival of a marriage?

We've already said that being his mother is a pretty dire predicament in which to find yourself. It's not what you signed up for; it isn't the relationship you wanted. It's a travesty of love, it creates toxic dynamics between you, and it can wipe out your sex life. Clearly, it can make a marriage miserable, and it's obvious that unhappy marriages are more likely to crash and burn.

But what does the research say? Let's look at the biggest factors that are recognized as being crucial to marriage—the ones that make a couple succeed or fail. How many of them are bound up with the Mother Syndrome?

Well, we can start with another survey by the always-helpful Pew organization.[10] In 2007 it asked people to rate various factors that make for a successful marriage—things like income, sex, and religion. The respondents were asked to rate each one as "very important," "rather important," or "not very important." Which factors were called "very important" by the most people? Well, if you guessed that the winner would be faithfulness, you'd be right. Ninety-three percent of adults rated it very important. Then came a happy sexual relationship (70 percent).

Number three was a surprise to the researchers. Pulling ahead of such old reliables as adequate income, good housing, and common interests, "sharing household chores" was chosen as very important by 62 percent of adults (64 percent of married working moms). That made it the success factor with the biggest rise since 1990. We think these good citizens are on to something. When household chores are not shared equally, you get the Mother Syndrome. So the third-highest factor in marriage success, if absent, leads to our problem. If you feel like it's a deal breaker, you aren't alone. Sixty-two percent of adults agree with you.

But these results can tell us more. We also have a claim on the Pew survey's number one and two choices. We saw in chapter 3 what the Mother Syndrome does to sex: it kills it. So if you become his mother, you've lost the factor (happy sexual relationship) that 70 percent of adults say is very important to a marriage's survival. Likewise for faithfulness, the top choice of respondents. When a husband sees his wife as a mother finding fault with him, it's very clear that he is more likely to look elsewhere. He wants someone who admires him, who treats him as an adult (and desires him); if he can't find that at home, he may fill the need elsewhere. Likewise for a wife who finds herself with a man-child who has lost his desirable qualities. So, 93 percent of adults think you need something (fidelity) that the mothered husband and his wife are likely to lose.

So much for success factors. Now let's look at the other side of the coin: an article on the top *problems* in marriage, the ones that cause divorce. We'll see that many of them can be traced to the wife's becoming her husband's mother. Thus the Mother Syndrome will emerge as the hidden factor, the unacknowledged key to many riddles of failed marriage.

A study of marital problems and subsequent divorce appeared in August 1997 in the *Journal of Marriage and the Family,* authored by sociologists Paul R. Amato and Stacy J. Rogers.

Their list of problems as reported by divorced people is led by

- communication difficulties
- general incompatibility
- infidelity
- not spending enough time at home
- disagreements over money

Extramarital sex was "the most commonly cited cause of marital dissolution."[11]

A look at this list reveals that every one of these problems can be laid at the feet of the Mother Syndrome. They cause it, result from it, or are exacerbated by it.

Let's flesh this out:

- **communication difficulties and general incompatibility:** Both can arise from the gulf, and the guilt and resentment, between the mothered husband and his wife, as described in our "Broken Dynamics" chapter. Seeing each other in this way can create an unbridgeable chasm that stops healthy communication and isolates spouses from each other. People can easily seem to be incompatible when they slip into these unwanted roles and poor mutual treatment.

- **infidelity/extramarital sex:** We've already seen that this can easily arise when the "sexual fallout" described in chapter 3 happens; the Mother Syndrome kills the intimacy between two people and leaves a man or woman pining for a real partner with romantic appeal.

- **not spending enough time at home:** Hmm. The circumstance where both husband and wife work sets the stage for the Mother Syndrome (just add unequal housework). Also, once the man is cast as "bad child" and the wife as "bad mother," he is much more likely to avoid home (maybe by spending longer hours at work) and to try to retrieve his lost dignity elsewhere.

- **disagreements over money:** Being the manager and the responsible one regarding finances can play a big part in making a woman feel like her guy's mom.

So, a typical study of marital problems turns up five things that are all strongly associated with the Mother Syndrome.

How about something more direct? In a 2006 article about household bargaining and divorce in the United States and Germany, Australian sociologist Lynn Prince Cooke says an unfair division of housework can be lethal to a marriage.

We can't do any better than Cooke's own words:

> If women find themselves unable to negotiate a favorable division of domestic tasks, economically independent women are able to then leave the marriage. . . . This suggests that the higher divorce rates since World War II are not reflecting just effects of women's rising employment; they reflect men's resistance to

> changing their domestic behavior in response to women's rising employment. . . . More than two decades ago, Huber and Spitze (1980) found that while wives' thoughts of divorce increase with their own employment, they decrease with husbands' increasing housework contribution.[12]

We believe that the move from "you aren't doing your share at home" to "I want a divorce" very often passes through an intermediate stage: "I am not okay with being your mother."

Having seen how big the Mother Syndrome is, we now turn to an interesting question: Why do so many couples not see it coming?

Chapter 5

How the Mother Syndrome Sneaks Up on a Couple

We said in the previous chapter that the home front is crucial in setting the tone of a couple's relationship. Who does the housework and child care—and who's in charge—can alter the balance of the whole marriage. So why don't couples watch out for this major threat to their wedded bliss? In this chapter we want to show how insidiously the Mother Syndrome wraps its cold fingers around a wife and husband, and why so many couples are blindsided by it. We'll understand the Mother Syndrome that much better when we see how it flies under the radar, right into two people's hearts.

What makes many couples sitting ducks is that they simply don't believe that the division of housework could matter that much. So what if they have a certain way of handling chores? Why should that poison the whole enchilada?

After all, the assumption runs, when a couple goes out to socialize with friends or see a movie or have a nice meal, that is the place where their true relationship unfolds, and it is untouched by what happens at home. Oh, and the bedroom too is somehow unscathed. When the lights are low and the moment is right, the bedroom will still allow the male and the female to be the ardent lovers they once were when they were dating, before the complex administration of a home (and children) raised its ugly head.

All this might make sense if a couple spent huge swaths of time somewhere other than where they live. And guess what: it *is* like that when people are first going out together. If you think of the life cycle of a typical couple, it begins in a world *where they are never in a shared home.*

Love in the Wild

Emma and Jon met in college. He lived in the dorm and she lived with two girlfriends in a small house two blocks away. They seemed to be always out somewhere, walking on campus, attending the classes they had in common, hanging with friends at the coffee shop or the amazing Mexican restaurant, or chasing their favorite college band from venue to venue. They weren't alone together that much, and when they were, they treasured it.

Sometimes, of course, they visited each other's places of abode. Jon's dorm roommate was pretty good about finding alternative places to crash on a Friday night, and so Emma would sleep with Jon in his ridiculous single bed that fit them only because they were in each other's arms. He didn't sleep over at her place as often, but he spent a lot of time there, because it was bigger and had the best zany, spontaneous meals, not hurt at all by the fact that one of Emma's housemates was a culinary major. Jon was more than glad to be a guinea pig at their many dinner experiments, and he and a couple of other males who were lucky enough to partake did their best to earn their membership with charm, wit, and copious bottles of wine.

So that's how this love affair started. If there were any domestic arrangements in Emma's house, Jon was blissfully unaware of them. It was just a place where a sweet, playful mist of feminine energy moistened his study-parched brow.

Then college was over and they still lived in separate places for a while, and it was hard to get to see each other because their jobs kept them apart and their apartments weren't very close. They had a passionate reunion in one of their places on many a night, sometimes just had time for a drink and then it was to bed, and bed was anything but domestic: it was a magic portal to a world where you couldn't tell the difference between the spirit and the flesh, but both were torrid.

So finally the apartness was too much and had to be solved. They wanted a "life" together, not just clutching each other in the wild night. So they found a one-bedroom rental house in the older part of town, not too far from the school where she worked and the commuter train that took him to the business district. And that's when domesticity finally reared its cunning head. They were on their way now, to a home of their own, which would have children in it before too long. What could possibly go wrong?

Everything.

Here's *why* everything can go wrong for so many couples. The passion and communication, the deep friendship and the sexual hunger they share, are not bred in a domestic environment. No, these couples meet and mate as wild horses ranging through the canyons. Our free-flying humans dream of a home together, but this dream is born at a time when they are never actually in such a bourgeois setting. And then they find themselves with a domicile to live in and run. And these two people who learned to love each other in an undomesticated world now find that their shared home is the main place where they see each other. The workdays separate them, their friends are harder to connect with . . . Suddenly, this is it.

As we remarked in the previous chapter, the fact is that home is where couples spend 90 percent of their together time, so *if you develop a bad way of relating to each other at home, then you've basically developed a bad relationship.* Even if you are that lucky couple that goes out together a lot, it's pretty hard to escape from the tone that is set at home—because you keep going back there.

Yet we found that both men and women—often unconsciously—make the careless assumption that the *apparently non-romantic* arena of housework/parenting can't really have any major effect on the "unrelated" and important area of romance/sex. Not to mention how it might affect the way they feel about each other as persons.

And so, as couples adjust to living together, an overlooked story often takes place, a shift in status that both people may not even notice until it's pretty far gone. At the time it takes place, neither person really intends it to happen: they aren't even aware of it, or of its huge implications.

Let's rejoin our story in progress.

Domesticated Love

Emma and Jon were now living together in their cozy rental house. Things were spontaneous and relaxed for a while, and then a certain ominous current seemed to grab them. To Jon's total surprise, Emma—his sweet, compassionate soul mate who had now found a good job teaching learning-challenged children—turned out to be a bit of a control freak in the kitchen. Her mother had run a tight ship, and Emma just naturally wanted to do the same.

At first Jon would joke with her and tease her and would try to make meals for them, but she had a way of letting him know that an omelet had to be stirred a certain way and that his dinner salad got soggy because he put the tomatoes in too soon. She was also a stickler about the handling of her Cutco knives; she didn't like it when he scraped the blade of the big knife across the cutting board to move chopped vegetables into a pan. Jon had always been able to cook for himself in his own place, but this new situation held a contrast: he was easygoing about how things were done, not too worried about details, whereas Emma had a clear, crisp conviction that every task has a "right" method. Trying to squirm out of the impasse, Jon would clown around and make light of things, but it seemed that the cold facts were always on Emma's side. So he was automatically trumped, because her way of doing things was fine with him, including the resulting meals, and his way of doing things wasn't fine with her. It was a no-brainer: for Jon, the path of least conflict was to retreat.

A similar thing gradually happened with cleaning and laundry, and Jon eventually felt it was safer and easier to let Emma do these things rather than face her dissatisfaction if he screwed up. Truth be told, Jon was a loosey-goosey guy who liked to have fun when he wasn't working and who had had loads of fun with Emma until now. What began to dawn on him was that a lot of the zaniness of their former life together had been because of the giddy mix of personalities that existed with her two frolicking housemates.

There was a subtle shift in their relationship, in that Jon felt a little put down sometimes, at home. As if he'd been demoted—he wasn't sure from what to what. He felt a sense of relief when they would go out with their friends and the old mojo would be working again, and he'd feel like the Jon of old with the Emma of old, having fun and hanging on to the vibe all the way back home and into bed.

Then Emma got pregnant and they got married and moved to a larger place that was farther from anywhere they liked to spend time with others. And soon there was a baby (later to be joined by another), and life got a whole lot more demanding. The first baby was a daughter. During the first year of her life, easygoing Jon developed a stomach problem, something he had never had in his life. How odd: foods he used to eat all the time would go right though him, and he would have a sensation in his gut that he described as feeling "like somebody left a clamp in there." Doctors were consulted and tests were done, and suddenly he was saddled with a diagnosis of a complicated set of food allergies. So now his meals had to be more carefully prepared, and Emma was just the gal for the job.

Though Jon dearly loved little Lizzie and was good at making her smile, relations between him and Emma were going steadily downhill. She was the boss of the place, the mistress of all logistics, and she would sometimes snap at him as if he was an incompetent child, because he just seemed to have a habit of doing things the wrong way, and she no longer had time to pretend to be respectful. He was developing a sheepish, hang-dog expression. His jokes annoyed her. He often looked guilty.

To top it all off, she was chronically displeased by his inadequate participation in housework and child rearing. She found him to be a shirker.

The rest is history, as they say: Emma was well on the way to becoming his mother.

The crucial point here is that at no time in this process did either Emma or Jon think they were making decisions that could somehow torpedo their relationship as romantic partners. They never suspected that they were caught in a gentle trap that would upend all the best things they felt for each other. It's true Jon's digestive problems were a glaring sign. The reason his gut deserted him was stress. He didn't know it, but the stress was from a shift in power that was going to threaten all he held dear.

The details and dynamics may vary, but the resulting pattern is the same in many, many marriages. In some cases the woman tends to *seize* control of domestic matters, as Emma did; in others she has it thrust upon her by the man's lack of participation. Either way, she gradually assumes the dominant role in various aspects of domestic life (food, cleaning, scheduling, child care), for a variety of reasons that we'll explore further in part 2. And the man goes along, because it's easier or because he thinks he's playing the expected role.

And here's the rub. In his mind it's no big whoop: *there's nothing important at stake.* But he's wrong: he has no idea how much he is losing besides the chance to do the vacuuming. By failing to fight for his ground or by shirking his responsibilities, he is ceding his equality in the household. And because *most of a relationship takes place at home,* this means he is actually losing his equality as a partner, and thus the whole ball game.

So the war is lost without a single shot being fired. That's because neither person realizes that their very survival as a loving couple is up for grabs. They have a common enemy: the tendency of couples to devolve into a mother-child relationship.

But instead of confronting this hidden enemy, they contend against each other. The battle is largely unconscious; the woman doesn't intend to take unequal power, but that is the outcome. She ends up emasculating the man, because a man who doesn't have an equal say, who is being ordered around, is not a man in his own eyes. Before he knows it, he's given up a whole major chunk of territory, and that has major implications, including sexual.

There's a special kind of pain for a guy that comes from being demoted in his own home. It isn't fun feeling like you are inept, especially in areas where you actually think you have something to give, which, as we will see in part 2, for men often includes more than women might think (child care is just one example). No one—woman or man—likes to be ordered around and feel disrespected by a supposed equal. And men, because of that famous male ego, are especially sensitive in this area: they can easily get their pride wounded, and a guy will stop trying rather than risk being made to look ridiculous—as a man or a lover.

That's a portrait of how the Mother Syndrome often develops. And seeing its backstory helps us understand why the predicament is so hard to dislodge. Because the typical couple walked unwittingly into the trap, never making any conscious decisions to downgrade their relationship, they are that much less able to see that things didn't have to be this way. She's become a mother to him, and it feels bad in so many ways, but neither person really knows how it happened.

Nor can they see a way out. Even though the situation is unpleasant, frustrating, and even painful, they both feel as if it has to be this way. In fact, what we've found is that typically both members of the couple are in a strange way *attached* to this bad way of relating to each other. Both are going along with this travesty of love. They enable each other. They are mired in it; it's what they know; they've learned how to live this way and they fear change.

And so they have a hundred ways of explaining away the status quo or justifying it or arguing that they have no choice.

Those rationalizations are what we're going to look at next.

Part Two

Reasons, Excuses, and Accusations

What keeps the Mother Syndrome in place?

The short answer is, men and women do. How? By believing things have to be this way. She has to do most of the work; she has to be a mother to him. Sometimes they blame each other for being stuck in this fix, and sometimes they agree on external factors that cause the problem.

But we say it isn't acceptable to be his mom, and it isn't okay not to be partners. So in the next six chapters we'll look at all the reasons, excuses, and accusations that help men and women stay in the grip of this formidable enemy. Though there is some truth in them, we'll show that ultimately they don't hold water (and we'll learn a lot about what women and men are feeling in the process).

That will clear the way for you to move the Mother Syndrome out of your life, a subject for part 3.

Chapter 6

"I'm Just Being a Good Wife"

Okay, you've become his mother instead of his partner, and emotional relations between you have taken a hit, including relations in the sack. Admittedly the situation sucks. So why do you and he persist in it?

We've heard lots of different answers to this question. Many take the form of accusations against the other spouse, but interestingly, not all of them do. Before we get to the blame game, we'll start with the most basic justification of all—one that wife and husband often agree on: "I'm just being a good wife." Slightly expanded: "Being the homemaker is part of what it means to be a good wife/mother." A variation would be, "I can't expect my husband to do woman's work!"

This idea has many sources, but one of the most powerful has to be a person's upbringing. Then the justification goes like this: "I was brought up to be the homemaker. He was brought up not to. What's wrong with that?"

Let's start there and see where it leads.

What Did Your Families of Origin Teach You—and Him?

As one woman, Celia, put it, "I was always close with my mom. We were pals—we still are. We enjoyed doing things together, and one of those things was meals. As a kid, I loved to go food shopping with her. We followed recipes together. We decorated the table for special occasions. I wasn't as turned on by cleaning, but I would even help her with that because I wanted her to be happy with me.

"And yes, she—not my dad—did all the cooking and all the cleaning, even though she had a part-time day job. As I grew up, I guess I was learning to be her. So when I got married, I just automatically followed in her footsteps. She never seemed to have a problem with how much my dad did around the house—which was basically mow the lawn, shovel the snow, and fix things. She would sometimes tease him about not being able to boil water, but it didn't seem to bother him. She never seemed like his mom. Yet I feel differently about my husband. I do feel like I've become his mother, and it definitely feels bad."

So it worked for Celia's mom, yet somehow it doesn't work very well for Celia. Going back another generation, many women say it worked even better for their mother's mother. Well sure, because back then things were different: the grandmother, in many cases, was a full-time homemaker. Granddad could be found in his workshop in the garage, smoking cigars and making model planes with real engines—but that was on weekends. On weekdays (when you didn't visit) he was all about his day job. Grandma was all about polishing the silver and making the world's best blueberry pie.*

But we're neglecting the male side. It isn't just women who take outdated cues from their upbringing. What did your husband learn from *his* parents? There are two ways a boy growing up may have gotten an idea that could last a lifetime:

1. He noticed what his mom did for his father. He noticed that she always had a meal ready for Dad when he arrived home from the office. That she set the table, served the food, cleared the table, cleaned and put everything away. He noticed that she picked up his dad's shirts from the dry cleaners, shopped for his toiletries when they needed replenishing. That she packed his lunch for work and literally polished his shoes. If his mom did all the heavy lifting at home and ran the place, with or without a day job, then why should things be any different for him when he got himself a wife?
2. But that's not all. What about all the things his mom did *for him* when he was a boy, and a teenager, and even as an adult visiting (or living at) home? Many men make a dubious leap here, from "My mom did *x* and *y* for me" to "My wife should do *x* and *y* for me." It's as if the two women are interchangeable.

Many men's autobiographies seem to feature three stages: "For my first seventeen years, life was sweet. Then I went through a

*This influence of one's upbringing can equally well be unconscious. Many women become like their mothers without wanting or meaning to. Because of what has been modeled to them, they just seem to slip into the role that they observed for so many years. And that's true of most of the influences we discuss in this chapter: they don't have to be consciously thought of in order to exert their power.

rough period for a few years—not sure why—where good food was scarce and my living space was a mess. But now I'm married and everything is golden again!"

As Claire put it, "My husband, Frank, grew up in a family where men were pampered and waited on like gods. His mother, Angie, doted on him and his two brothers and took care of their every need. It's true she encouraged them to be manly out there in the big bad world, to be brave and win at sports and hold their own in fights, but when they came home with a dinged elbow or grass-stained jeans or a hungry tummy, it was her job to salve their wounds and kiss their heads and clean their clothes and feed them steaming plates of lasagna. They were her warrior princes! She would have thought it was sissified for them to raise a hand in housework of any kind. Frank worshipped his mother, and when he looked for somebody to love, he wanted to worship her too. And I was the lucky girl. Unfortunately, in his vocabulary, 'worship' means the way you feel about a woman who spoils you in every way."

The problem can go beyond what expectations your *husband* may have gotten from his mother. There's also your own troubled scorekeeping, where you find yourself looking bad compared to her. What makes this scenario especially aggravating is that a mother-in-law can have an unfair advantage. By the time you've settled down with her son and get to visit her house, her kids have usually grown and she is cruising through the calmer years—no mess, no fuss. But when she inspects your premises, she is catching you at a more hectic time in life, with more going on, greater demands on you, and maybe little humans wreaking havoc as best they can. As Mariah said, "I don't want to channel his mother; God forbid I should turn into her. But on the other hand I feel I have to compete with her as far as homemaking and all that . . . she runs a tight ship and when she visits us and looks around, I cringe."

So we face two questions. Why do women feel an obligation to do as the older generations did? And why doesn't that feel right anymore?

"Woman's Work" as a Law of Nature

People imitate what they see when they're growing up. At first glance this seems like a strong defense. After all, both genders get a lot of our ideas that way, right? We learn in school and we learn in the home. And when it comes to how a man and woman should be together, we learn that at home too.

Or do we? We rebel in many ways against our parents' lifestyles; we learn from our peers; we have different attitudes and ways of relating. We improvise to fit new situations and new pressures. We dress differently. We talk differently. We enjoy different toys. We connect with each other in new ways. We start having sex earlier. We listen to different music, on media that didn't even exist when our parents were young. It's pretty clear: in many respects we are free to carve out our own ways of living. So why, in this area, do so many women (and men) honor tradition?

It has to be because they think that's how it *should be*. A woman isn't imitating what her mother *happened* to do: she is seeing her as the emblem of some general rule—a rule that should be etched on a fine oak plaque and polished with Pledge: "Woman was meant to be the homemaker."

Meaning, a man cannot be expected to do *woman's work*. That would violate his natural destiny, which is to bring home money, watch TV, fix the screen door, watch TV, haul the garbage out to the curb, and watch TV. A woman is fulfilled by providing a warm, comfortable home for her husband, with a nice roasted bird on the table (which he, of course, should carve, because after all, he knows his way around a carcass and a knife).

If you say so. Men are hunters, women are gatherers. Women bring a few blueberries in from the yard, then they stay home and vacuum the cave while men are ranging far afield, driving woolly mammoths off cliffs. There's a word for men who like to dust and exchange recipes: *gay*.

Let's be clear: we aren't presenting any of this because we believe it. We're highlighting this argument because a surprising number of married couples still seem to buy into it, and it helps lead them down the thorny path to the Mother Syndrome.

Take that notion of women's work. It would seem incredible that after the Women's Movement and the rise of women into every hall of higher education and employment, this hoary holdover from the fifties could still be hanging on. But it is.

The Unexpected Twist of *Leave It to Beaver*

Is June Cleaver (mother of Theodore "Beaver" Cleaver in the 1957–63 sitcom) really to blame for all this? Well, maybe. In the 1940s, during World War II, women had entered the workplace in droves, staffing the factories and offices while the men were away. In 1945 the war ended and, with men returning to the job market, women were sent back home and asked to be feminine in a more constricted sense, by dressing nice for Dad when he came home from work, regaling him in baby-doll nighties like you see in *Mad Men,* and getting pregnant early and often. And yes, June Cleaver was the poster girl for the 1950s wife.

But that isn't the whole story. There's another nugget that needs weighing. Because if you watch *Leave It to Beaver* reruns,

June didn't come off as her husband's mother. Ward Cleaver came home from work every day and was treated as an equal—at least. Sure, June did all of the housework and most of the child rearing—because she was home all day. It was a sunny time, when one working stiff could handily support a wife and family. This was not the ideal arrangement; being a homemaker left many women seriously unfulfilled. But in some ways it was a logical division of labor. And it didn't stop couples from staying together more often than they do today.

At least as portrayed on TV, June Cleaver didn't resent her husband's more worldly, more interesting life, and she didn't mind bringing him his slippers and a nice glass of milk (a TV euphemism for stronger spirits) when he got home. Maybe that was because the focus of both parents (and of the show) was the kids. Ah, those kids: Wally and Beaver, and on *Father Knows Best,* son Bud Anderson and daughters Betty and Kathy, appropriately nicknamed Princess and Kitten by their doting parents, Jim and Margaret. Kids abounding, kids watching the show, baby boomers growing up without the poverty and war their parents had known, buoyed by a strong economy and by this strange new animal called television, which made them feel as if they were the center of the universe. Wally and Beaver were boys, but in the *Father Knows Best* family, Betty and Kathy got just as much attention and seemed more viable than their faintly troubled brother, Bud.

It was too plain to see: Betty and Kathy would go to college and would see no reason why they shouldn't have careers. That was the fly in the hand lotion. Although Margaret Anderson seemed placidly content with her own lot, even she was raising daughters who seemed headed for something other than homemaking. And she was just a sitcom creation with no past, no backstory. But the women who watched her on TV were real. They remembered the war, when they had tasted hardier challenges than dusting and baking. They followed Betty Crocker's recipes, but they also read a book called *The Feminine Mystique,* by quite a different Betty (Friedan), in 1963, the final year of *Leave It to Beaver.* So these women, who chafed under the yoke of homemaking and never made it into TV shows, fired up their real daughters and filled them with a dream of equality.

And thus it turned out. Unfortunately, as women took their place in the full-time day job world, someone forgot to send the memo that the old homemaker role didn't make sense anymore.

After all, it no longer seems in any way improper for a woman to do pretty much any job a man might do. The only limitations are brute physical ones, and even those seem to be getting blurred. A woman can do "man's work" and still be a woman. So why do some people still think that a man shouldn't be expected to do "woman's work"? We see you, Mr. Double Standard, rearing your head again. We don't define a woman by some supposed girly inability to venture where men go. We don't think she can't be tough enough to be a trial attorney or a soldier, a crisis manager or a leader. She has left June Cleaver somewhere in a clunky television cabinet.

So maybe it's time for men to step out of the convenient shelter of the fifties male and get in touch with the homemaker within.

If and when they do, they're going to run into an unpleasant surprise. So we might as well deal with it now. Many men (and women) believe that getting married will make a guy's life easier, even a guy who intends to pull his weight. (After all, he's now sharing the work with someone else!) If we're really going to say that men should do "woman's work," we need to face an important fact: men and women have very different assumptions about *how much work* that is.

Does Marriage Mean Less Work?

Let's compare two likable singletons, Jake and Jilene. They're both thirtyish. He lives in a one-bedroom apartment; so does she. They both have jobs and are living viable lives. Although they don't know it, they will soon meet and start dating, and within a year they're going to tie the knot.

Right now they each do their own cleaning, cooking, and so on. So let's ask:

- In their separate places, which one does the most housework?
- When they get married, will Jake's workload go up or down if he shoulders half?

We would argue that if Jake is a typical guy, he does a lot less work taking care of his one-bedroom apartment than Jilene does taking care of hers. That's because she shoots for a higher domestic quality than he does. She keeps the place cleaner: her kitchen is usually immaculate, she scrubs the bathroom once a week, she vacuums, she dusts, she changes her linens often and does a lot of laundry. She also works on interior design and decoration, is always making changes and improvements in paint job, curtains, furniture, accessories—details. In a word, Jilene puts more love into her home. She is more house-proud. And she makes better meals with more variety, which require more planning, shopping, prep, and cooking time.

Jake, by contrast, does the dishes only when he runs out of dishes to use, has never scrubbed the sink with Comet, has never deep-cleaned the stove or oven, changes his linens only if a woman might stay over and he has any clean ones, does not even notice the dust on his bookshelf, and tackles one or two loads of laundry every couple of weeks. Decorating? Sorry. Accessories? He bought one lamp. Meals? He often eats fast food or gets pizza delivered; there are no recipe books in his kitchen. He sometimes heats pasta sauce from a jar, he can fry an egg, and he has the toaster set to exactly the right degree of brown.

Now, most guys are more like Jake than Jilene. So when a guy marries, he's opting into a situation where if he does half the work, he'll have *more* work than before. The first shock: he'll find a whole lot of cleaning goin' on that didn't exist in his former life. As in laundry. There isn't twice as much laundry; there's five times as much (because a woman has more clothes that require a greater variety of treatment). Same for food: there isn't twice as much meal-related work as he had before; it's a higher factor. In every area of homemaking, his 50 percent share of what now needs doing is greater than 100 percent of what he used to do. The so-called economies of scale don't have the expected effect here. Then add children in; they bring with them a whole boat-load of work that was completely absent before. Half of that is no small amount.

Someone might interject here, *Wait a minute, aren't you promoting the very stereotype that you claim to oppose? Aren't you saying that women are more into homemaking than men?* Well, yes and no. There are two different questions here:

1. When a man and woman live together, should the woman do more work?
2. Do women have higher ideals than men when it comes to what a home should be like?

We're saying no to question 1. No surprise: that stereotype, we reject.

Question 2 is trickier. It seems clear that a woman living alone usually achieves a higher level of homemaking than a man alone. Her sense of what a home should be, what sort of environment can bring her joy and satisfy her nesting dream, seems to be cleaner, nicer, and more beautiful. We don't know whether this is the result of cultural indoctrination or whether it's hardwired. In any case, one can say women in our culture want a nicer home without committing the sexist mistake of saying women should do more of the work. If a guy wants to live with a female, maybe he has to buy into her standards. And maybe part of the reason many men want to be married is that they actually crave the kind of home that will bring. So maybe men's standards aren't so different in the end.

In any case, the dude who thinks he can ease off on the throttle, enjoying a cushy deal now that he has a new woman in his life, is sadly mistaken *if he means to do his fair share*. To get married is actually to sign a contract to work harder, not to slack off and take it easy.

"Real Men Don't Do Housework"

At this point, the hard-pressed male is running out of options. But never fear: there are still traditionalist women who have his back, and they have one more card to turn over, a very pesky wild card. It builds on the notion that men shouldn't do women's work, but it takes it a step further by predicting dire sexual consequences for those who try it. In that way it directly challenges what we're saying in this book, which is that men *not* doing enough housework puts a damper on sex.

Here's what these wives say: "I don't want to turn him into a woman. Then he *really* wouldn't be sexy." The idea here is that there are two types of men:

- men who are sexy, virile dudes
- men who are good at "woman's work"

And you can't have both. So when a woman chooses a husband, she has to decide which she wants. The price of having a manly man is having to do the homemaking yourself. And the last thing you'd want to do is turn Mr. Testosterone into a wuss.

We have two answers to this gambit.

First, it's just another way of coughing up the same old stereotype that doesn't make sense anymore.

Second, recent scientific research has shown that this fear is unfounded. Women who see their husbands pitching in at home and even learning some new skills actually find their men sexier. According to several new studies, when a man learns to cook or clean better, takes over more household responsibilities, or becomes more involved in child rearing, his wife gets a warm fuzzy feeling that includes sexual attraction.[1] That is because he is actually *giving* something in a currency that she values. He is making an effort. And that can bring the passion back in a hurry. Because it shows real love. And partnership. And those things are *romantic and sexy*.

It may not seem obvious that a guy's housekeeping could lead to a rekindling of the sexual fire, but it does. Things that don't seem romantic or sexy at first blush can actually lead to a woman who wants to pleasure her man. The reason for this is monumentally simple. We saw in part 1 how your healthy (equal, caring, respectful, sexy) relationship has been wounded by your feeling like his mom. So it stands to reason that anything he does that makes you *not* feel like his mom is going to help you get the good stuff back—including the sensuality. When he "mans up" and takes on his fair share of the domestic load (whether it's cold-cold or warm-cold), you stop feeling like his mother. That leaves you free to feel like his wife, his friend, his lover. . . .

What could be more manly than a guy who takes initiative, who steps up and does what needs doing, and makes your life easier, and wants to be on the same team as you? A guy who lies around expecting to be waited on is not *adult,* and one of the conditions of being manly is being adult.

There is a kind of sacred membrane around the area of "women's work," a barrier that many people still think a man should not penetrate. In this chapter we've had a first look at where it comes from, and we've tried to undermine some of its supports. But really we've just begun to see what we're up against. The same deep root sprouts up in many different forms, and the upcoming chapters will tackle them one by one. We'll turn next to the man on the pedestal.

Chapter 7

"He Needs Me to Cater to Him"

This is a promising excuse for becoming a guy's mom. At first blush, it sounds like it's all about giving. A person has needs, you fill them: what could possibly be bad about that?

Variations on the theme:

- Mimi says, "Fred heads out of the door by 8:00 a.m. and has a full day dealing with customer complaints. He barely has time to take a pee. By the time the poor guy gets home, he's totally tired. He needs to relax and watch some tube."
- Gabi says, "When I took my marriage vows and said 'I do,' I really meant it. I do want to make sure that my man is well taken care of. So what if I'm doing all the work? I do it because I love him."
- Helena says, "I watched my mom taking care of my dad and saw how content they were with one another as the years went by. Even though I felt that she sometimes sacrificed her own needs,

> I understood why. She wanted to make him happy. When he was happy, she was too. I want to make Fabio happy, no matter what it takes."

This is the all-too-familiar situation in which the male is put on a pedestal, and love becomes a service industry, dedicated to making his life easier.

But it raises a few questions. If his needs rank so high, what happened to yours? If you're both working day jobs, why is he the one who gets to be "too tired"? Why should giving be a one-way street? This explanation doesn't honor you and, truth be told, it doesn't honor him. Because it paints him as a guy who exploits his partner for his own ease.

Of course, that won't stop some men from taking a ride on the Pampered Prince bus, if they sense that you'll drive. So when a wife offers this excuse, her mate is likely to agree. It's hard to resist a vacation from effort, if it is offered. A guy can get used to it, can then get to expect and even insist on it. Spoiled children are the most demanding, after all.

Three Roads to Good-bye

But eventually the ride takes a turn for the worse. When one person is doing all the giving and the other is doing all the taking, one of three scenarios is likely to play out.

Scenario One: Complacent Cal

Cal and Penny have been married for ten years. Every day at exactly noon, Penny calls Cal at the office to ask how his day has been. She asks that he call her when he leaves the office so that she can time her casserole to perfection. When he arrives home and walks into the kitchen, he expects to see the table laid, as always. She suggests that he "wash up" and come to dinner. Once he's seated, Penny places the napkin on Cal's lap, serves the food onto his plate, and waits for him to taste it before serving herself. If it's too bland, she adds salt. If he needs something to drink, she'll pour his first. If there's only a small amount of juice left, it's his. Penny anticipates Cal's needs and desires even before her own.

Complacent Cal lives in a predictable place. He knows what to expect and what is expected of him. His world is neat and organized. Cal can do nothing wrong in Penny's eyes. If he shows disappointment in her for overcooking the meat, she apologizes and offers to make him something else. When he complains about the lumps in his strawberry jam, Penny uses the strainer to make sure the lumps are all gone the next time.

Then one evening, Cal and Penny are at another couple's place for dinner. Also invited is a newly divorced friend they haven't met before, named Sally. She is an entrepreneur with lively stories. Cal is thinking how crazy Sally's husband must have been to leave her. He finds her interesting and exciting. In the next few days, he can't stop thinking about her. He finds a way to get her phone number from their friends and arranges a social get-together in the guise of a business meeting.

At the "meeting" Sally quickly takes Cal out of his comfort zone. When he goes ahead and orders some wine, she says, "Weren't you going to check with me as to what I like?" He apologizes, feeling jerked to attention for the first time in years, and asks her if she would like red or white.

"That's it?" Sally says. "It depends on what kind of red, what kind of white, and what entrees we're both ordering. How much do you know about wine, anyway?"

Cal recites something he heard about chardonnays being oaky. It quickly emerges that Sally has gone a bit deeper into wine country than he has, and to be sure she'll like what she gets, he asks her to order. When the cabernet franc comes, she tastes it and gives the green light, and the waiter pours them both a glass. Cal says it's nice and Sally replies, "Is that the best that you can do?" Cal gives her a more elaborate tribute to the wine and she leans over and touches his hand, giving him an instant erection.

The meal proceeds like this, with Cal working hard to show Sally what he's made of. By the end of it he is enthralled and in an advanced state of lust.

So that's scenario one. Man comes to take Woman for granted, gets bored, and feels like she isn't an exciting challenge anymore. How could she be, when he doesn't have to lift a finger to earn her approval, while she does so much for him? In a chilling phrase, she's "too easy." Then he meets Other Woman—someone who jolts him into full consciousness and expects him to dance in the rain and do cartwheels to show how much he admires her. He is smitten, and before long, he moves on.

Scenario Two: Guilty Gus

Gus and Gloria have been married for eight years. Near the end of their phone calls, Gloria always says "I love you." With a slight hint of satire, Gus says, "I love you too. Gotta go." Little do they know that this exchange is a prediction of what is going to happen in their life.

Even though they both have day jobs—she works at a library and he's in the police force—they both assume that she will take care of the home and kids, because a cop's life is hard. (The fact that Gus has a desk job in IT doesn't seem to lessen this fact.) They met when they were both in their thirties, both having given up on love, and Gloria is never going to forget to be grateful for their good fortune.

Like Penny in our previous tale, Gloria does everything for Gus, including his share of the child rearing. As the years have gone by, she has aged more than he has and has developed that gaunt, slightly haunted look that many overworked wives have. Still, she is always cheerful, even solicitous, with him, and incredibly, it seems that for her the romance is still alive. On the rare occasions when Gus remembers to thank her or praise her, she positively glows, and she still wears sexy nightgowns for him, but they don't quite mesh with the worn patina she presents. A dream is still alive in this household, and Gus is sometimes painfully aware that it abides in her soul, not his.

On Valentine's Day, Gloria sends flowers to Gus at the police station, and his buddies rib him about it. They ask him if he got anything for her, and he admits that he spaced out and totally forgot. He vows to pick up a card at the supermarket on the way home. But his real reaction is a gritting of the teeth, a wish that she wouldn't hit him with these gestures of adoration and would just let him be. It grates on him, makes him too aware that he doesn't feel what he should for Gloria, doesn't feel what she dreams that he feels.

The same thing happens on his birthday: she hires a sitter for the kids and takes him to a fancy steak house, where she's arranged for a cake and for the servers to sing "Happy Birthday." Her birthday gets shorter shrift; it always seems to come when he is jammed up at work, and he always says they'll plan something down the line. When he does this to her, he feels a grim shot of remorse moving through him, combined with a strange annoyance that he can't explain.

How can he be angry at a saint?

Yes, the problem for Gus is that he has a conscience. Too much good treatment for too long a time can be tough on a good man. One day after her uncelebrated birthday, he opens his eyes in bed and sees her by the mirror, arranging her thin blond hair and being ever so quiet so as not to disturb him. Something cracks within him and he knows with awful certainty that he is unworthy. He doesn't deserve this abject generosity, doesn't deserve to be waited on and adored. It makes him terminally nervous. He feels like a heel. "She loves me too much," he thinks. "I can't catch up; I can't make myself feel what she feels. I don't love her, and she deserves someone who does."

Guilty Gus is being a little shallow in his analysis here. The truth is that all the pain and remorse he feels, and the gnawing pity for how hard she works and how worn she looks, springs from his heart. He does love her. But he makes a common mistake: he confuses *not loving someone enough* with *not loving them at all.* Still, Gus vows on this morning that he must have relief from this situation.

It never occurs to him to go all out and surprise Gloria with an amazing belated tribute to her birthday—to outdo her in the "thoughtful" department for a change. Because he thinks that would be insincere. He is stuck with the inadequate love that is all he can muster, and there's no point in faking something more. So he doesn't find out what would happen if he invested a whole lot more energy in pleasing and serving his wife, how that might restore her confidence, put a spring in her step, and even make her more valuable in his eyes. If he took the trouble to make her important, she would *become* important to him.

It also doesn't occur to Gus that maybe the saintly Gloria has cast a net of emotional debt over him as a way of keeping him in line, and that she, perhaps unconsciously, finds regular ways to press his buttons of gratitude and guilt. Could his Mother Teresa have her own sneaky way of asserting power? (We'll return to this idea in the next section.)

No, Gus is only aware of the cold, empty, mean way he feels about himself in relation to Gloria. He can't go on feeling like this much of a cad. So he begins to plot his exit, and one day he is gone.

Scenario Three: Rebel Rita

Rita was a full-service wife too, but she had inexhaustible energy and high spirits and never lost her ability to engage with the world and have fun with her eclectic circle of friends and her husband, Clay, while raising their two kids and doing pretty well in real estate. She simply was Supermom.

Clay was a good-time guy who did remember his wife's birthday and on suitable occasions would arrange a gala party for her. He was also lazy and hardly lifted a finger around the house, but he had zero talent for guilt, and this helped things stay on an even keel. He was very clever at the smelter engineering he had learned on the job, brought home a good wage, and when he reposed like a smug cat at home, he still had a kind of virile quality. Rita teased him about his indolence, but he only seemed to bask in the rays of her mock anger. After thirteen years of marriage, they had also not lost their spark in bed, because they were both highly sexed and were exactly each other's "types."

So what could go wrong?

What could go wrong is that Rita got Lyme disease. It was

probably caught during a jaunt in the woods with her eldest daughter, but it wasn't nipped in the bud, and it led to a debilitating and drawn-out bout of something resembling chronic fatigue syndrome. The indomitable Rita was for the first time laid low, and it was during that period that she began to see Clay in a new way.

He didn't know it but this was his big test—his final exam for husbandhood. And he failed it, because it turned out that he really was lazy and self-indulgent, and he let the house and the kids slip out of kilter and actually complained that Rita wasn't pulling her weight—as if anything besides real disease could stop that dynamic life force. Rita's friends, male and female, came over to help, and Clay was sometimes testy when they didn't do things the way he was used to. As she lay weakened in bed or struggled to wipe a sink or make toast, Rita saw their past in a new way. She saw that she'd been taken for granted and that unselfish love had never been part of Clay's repertoire.

He morphed, in her eyes, into what he had always been—a spoiled brat. A child exploiting her, taking advantage of her largesse, surfing on the wave he had luckily found.

So Rita made herself a promise that she would leave this unworthy guy, if she ever got her energy back, and find someone who would bring to her the same kind of love that she was so capable of giving. She found a new doctor who tried a new treatment and put her on a strict dietary regimen, and in six months she crawled out of the hole and began to be Rita again. Clay was overjoyed to see her return, but she knew his relief was for the wrong reasons. He had even complained that she'd lost her sexual oomph while sick. He could see it was back now but was surprised to find it wasn't going to visit him anymore.

Rita found a cool condo—it wasn't hard, since she was a real estate agent—and took the kids. She let him have the house, which he ended up selling two years later. His real estate agent was his ex-wife.

Rita's case is an extreme one, where an epiphany arises out of a major illness that suddenly opens a woman's eyes, but there are much more mundane ways that a wife can reach the same conclusion. In most cases the problem isn't masked; it just unfolds and unfurls until it becomes untenable. In part 1 we explored how this can happen, how a wife can get tired of being exploited, sick of unreciprocated effort that is literally thankless. So she starts to see her husband as an unworthy child, develops anger and resentment, and finds ways to punish him; or she just loses patience and moves on.

The only way to avoid one of these three scenarios is for both of you to stop the bus and get off. That's what we'll help you to do in part 3.

The Darker Motive

But we haven't gotten to the bottom of this excuse yet. It has a darker layer, a more desperate motive that came out when we asked women about it. Instead of just saying, "He needs me to cater to him," some went on to add, "and besides, I'll lose him if I stop taking care of him." Here is how Trisha revealed the backstory behind this fear:

Tisha's story

> Sure, I resent Ron sometimes, and our sex life is kind of scarce, but if I don't give him a comfortable home life, I worry

that there'll be nothing else to hold him. I mean, we aren't as affectionate as we used to be—let alone romantic. When we were dating, we used to love spending time together, we had great talks—and we were hot in bed! So there was plenty to keep him hooked on me. But now it isn't like that. So I've found other ways to keep him attached. I make his meals, I keep his world spotless, I schedule everything and take care of the kids, and that means he needs me. It isn't his fault; I chose it.

I worry about losing him. There are very attractive single women where he works, and Ron is a good-looking guy. I'm not as svelte as I was. And he sometimes seems bored with our routine. When I hooked up with him, he was separated from his first wife, and the things he told me about her come back to me now—how she wasn't his soul mate, wasn't really his type—and I worry that he could say the same things about me to someone else.

I think back to how hard it was to find a guy, hard to meet people. It was just a fluke that I met Ron. I don't want to go through that again. And I don't want to be alone.

Why Insecurity Doesn't Win

You don't have to be a psychologist to see that this rationale is based on insecurity. Trisha doesn't really think she merits a good partner and doesn't think she could find one if she had to go looking again. So she's let herself slip into a *settling* stance. Settling usually means choosing a guy who isn't everything you want because you can't get the one who is. So it's about comparing one guy to others. But it can also happen within one relationship, when you accept less than your spouse *could* give because you believe you can't get anything better from him. You lower your expectations of someone just to avoid the awful fate of losing him.

But that means that the sacrifice you're making isn't going to work anyway. It won't keep you from losing him, because you've already lost him. That horse has left the barn, because you don't have the kind of relationship with him that you wanted to have. The romance has drained away; you feel alone in your many responsibilities, and your bridge to him is fear, not love.

In our example, Trisha is trying to *earn* Ron's love because she doesn't feel he would give it freely. Why? Because she isn't worth it. Clearly Trisha has some cracks in her self-esteem, and it just may be that Ron has found ways to open those cracks a little wider, so he can have more power over her. So maybe he casually mentions these good-looking women who hover at his place of employment. And maybe he teases her about having gained a little weight, and that's supposed to be okay even though he has gained more pounds than she has during their seven years of marriage.

Now, Ron shouldn't be acting like that. But Trisha's way of dealing with the problem has made it worse. By trying to make Ron dependent on her services—to "keep him attached," as she says—she has shifted the terms of their relationship to a Faustian bargain: *If I let you exploit me, will you stay?*

She may not have come out and said this to Ron, but in her mind it's a done deal, and that means she is now defining her man in very unworthy terms. Because any guy who would consciously agree to this logic isn't worth having. Any guy who would say, "That's right, if she doesn't continue to do all the heavy lifting, I'll walk," is an unworthy individual who doesn't care about her.

Her fear of losing him makes our first two scenarios even more likely: he gets bored with such an undemanding love and moves on, or he gets guilty and leaves. The third scenario is also possible, though it might take more time: she gets disgusted with him (and herself) and ends it.

But it doesn't have to be that way. If you and your spouse are in a situation like this, you can still spring the trap. Lots of people have insecurities, but that doesn't mean you have to give in to them. Power shifts happen between two people, but they aren't always deliberate or evil. A Trisha can be braver; a Ron may have a lot more to give; and love waits to grow again when the weeds are pulled. The servant-mom can gird up her pride and stop being a servant-mom; and when she does, that will often knock the pampered male off his pedestal and wake him up in ways you might not expect.

The takeaway here: fear of losing someone is not a good reason to replace a healthy relationship with a dysfunctional one. Fear has to be dealt with directly, not deflected into a set of misbegotten behaviors that become more and more entrenched.

In part 3 we'll talk about how to face this fear and how to show it the door along with the mothering habits it seemed to justify.

Chapter 8

"It Won't Get Done If You Wait for a Man to Do It"

Ah, men. They just don't seem to be up to this housework stuff.

You can't get your guy to do it, and when you try, you're perceived as a nag, so then you go ahead and *become* a nag (might as well, since you're being accused of it). And that gives him an excuse to ignore you: who wants to obey a nag?

And who wants to *be* one? Not you. You didn't sign up to be a cross between a drill sergeant and a party pooper. Even if he grudgingly does what you ask, where's the joy? As one woman put it, "I never wanted to have to tell him what to do. The whole idea is I want him to volunteer. I want him to be my partner, like we're on the same team . . . I mean, if it's coming from me, then even if he does it, it's really *me* doing it by making him do it."

So you do the work yourself.

But why is any of this necessary? Why don't men roll up their sleeves and dive into the joys of housework? We're through with noble answers that spouses often agree on—role models and men on pedestals. Let the blame game begin! In this chapter we'll look at three accusations that women level at the hairier sex.

1. Men are just naturally lazy. Like boys.
2. Men can't see what needs doing anyway. Because they're just naturally messy.
3. Men are always focused on their own agenda. They aren't team players.

These are not kind words. But hang in there: when women are asked to back them up, they say some pretty interesting things.

For example, when women speak about men being lazy like boys, what they mean is that a man makes way too rigid (and childish) a distinction between work and play. Work is what he does when he has to, like at his job, and play is what he does the rest of the time. When a guy gets "home from work," the last thing he wants is *more work.*

Work bad, play good.

Maybe the concept goes back to boyhood, when he had to get school out of the way so he could have something called . . . fun. But at least fun meant *activity,* running and pedaling and throwing, or at least dynamic engagement in a video playground. For older guys, on the other hand, playtime seems to mean steering clear of any real effort in favor of watching a screen, drinking a beer, lounging around.

Whereas women can't seem to stop doing.

As one guy put it, "I observe her during her so-called leisure time, and she's hunched over her computer editing photos, or she's organizing drawers, or she's labeling her homemade spices. Her idea of taking a break from work seems to be doing some *other* kind of work."

Even when women choose an activity that men would accept as relaxing, they often simultaneously do a little work—like folding laundry while watching TV. As we saw in chapter 4, researchers have actually found a way to count this "secondary" labor as part of the total hours worked, and it makes a difference.

Not so for the brave members of the male sex. For them life is a study in contrasts: a dude forces himself to toil all day because he isn't rich and needs a paycheck, and then, to make it all bearable, he slides into reward time. That's when he is totally passive and he consumes things—mainly food, drink, and entertainment. If he didn't have this solace waiting for him, life would be unbearable.

Much To-Do about Nothing

It isn't too surprising that this philosophy reads as laziness to women. But that's just the tip of the iceberg. Here's one woman's theory about the nefarious secret of a man's to-do list.

Angela's story

> A man's to-do list isn't like a woman's. My list is written out or typed, on paper or on a screen, and it works in a wonderfully simple way: *it reminds me of tasks so I can* do *them.*
>
> But here's what I realized one day in a lightbulb moment. My husband Dan's to-do list, which he keeps in his head mostly so I can't critique it, has a whole different mission. It is to *save* him from doing things!
>
> Here's how the system works. Somewhere in the male brain, an operating principle is hardwired. It says *a man must not start*

work on any item on his to-do list until he has completed all the items above it. What this means is, my Daniel can't begin to work on any of the other things he should do until he's finished the top one. (No multitasking for him!) So all he has to do is make sure item one is *impossible,* and he's home free (literally: home, free). That step is made easier by a second rule that lurks somewhere in his brain porridge: *I shall not start on something unless I can complete it during the same session.* It wouldn't do to get partway and have to continue some other time! He might never finish! That would be way too chancy. So he needs a *big chunk of continuous open time*—not easy to find for our busy guy. But wait, there's more. *A real man won't tackle a task if he isn't at his very best.* He must be capable of bringing it off in fine style.

Take last Saturday afternoon. There were a whole bunch of chores that needed doing. The kitchen was a mess, dirty dishes overflowing the sink. The garage needed cleaning out: we couldn't even fit the car in it anymore. And the windows needed washing.

So my brave warrior sits on his couch and surveys these possibilities. . . .

Problem one. The top thing on his to-do list is his income taxes. He got a six-month extension, but that deadline is now only two weeks away. He can't very well do less important things when something so crucial is crying out for his attention! *Problem two.* It would take him at least six hours—maybe even double that—to organize all the paperwork and fill out the forms. But the football game starts in two hours! That isn't a big enough chunk of open time. *Problem three.* He's a little tired today. He watched TV until two in the morning and didn't sleep that well. Even if it were acceptable to start something when you don't have time to finish it, you certainly don't want to start it when you aren't at your best—God forbid!

So for the most innocent reasons in the world, my tiger can't do any of the household cleaning chores that need his attention. His mind is focused on that tax job, and his noble loyalty to it (even though he can't do it right now), his refusal to mingle it with lesser tasks, stands like a mighty wall of virtue and prevents him from accessing the damn garage!

Men's Convenient Blindness

So much for laziness. What about the ancillary charges? Are men really unable to perceive what needs doing around the house?

Gina says, "It's all about men seeing what they want to see. I think if there was a dead dog on the couch and my husband wanted to watch the football game, he would move the moldering mastiff to one end and sit down at the other. He would drink his beer and watch the game and maybe even rest his bottle on the dog's furry back. No, I'm serious! He has an amazing ability to not see a problem if it would distract him from what's on his mind. So I end up being the one who removes dead dogs. And a lot of other things."

Susan adds, "It's like men have tunnel vision. I mean, there's clutter and dirt to see, for anyone who has eyes. But my man is protected against that scary knowledge by his one-track, horse-with-blinkers-on, tunnel vision. He can walk into a room strewn with toys and dishes and only see the magazine he came to find. His attention is like a flashlight beam; the rest of the room is dark! That's my cross to bear: I *see* the clutter and the mess."

But wait: men have an answer here. They are perfectly capable of seeing what is in front of them, but they *don't always think it's a problem*. This came up earlier, when we compared the housework Jake did in his one-bedroom apartment to what Jilene did in hers—when they were both still single. Jake did a lot less, presumably because he was content with a lot more clutter, dirt, dust, and lack of decoration. In other words, men have a higher threshold for when cleaning (and froufrouing) needs to be done.

J.M. had a friend once—a brilliant, funny dude from New Jersey named Rob—who had a theory about bathtubs. Of course, he was a PhD student who studied relativity, so he was good with theories. Anyway, Rob said that a dirty bathtub is a sign of good hygiene. He lived with three other guys and they wanted him to take his turn scrubbing the claw-foot down the hall, but he wouldn't. Here's what he told them:

"When you take a bath, you sit in the hot water and dirt moves off you and onto the walls of the tub. That's *the purpose of bathing*. That's progress! That's good! Eventually you are clean and the tub is dirty, and as more people take baths, more and more dirt moves off humans and onto the tub, until the walls are coated with a goodly amalgam of crud. What is wrong with *that*?"

Okay, so that takes the threshold thing a bit too far. Even Rob knew he was being devil's advocate, saying it would be fine if you were eventually bathing in a mud slick. But in general, do men have lower standards? Are they somewhat blind to dirt? Maybe, but there's more to men's inaction than meets the eye.

"Better Not to Do It Than to Do It Wrong!"

Pete wrote us an email:

From: Pete Perfectionist

Date: Recently

To: Sara and J.M.

Subject: The Bathroom Job I *Would* Do

I am *really good* at cleaning the bathroom! I get right down to the crud on the back of the toilet (hidden behind the seat), and I know how to scrub a sink with bleach. *Tubs* are painful, because I have a bad back and a blown-out knee (from high school football) and it's really hard to get down and reach the bottom and the sides. (Actually, the whole room is hard, because everything is too low. Sinks really suck: they're too low for grown men.) So I have to bend my back a lot, but I *am* good at it.

The problem is this: it takes me at least an hour to clean the bathroom. I know, because earlier this year when my wife was coming home from a ten-day trip, I did it to surprise her and, okay, because it had become kind of disgusting.

But my wife—somehow she can go in there on a day when we're expecting guests and wave around some kind of wand and some kind of sprayer and ten minutes later she's done the whole room, even the tub. Of course, she doesn't do it as well as *I* do . . . but I'll admit, it *does* look better than before she went in.

So I don't think about cleaning the bathroom unless I have a good hour—and a good amount of energy!!—to spare. But when do I have

> that? Never! At night I have to eat dinner and watch TV; on weekends there are errands to run and yard work if I can get around to *that*. . . but my back is *brutal*.
>
> Also there's an issue of timing. Cleanness lasts a good long while—days or weeks usually. I'm not going to clean a room before its time. But when it still looks fine to me, my wife is already horrified by it. So she always gets the drop on me—I mean, it's like the Old West and she is quicker on the draw.
>
> So here's what she doesn't know, though I can't prove it: I *would* clean it—to within an inch of its life—if it got dirtier, but it never does!

There's that male to-do list again. Cleaning the bathroom is on it, but can a guy help it if somebody else gets to the job first? And why start if he doesn't have a good solid hour to spare?

And here it must be admitted, guys, that women seem to get a whole lot more done. Why?

Women don't insist on perfection if that would mean not even doing the task.

We've seen how men embrace the divine principle of perfectionism as a reason why they can't tackle a certain chore right now (or ever), because enough time isn't available to execute it perfectly. Women are willing to compromise to get the job done.

This point was nicely proven on a day when Jay and his wife were about to pick up a good friend and go to a political rally. For his own comings and goings, Jay drove a reliable six-year-old Honda, whereas the official family vehicle was a shiny, recent-model minivan, which his wife, Nicki, kept in spiffy shape. The interior of Jay's Honda resembled a dumpster with seat belts. In his defense, it's hard to dispose of things in a careful way when you're hurtling along the highway at seventy miles per hour, whether the thing you're supposed to be stowing is a McDonald's Big Mac container or a sheet of paper with directions on it that have allowed you to navigate out of the suburban maze you had to penetrate for a visit with your long-lost college buddy.

Jay never liked to take his eyes off the road because he had almost been killed by a turning truck while trying to adjust the nearly defunct heater in his car. So when he had anything to toss, a banana peel or a Kleenex or an empty water bottle or a receipt or a CD that wasn't pleasing him or a towel he had just wiped the windshield with, he simply threw it over his shoulder.

Jay had a plan for dealing with the state of his car. One day when the stars were in a rare alignment, perhaps during a visit from Halley's comet, he assured himself that he would sit in the car and go through every item in it and toss the garbage while making sure no valuable thing was not saved. Now, back to our story. The minivan was in the shop, but they'd agreed to pick up their friend Amos in twenty minutes, so something had to be done. Nicki looked at Jay, shook her head, picked up a green garbage bag, and strode out to his car. Into the bag she quickly stuffed every item that wasn't attached to the interior and some that were only bonded to a surface by dried coffee. Then she threw the puffed-up garbage bag in the trunk. It would do.

Nicki was fully capable of detailing a car interior if she was of a mind to. She was capable of perfection that Jay could only dream of. But she was also capable of cutting corners when the show had to get on the road. And here's another point.

Women are willing to start a process even if it might be interrupted.

In fact, women (especially women with children) don't have a choice but to become adept at resuming a task after interruption. Just listen to a typical moment in a mother's day:

Rosanne was stirring some muffin mix as she spoke to Louise on the phone. "So, as I was saying, Karl has been acting kind of strange. When he came home from the office yesterday, he seemed in a bad mood, but when I asked him what was happening . . . Yes, Meghan [turning to her six-year-old daughter], what do you want my help with? . . . Hold on a sec, Louise, Meghan is having a goldfish problem."

She followed her daughter into the bathroom, where a goldfish was spasming its last seconds on the floor, having leapt out of the sink that Meghan had temporarily put it in while she cleaned out its home bowl. Holding the cell phone in one hand, Rosanne picked up the fish with the other and put it back in the sink, which had four inches of water in it. Meghan said, "Thanks, Mommy," and Rosanne returned to the kitchen and put the muffins in the oven while reengaging with Louise.

"Where was I? Oh yes, about Karl. Yeah, he does get into those moods occasionally but this time is different. I wonder if it has anything to do with . . . can you hold for another second . . . I'm getting another call in and I can't identify the number . . ."

The call was Karl, using a client's phone. He asked Rosanne to go to his desk and turn on his laptop so he could access "Go to My PC" from the office.

"Sorry about that," Rosanne said to Louise. "You there? Oh, you had another call too? Well, good that I didn't make you waste any time on hold. Doesn't seem like we can ever complete a thought. *C'est la vie.* Listen, I want to finish this conversation later. I'll call you."

In other words, women aren't allergic to multitasking.

They also seem to be very willing to treat a problem as their own, even if it was created by some other resident, such as a child, a husband, or a goldfish.

That is why Joy was so unjoyous about something Chris didn't do.

Joy's story

> I've noticed something pretty weird. My husband, Chris, tries to separate *his* mess from everybody else's. He only wants to deal with the part *he* is responsible for. *It's like he's in denial of the fact that he joined a larger team!* I mean, I just wade in and do everybody's stuff. But he doesn't want any more work than he had when he was on his own. It's almost a legal argument: *anything I didn't have to do when I was single must be caused by someone else. Therefore, it is not my problem.*
>
> Reminds me of the famous *Godfather* line. "It isn't personal, Sonny. It's business." (Said by Michael when he wants to kill the policeman who roughed him up.) Sometimes I think that Chris thinks, *My dirty stuff is my business, and I take care of it. But I don't mix it with other people's personal shit, like their dirty stuff.* Give me a break, Christopher. This is *all* business!

The first time I saw this was shortly after we moved in together. One afternoon Chris came to me and said, "Honey, do you know where my laundry thing is?" He meant the white hamper in his closet, where he throws his socks, T-shirts, and skivvies when he undresses at night. At the time I was impressed that my guy took care of his own dirty underwear.

I said, "It's down in the laundry room. I took it down there this morning."

"Okay," he said, with a quizzical look that I didn't pay attention to at the time, and he disappeared down the stairs. I thought, *This guy pitches in. I got me a real catch!*

That day was hectic and we went out in the evening.

The next morning he came out of the shower, his pecs gleaming, and seemed unable to find any underwear.

"It must be in the dryer," I said. "I'll run down and get you a pair."

But he winced and shifted on one foot. "Maybe not," he said.

"You didn't do your wash yesterday?" I said.

"The washer wasn't available," he said. He avoided my eyes.

It took a second or two for the bad news to compute. "Wait a minute. You're not saying you didn't unload my wash?"

"Didn't want to touch it."

"It's still in the washer? It's still *wet*?"

"Well, not really wet. Kind of moist." He looked sheepish and slightly terrified.

I thought, *Okay, you couldn't lay a finger on* my *wash, even though I made dinner for you and your friends from work yesterday and I cleaned the bathroom you use and dusted the downstairs and the list goes on . . .*

The Defense Digs Deeper

Things are looking shaky for our male defendant. It looks as if he's going to have to admit to laziness, an unwillingness to pitch in, or a lack of initiative. He is also looking bad on the ancillary charges of not seeing what needs doing and not thinking like a team member. His excuses aren't holding up very well. "I *would* clean the bathroom, but she gets to it first" sounds like a cop-out. "If I don't have time to do it perfectly, I don't do it" sounds either obsessive-compulsive or phony.

What else you got, guys?

Well, the defense does have a couple more moves. The first one goes like this:

"A home should be a place where you can put your feet up on the coffee table and relax, not always be hounded by endless duties like arranging shoes in nice neat rows, making sure that the toilet paper rolls are stacked just right, and checking that every item of children's clothing has their name on the label. By trying to be Supermom, she makes her own life, and everybody else's, impossible."

Nice try, guys. You've managed to appeal to a principle that sounds good—the glorious beauty of relaxation. But the prosecution has an answer: all the labor and effort of homemaking *has* to be *done*. It can't just be laughed out of court. The reason many women are called supermoms is not that they needlessly invent annoying tasks, but that they recognize what things need doing and try to do them all—on top of working a full-time day job. Because if a woman doesn't take care of the tasks right away, then they will just have to be added to tomorrow's work pile and that's never a good idea. So she lives by the motto of not putting off for tomorrow what she can do today.

So it won't help a man to say home should be a place where you can relax. Or it *would* help, if he said it to his *wife*!

"Okay," the men say. "It isn't fair for one spouse to relax while the other slaves. We'll admit that. But what's wrong with *both* spouses relaxing more, and come to think of it, what about the other things we have on our plates? Because we kind of misspoke when we made this all about relaxing. Do all these housekeeping tasks really need to be done, this many and this soon and this often, to the exclusion of whatever else a guy might be thinking about?"

There's a valid point here. When a man and a woman move in together, they each bring their own priorities, concerns, needs, and, most important, *ways of looking at things.* The same room can appear functional and pleasant to Rick and horribly disordered to Rhonda. How you see things determines whether you think any remedial action needs to be taken.

Are men really so lazy? Not when they're passionate about something. Take householder Curtis, who on a Saturday is shopping for, and then building, a backyard storage unit to take care of the stuff piling up and choking the garage, which is something he cares about because no one can find anything and the garage has basically been lost for other uses. The project runs into the dusk because the instructions weren't so clear, but he keeps going and gets it done. And the next day he carries out a total reorganization of both spaces, throwing out a whole lot of junk in the process. No sloth there. A lot of diligence. Most people will appear lazy if you judge them by the tasks *you* think they should be doing, rather than the tasks *they* think they should be doing.

If you're thinking the house needs dusting, that's what's on your mind, but he may have a lot of things on his mind too, and that may not be one of them. You can't just disqualify a guy for having things on his mind. He wasn't born with your thoughts in his head. He has to *learn* what things concern you, because he's a different person. To just *expect* your man to share your own knowledge and perspective isn't reasonable. It would be like him expecting you to know everything he knows, as if through osmosis.

The problem, women say, is that they do what needs to be done, even if they'd rather not. Of course Curtis isn't lazy when it comes to shopping for and assembling a backyard storage unit, because it's something that turns his crank. It would be a completely different story if he had to get up to mop the kitchen floor or organize the cupboards.

There's a big assumption lurking behind everything we've just covered: if a man disagrees with a woman's opinion of what needs doing, he's wrong. A woman's view of how the house should be kept trumps the man's. Well, that may be true, but a trump card is no good unless you play it. Which in this case means, educate him about your standards. Don't assume he's lazy; assume he sees things differently than you do, and that this could be changed if you explain how you see them.

And maybe, just maybe, be prepared to give a little ground. We said in chapter 6 that men are actually attracted to the kind of (nicer) homes that women create, but he may still disagree with some of your goals and may prioritize things differently than you do. And he may not always be wrong.

So a man may *seem* lazy, oblivious, or one-track when he is simply not driven by the same motives you are. Spouses need to *learn* each others' viewpoints, learn to understand them and be given time to assent to them or not—to decide and declare what they agree with and what they don't. It's the often-neglected process whereby they *absorb* each other's values, and it's part of what forges a true partnership. They don't walk into the relationship sharing the same agenda.

If you take the time to inform your mate about how you see your home environment—what pleases you and what bothers you, what ruins it for you—he is much more likely to take your side and fight for your causes. You don't have to approach the topic in a preachy, self-righteous, or angry way: treat it more as an amusing, somewhat exotic tour of another mind (yours). And get him to give you a tour of his. (We'll lay this plan out in a very practical way in part 3.)

Meanwhile, there's one more factor that can make a man shy away from a task. It can easily be mistaken for laziness, but it's really very different. Remember when Chris stood in the basement staring at Joy's wet wash and did nothing? He may have fallen victim to a common malady: fear of doing it wrong. That brings us to the next charge that women level against men—and it's a doozy. If not dealt with, it could cancel any progress we've made on the laziness front. That's because it says that even if men *weren't* lazy and were ready to pitch right in, it wouldn't do any good. Because men are incompetent. The next chapter is about that.

Chapter 9

"Even If He Does It, It Won't Be Done Right: Men Are Incompetent"

In the last chapter we saw husband Chris staring at wife Joy's wet laundry in the washer and doing nothing. Joy's infuriated reaction was to declare him lazy: he just couldn't bring himself to pitch in and take care of her wash, which also stopped him from doing his own. What a deadbeat.

Except we suspect Chris isn't a deadbeat. There's another factor that stops men dead in their tracks, and it may have been what made Chris balk. It plays right into the female accusation that is the subject of this chapter, so we're going to start with this common male predicament: *men are afraid of screwing up.*

Why Men Accuse Themselves of Incompetence

We turn at once to a tragic tale told by a dude. Not Chris, but a guy named Gary in a very similar situation.

Gary's story: How I Lost the Ability to Do My Own Laundry

I used to do my own laundry, before I lived with Reese. I didn't have my own machines, so I would go to the laundromat, and I was *good.* Got it all done in less than two hours, scoped out the chicks, ate a gyro sandwich. Didn't spill the tzatziki sauce on my warm towels.

Then I moved in with Reese and I made a crucial mistake. She started doing my wash along with hers, and I *didn't stop her.* All I had to do was say gently, "Hey, hon, you don't need to do that, I'm fine." Actually, that wouldn't have worked. There must be *something* I could have said. Or maybe there wasn't. She likes to do things for others. So she *mixed her world with mine.* She mixed panties with jockey shorts. That should never be. That was the beginning of me becoming "the Incompetent One."

Here's the situation now. Reese throws her clothes in with mine in the same hampers, so I can't do "the laundry" unless I do hers too ('cause after all, it wouldn't look too good if I took my stuff out and ignored hers). But hers is way too complicated. She has all these different categories that I don't understand, and different things she does after washing, and if you do the wrong thing, the article of clothing is ruined.

She comes downstairs and I'm sweating over a hot dryer and she says terrible angry things that mean something, but I don't know what.

Here are some words she has said to me that went right over my head:

"YOU PUT THIS ON A *FULL-SIZE* HANGER?"

"YOU WALKED AWAY FROM THIS AND MOWED THE LAWN? THIS IS THE DELICATE-COLD CYCLE!"

"YOU STARTED WITH *THIS* PILE? IT'S *SUNDAY NIGHT*!"

"YOU PUT *THAT* TOP IN THE *DRYER*? I GOT THAT AT *NORDSTROM*!"

Guys, can *you* understand this stuff?

But the worst thing she ever said was soon after we moved in together. It involved the word "felt." I was down in the laundry room, and I thought, I'll surprise her and do all her wash! There was a pile of clothes on the floor, and some towels. I did the towels on HOT (a woman at the laundromat taught me that), then I did the other clothes on COLD, mostly jeans and T-shirts. I put everything in the dryer.

Then I spied them. They were on a utility shelf next to the dryer, with pieces of cedar wood. They were colorful; they were sweaters.

I thought, *She won't believe it if I do these too!*

I was so right.

I put 'em in the washer, on hot because sweaters are sort of like towels, and when they were done, I slung them in the dryer on hot too.

She came down as I was pulling one pink and blue sweater out of the dryer. It seemed smaller.

She said, "Oh no."

She looked over at the utility shelf and then actually sat down on the cement floor.

She moaned. "Oh, honey." A tear rolled down her cheek.

Then her mood changed and she stood up. She made one of those utterances that perplex me. *"You went to Kmart with me!"* she screamed.

"I did?" (Wondering how that could be a no-no.)

"You watched me buy that drying rack! The one right over there. I told you my plan!"

"You did?"

"You don't listen." She yanked the sweater out of my hand, then reached and took another from the dryer. "*Look* at these! They're my beautiful Shetland wool sweaters that my parents brought me from Scotland. *Look* at them! Do you see what size they are? They're like baby clothes now! And they've felted. They've *felted.*"

"Honey, I didn't know," I said. And it was true. I had no idea what felting was, but it couldn't be good.

"I set them aside," she said. "I told you I was going to handwash them. In that tub. See that tub?" She started to cry again. She was wracked with grief and rage.

I felt like a five-year-old. I wanted to die.

And I tried to learn. But there is no consistency, none at all. Some things she hangs up (and for some it matters *how* they're hung up, for others it doesn't); some she dries for twenty seconds and then hangs up; some she dries for longer times and pulls out at the right moment. Then she has a special way of folding each item; some are okay wrinkled because she knows she's gonna iron them, but some it's a *disaster* if they're allowed to wrinkle! Am I gonna touch any of that? No way!

So now I don't do *anybody's* laundry, not even my own. And sometimes she says to me, "Honey, couldn't you at least empty the washer and put in the next load?" And I think to myself, *Yeah, sure I could, if I wanted to risk death and dismemberment.*

She even folds my underwear and when I find it that way in

> the drawer, with the socks all nicely matched and paired, I am touched and horribly guilty, but what can I do about it?
>
> I used to be a guy who could at least do his own laundry.

We authors sympathize with Gary (at least one of us does). He had the best intentions in the world. He isn't lazy; he wanted to help. But he has learned the consequences of getting in over his head.

Thus men, refusing to admit to laziness, plead inability. But that's an even deeper hole than laziness, in the eyes of *both* sexes. Laziness you might overcome, by rolling up your sleeves and giving a damn. But incompetence? It provides a very powerful, unchangeable reason why a wife has to be a mother to her husband. So by copping to it, guys are helping to entrench the status quo.

It's the "We just can't do this kinda work! Poor us! So quit givin' us a hard time!" defense.

Also offered by Melvin, who had this to say about dusting:

Melvin's story

> How do you dust? I tried to dust the living room once. I'd never realized how much bric-a-brac we had everywhere . . . photos and statues and rocks and boxes with precious things in them and a ceramic shoe. And a lot of books. I brought a cloth with me. But I didn't know what to do with it. I mean, obviously you're not going to pick each thing up and individually wipe it all over. Are you? That would take forever.
>
> The weird thing is, I think I've sometimes been in the room while a woman was dusting. It may have been my mother or a cleaning lady or my main squeeze, but I was there. So I should know how it's done.

It seems to me my mom used to go around the room with some kind of polish or wax, like a furniture polish. Was it called Pride? Or was it Pledge? She would have this nasty-looking thick cloth wadded in her hand and it had a big dark stain on it from rubbing things, and I would almost swear she used it on everything in the room—I think she dusted with it. But that makes no sense to me. Why would you use a furniture polish on a book? I must be wrong.

The other thing is, whenever I have tried to dust, I found that I was just knocking all the dust into the air, where it could just settle again onto the objects. So I went around with a canister vacuum using the little round brush attachment, and tried to *pull* the dust off the knickknacks. That didn't work very well either. I broke Beethoven's nose.

Why Women Believe That Men Are Incompetent

Melvin is willing to admit he has a problem. Some guys aren't. But never fear: if men resist the accusation, women are ready to ram it home. The wives we've talked to are eager to document the ineptness of their husbands in all its glory. When a guy tries to "help," they say, he just makes things worse.

So why, according to women, are men incapable of "doing it right"? What are their underlying cognitive flaws?

According to women, there are two.

1. Men are not detail-oriented. They can't handle anything complicated. They don't notice the little details and niceties that are crucial to doing a job right. Take laundry, as we just did. A man can't master it. Better to keep him away from it.

2. Men lack the requisite skill sets. They simply *don't* know how to clean or dust, make a bed or pack a suitcase. Or how to prepare a tasty, nutritious, interesting meal that you haven't already eaten this week.

These points are not mutually exclusive: mastering a skill set is partly about knowing how to handle details, and knowing they're important. Gary's shocking botch of the laundry says it all.

Or not quite. We need to hear this from the female side. Here's what Lana experienced one day.

Lana's story

This morning I switch awake like a lightbulb and hit the floor running. Even though we are only going away for two nights, I feel like I've packed for a month. With a two- and a five-year-old you never know what you're going to need. But I'm done: I've got three people's stuff bagged and zipped. My husband, Ty, on the other hand, has just eaten a leisurely breakfast and is on the phone to a colleague. He can't understand what I'm so stressed out about. I've told him I'm not going to pack for him, but at this point I'm willing to finish the task if he has at least *chosen* the clothes and sundries he needs for the trip.

Looking around the bedroom, I see that Ty has in fact thrown a few items over a chair, but he's left out a pair of shoes that I'm sure he'd want to wear, any kind of dressy outfit, and his favorite pajama-substitute sweatshirt, which is hanging over the doorknob, and he hasn't gone near his toiletries, which are scattered all over the bathroom. I contemplate teaching him a lesson by just leaving all these items behind, but I don't want

> to be that evil. He has told me in the past that he finds packing traumatic and confusing, and it crosses my mind that he *simply doesn't know how to do it.* Since his wardrobe choices are already so random in daily life, the concept of *predicting* what he'll want to wear on a future day in a novel situation is way too obscure. He also is not good at stowing things in such a way that they will stay in place and not tend to open and spill, so toiletries are a major challenge, always. Finally I give in and plan his next two days for him.

We might ask in passing, *Why does Lana give in?* It's partly to protect herself. She goes ahead and finishes the job for Ty because she knows she would be more miserable on their trip if he were unhappily searching for things he needed, or if he couldn't sport a nice shirt and pants for dinner. After all, she can't make wardrobe suggestions if she hasn't packed the items she wants him to wear.

Habit can also play a big role here, allowing the assumption of male incompetence to become more and more entrenched. Lana's intercession becomes a crutch that makes Ty weaker. She has trained him not to really worry, because he knows that she has his back and that the details he doesn't admit he cares about will magically be taken care of. He is sure that she will tie up the loose ends, cross every *t* and dot every *i*—because she is so very skilled at that. And the more he counts on her, the harder it is for her to cut him loose.

That's the tale of a woman whose belief in her husband's ineptitude becomes self-perpetuating, so he can't even manage his own life. Now let's look at a wife who starts off being more optimistic and bravely seeks her husband's help with an ordinary parental task.

Teena's story

Last week I asked my husband, Ryan, if he could give me a hand by organizing the kids' schoolwork—the pieces I've saved for them to look back at some day when they are adults. The stack had been accumulating in my study for eons, till I moved it recently to the rocking chair so I'd remember to work on it. (I guess Ryan never saw it because he never *needed* the rocking chair.) I love organizing, but it is very time-consuming and hours are exactly what I'm short on. So this was one moment when I felt willing to sacrifice that pleasure. The job would get done, and hey, maybe my husband would actually notice some of the creations our amazing children have brought home!

He picked up the pile of loose papers and disappeared into the dining room.

Twenty minutes later, he reported to me with a smile. He was done.

I couldn't believe it. I figured it would take me at least a couple of hours to sort through all that stuff. Could it be that I'd just discovered a major talent in him? Unnoticed by me, he has a genius for rapidly sorting documents into categories? With hope in my soul, I sat down at the dining table and examined what he'd done.

What was this? Most of our older daughter's work was in our younger daughter's stack and the papers were not even separated by subject or year. Then I saw the Post-it next to each pile and realized what he had done. They read "good" and "not so good." Great, he's rejected half of the collection!

It was *all* good stuff, brainiac—that's why I saved it! I gritted my teeth and tried to remember the rules of Encouragement 101, but I'm like, *This has just made the task harder!* Inside I am starting to seethe. But I say, "Thanks for your help." He looks at me a little curiously, like a child who suspects that an adult is being insincere. But then he grins and heads for the fridge to get a beer.

Are Guys Really So Helpless?

Okay, we've given male incompetence a run for its money, and we've seen both sexes buy into it as an excuse. But now it's time to step back and look at this skeptically.

Take detail orientation. Is it true that men are lacking in this department? Are they fated to be bad at picky household tasks?

Have you ever seen a guy work on a model ship or a sports car engine? How do men do in professions that are all about details? Ever heard of a finish carpenter?

Hmm, how about brain surgery? That seems to require a pretty fine focus. Then there's astronomy, archaeology, zoology—men haven't done too badly in these fields. Guy named Darwin did okay at zoology. Sorting fossils makes sorting laundry look pretty simple.

Science is all about details; so is engineering. Put them together and you get NASA, producing vehicles that can reach outer space, support human life out there, and make it home again. Check out the movie *Apollo 13* if you haven't already: the superb true story of a crippled mooncraft trying to make it home, with the guys on the ground trying to figure out how the guys in space can cobble together an air cleaner out of the chance materials that happen to be available on the spaceship. Their grasp of details is mesmerizing.

Okay, men can handle details. So what is the problem? For a clue, let's look back at two of our stories. Gary, at the beginning, made a few attempts at laundry and was found disastrously wanting by his wife, Reese. We talked to Reese and it was clear that she does have a definite, well-worked-out system. As she told us, "I know which items have to be hung and which have to be laid flat. I know the size of hangers to use so that there aren't huge indentations in the shoulders of the kids' T-shirts. I know which pile I should begin with so the essentials are ready for the beginning of the week. Oh, and I don't start the delicate cold cycle if I'm not going to be around to take the items out of the washer right away."

And that doesn't even get into the subtle distinctions she makes with her own clothes, which Gary found so inscrutable. As he said, "Some things she hangs up (and for some it matters *how* they're hung up, for others it doesn't), some she dries for twenty seconds and then hangs up; some she dries for longer times and pulls out at the right moment. Then she has a special way of folding each item; some are okay wrinkled because she knows she's gonna iron them, but some it's a *disaster* if they're allowed to wrinkle!"

Clearly Reese has an admirable mastery of this area, but we have to ask: Was there ever a time when she sat down and explained it all to Gary? She certainly let him know when he screwed up, but did she even explain *why* those were mistakes? Is that any way to learn what is actually a complicated set of procedures? Gary, as it happens, fixes automobiles for a living. And cars keep evolving, and Gary keeps up with them. Hardly a guy who can't cope with details.

Then there was the case of Ryan the paper sorter. It emerged that Teena had definite goals for the organizing of the kids' schoolwork. She wanted it sorted by daughter, and then by year, and then by subject . . . and we wouldn't be surprised if that wasn't all. Ryan dove in and noticed that some of the work seemed truly memorable and some fell short, so he sorted it into those two categories. He thought his job was to *critique* his daughters' productions. Thing is, Reese never shared her plan with him.

A guy can't engage with the details if he doesn't know what those details are.

Beyond Incompetence

Okay, we're making some progress. If men are not so much incompetent as lacking in training, that raises a new question. Who is at fault here? What (or who) kept this priceless knowledge from filtering into these male brains?

First, men are afraid of looking stupid. We pointed this out before, as a reason why men don't do certain tasks. But it's also a reason why they don't try to *learn* how to do them. They would rather stay out of class than be branded as a doltish student, and they don't overlook the evidence of past experience, especially if it teaches that failure is, in the eyes of their instructor, very likely. The art of backing down is one that is drilled into boys from an early age. You engage in combat with another male, and if you know you're bested, you don't take that guy on again. That's how you avoid even more loss to your ego and damage to your body. And after a while you learn to size a dude up, and if you're sure you can't take him, you back away from any potential confrontation. A similar instinct for self-preservation can lead a man not to ask questions about areas where he is likely to incur his wife's scorn and anger. But this backing-off instinct is perilous, because it's very hard to reverse once it happens.

What exacerbates this problem is that women too often

assume men should magically know things they don't know. They also make the natural inference that if a guy has been exposed to something all his life, he must have noticed it. Like Kevin, in our recent story, must have noticed how dusting was done.

We heard of a man who bought his first house, in which he lived alone. That is, until he met a wonderful woman online and she elected to move in with him, since her apartment was small and he had lots of space. When she moved in, she brought along with her an alarming array of items used in cooking. The day they were unpacking her stuff, she was busy in another room while he tackled her kitchen boxes. She took a break and found him in a state of perplexity. He had unloaded a huge array of herbs and spices in little jars and bottles, and had discovered that if he lined them up in rows like toy soldiers, he could get them in the now-overflowing cupboard, but he could only get *at* the ones in the front row!

Then she saw some plastic parts lying on the table, where he had left them because he didn't know what they were. As he watched in wonder, she quickly assembled the flat disks and the little uprights, and soon there was an interesting revolving structure with two surfaces. "See, honey?" she said. "We can put this up in the cupboard and then we can put all the spices on it, and look—all we have to do is turn it and we can reach any spice!"

He was amazed, elated, euphoric. "That's incredible," he said. "I've never heard of this. What is it called?"

"It's called a lazy Susan. You've never heard that term?"

"I've heard it but I thought it was some kind of cake pan."

"Honey, your mother has, like, five of them on her kitchen shelves!"

So a woman often assumes that a guy must know the difference between dishwashing liquid and dishwasher liquid; that he must know that real bleach has a different effect on colors than OxiClean (because she has sat beside him while they watched the commercials on TV), and that milk has to be watched when you're heating it.

In fact, most humans make a pretty rash assumption that what is obvious to them must be obvious to all others. Men do this too. They do it to women and they do it to other guys. Men who know how to fix cars cannot understand how a guy could keep driving down the highway when his oil light was on, treating another quart as something to add to his to-do list. Men who understand electronics are scandalized when another man (or a woman) plugs in a computer without using a surge protector. People are constantly amazed (and incensed) by the disastrous mishaps of others that were caused by not knowing an "obvious" fact.

But we are talking about the domestic realm, and the esoteric lore that would avoid so much mischief if it were only passed on is often securely locked in the heads of women. Another factor that keeps men from learning household skills is this: both sexes are influenced by the stereotypes we looked at in chapter 6, so they tend to *expect* male incompetence at "women's work." When you don't think you have an apt pupil, you are likely to do a half-assed job of instructing him or not try at all. But lack of skill is not a proof of inability to learn. It's just an opportunity for a teacher to draw the wrong conclusion and cop out on her job. That's why so many mothers are so good at teaching their daughters the skills of the household: they already believe in advance that their daughters are going to have an aptitude for the work. The belief that it's inevitable, and even adorable, that a son won't be good at this stuff pretty much seals his fate.

Of course, there's another trusty obstacle to learning, and that is the belief on the *student's* part that he won't be any good at this. The stereotype of "women's work" also wreaks its sneaky magic in men's brains, so they become programmed to be dense in this area, and even to resist it on grounds of male dignity.

How Women Gatekeep on the Domestic Front

Having heard all this, some women would boil things down to a simpler explanation. The reason men are so blissfully free of the domestic skills they need is short and sweet: "They avoid learning how to do things, because then they'd have to do them."

This really amounts to a rerun of the laziness charge, and this time it elicits a stinging response from the male side. "She doesn't really desire my help, as proven by what happens when I actually pitch in. Instead of explaining what she wants, she just jumps all over me for doing it wrong. I am programmed to fail the test. So naturally I stop trying, kind of like a high school kid who drops out because he's discouraged by his lousy grades."

Or in more incendiary words, "She's an obsessive-compulsive control freak. I *have* to give in and let her do everything. Because she wants it done exactly 'right,' which means *her* way."

Interestingly, this accusation by men is taken seriously in the academic research. So much so that sociologists have a name for the way women sabotage men's attempts to engage with the very jobs that men are accused of shirking. It's called "gatekeeping." Many husbands who want to do more at home are faced with wives who won't let them in. Scholars list a number of ploys that women use to program men for failure, as a way to keep them at a distance. Examples include setting too-high standards, accusing men of incompetence, and redoing a task after the man has done it. We discuss all of them in these pages, as well as the gambit of not offering any effective training.

Sociologists are puzzled by this illogical behavior. If a woman is lucky enough to have a guy who wants to do more at home, why *would* she try to keep him from participating, when common sense (and economic theory) says this would lighten her burden? Scholars give several explanations.[1] One is that many women are unable to get enough validation and power at their day jobs, where they often make less money than men and are considered less reliable because they have (or may have) children. So they compensate at home by taking over and maintaining control. Another explanation is our old friend from chapter 6—women tying their identity to a certain definition of a good wife/mother. Sociologists call this "doing gender." A woman judges herself, and feels judged by other women, according to how sparkling her house is and whether her kids' outfits are trendy, appear uncreased, and actually match. And it's not just about fear of looking bad in the eyes of one's peers. A person's ego is tied up in a positive way with her or his gender identity. So a wife may assert her womanliness by not letting a man encroach on her domain, just as a husband may cling to the manliness of not doing housework.

We think there's truth in both these theories, but there's a simpler explanation that leads to a more hopeful prognosis.

Rod's story

My wife, Kirstin, got a hotel management job. For her first six months, during the tourist season, she had to work really long hours, leaving at 9:00 a.m. and getting home at 8:00. I was working part-time (while looking for something more) and I just kind of took over a lot of the housework: I did all the food shopping, meal making, and cleanup. It took me a while to get up to speed, but pretty soon I knew which supermarket had which bargains and I was making great meals and giving her lunches to take with her to work. She would come home exhausted and find a nice supper waiting for her in a clean kitchen.

Then the off-season came and her hours went back to normal, in fact less than eight hours a day. And a weird thing happened. I found myself shooing her away from anything she tried to do in the kitchen. I didn't like the way she did the dishes: she used too much detergent. One day she was boiling water for coffee and I saw her take the half-and-half out. I was frowning at it, about to suggest that she leave it in the fridge until the coffee was ready (to increase its shelf life), when she put a defensive hand on it and I backed off. Then one evening I came home with all the ingredients for a salad. We were both ravenous and I could tell she wanted to speed things up. She put some almonds in the toaster oven and turned it on. This wasn't okay, wasn't the way I liked to do it. I pulled the almonds out.

She said, "What are you doing?"

I said, "I like to preheat it first so the nuts don't get burned."

"Well, I like to give them that toasty edge. But fine." She left the room.

I had peppers, a tomato, and an avocado waiting on the island to be cut up, but I was busy washing romaine. She came in and said, "I know there are rules, so I guess there isn't anything I can help you with. I might not do it right."

> That's when I realized I had become a kitchen dictator, and I hadn't been subtle about it. I felt like a jerk. I said, "No, there are no rules, please go to town on those vegetable and let's get this thing done."

So there you have it: a husband putting up the same kind of roadblocks that wives often do. That suggests that maybe gatekeeping isn't so much about gender. Perhaps the motive is more ordinary and human: the lust to defend one's territory. When you do most of the work, you get invested in your own modus operandi—whether you're a man or a woman. You figure out the best method of accomplishing each task, you create an order that works for you, and you don't want it tampered with. We all get attached to our own ways of doing things, and then we irrationally think that someone else's way isn't as good. When you think of it like that, it gets a little easier to let someone else in. It clears some of the gender baggage out of the way, so you can catch yourself in a more self-centered foible and tell yourself to knock it off.

Regardless of causes, though, the most important takeaway here is simply that gatekeeping exists. *Women bear some of the responsibility for men not doing their share at home.* So you may want to take a hard look at the extent to which you could be actively discouraging your spouse from taking more responsibility. Maybe he isn't quite as much at fault as you've been thinking. And in order to get him more engaged and make him more of a partner, you have to reconcile yourself to giving up some control.

Let's sum up what we've learned in this chapter.

There is not one household task that a man can't do well, if

1. His wife is ready to teach him in a gracious way.
2. He is ready to learn.
3. She is willing to surrender some control, fight off her gatekeeping instincts, and accept that he will inevitably, in some ways, make the job his own, and she might even learn something too.

That's two conditions on the wife and only one on the husband, but believe us when we say that point 2 is just as big as points 1 and 3 combined. In part 3 we'll address them all.

Chapter 10

"Our Lack of Sex Has Nothing to Do with My Mothering Him"

Browsing through the Hallmark birthday cards in the gift shop, Nella came across one that suited her and Alec—and thousands of other couples—perfectly. On the front was a sketch of a formally laid dinner table at a restaurant, with words that read, "After your birthday dinner tonight, we should go home early and . . ." The punch line inside read, "Yawn, yawn, snore, snore." She didn't need to look any further. When Alec received the card and read the opening, he looked up at Nella and winked. "Yeah!" he exclaimed, thinking that he was going to get some loving on his special day, but then went limp when he opened the card to read what he knew to be the truth.

The Real Reason We Aren't Having Sex

Alec has heard all the excuses in the book—probably the least of which is the clichéd "Not tonight, honey, I've got a headache."

The most typical response from Nella, when he gets up the courage to make even the slightest advance, is, "I've had such a long day. I'm so tired." Most of the time he doesn't even try. Why bother when he knows what the outcome will be?

And the "tired" excuse isn't just for Alec; Nella also used it to explain her behavior to us. Nella is like a mother to her husband, but she doesn't want to admit how that role has affected their sex life, because that would be a reason for changing things. And like many women, Nella doesn't think she *can* stop being Alec's mom and resists trying. After hearing the ideas in chapter 3 about how sex and intimacy can be crippled by the Mother Syndrome, Nella played the "tired" card with us.

"It's the honest-to-goodness truth," Nella said. "I *am* tired by the end of the day. That's why me and Alec don't have sex anymore. It isn't because I do mother things for him, though I do." Even though she gave up working at the bank years ago, she says that she barely has a moment to catch her breath between running errands and arranging car pools and appointments, making dinner and keeping the house in order. By the time she drops into bed, the last thing she feels like doing is more work.

Yes, sadly, sex has become work. But it shouldn't be that way. Sex should be playful pleasure. A reward after the real work of the day is done. And if you're really tired after a long day's work, then your partner might even be willing to oblige by being more of a giver than a receiver. Maybe all you have to do is lie there and let your body take over. If you're really into being with your mate, your body's amazing physiology will respond all on its own, without your having to put much thought into it. You can pretty much be on automatic pilot.

Good sex can be rejuvenating, along with its other benefits—like a release of tension and stress and a portal to a better night's sleep with a happier sense of your partner. If you think back to the premarriage or living together phase of your relationship and remember a really physically exhausting day, you may recall still looking forward to connecting on a sensual level after your time apart. Back then sex was a pleasure and part of your leisure, even when you were really tired. One woman, Joan, put it this way: "When Rick and I were living together a few years ago, it used to seem to me as if I had two separate tanks of energy or fuel in my body. One of them was for everyday activities, work and meals and even entertainment. And after a long day it would be time for bed, and that tank was *soooo* empty. I would feel so totally exhausted that I barely had the strength to take off my makeup and brush my teeth. I just wanted that mattress and those covers; just let me lie down. But then we're in bed and one of us touches the other, and it was like a new wave of energy came out of nowhere. Like there was a reserve tank that hadn't even been touched by the day. It was still full."

So, is your lack of desire really because you're so tired, or could it be that you feel disconnected from someone whom you're often resentful and angry toward? Someone who you feel depletes you emotionally. Perhaps when you say, "Sorry, hon, but I'm so tired. I just want to go to sleep or read my book," what you really mean is, "I'm so tired of being your mother, so tired of doing more for you (and the 'other' kids) than for myself. Now all I want is to be left alone." You may not even be aware that that's what is going on, but the next time you turn the other way and mention being tired, think about this. Ask yourself, "If I set aside the tiredness, what else might I be feeling?" Angry, annoyed, frustrated, resentful, irritated, or even hopeless might be on the list.

We understand that even if you acknowledge the most significant reason for turning away, you may not be inclined to tell him how you really feel. Just to say you're tired is so much simpler and more seemingly legitimate an excuse, one that he is mercifully unlikely to argue with. It means that you'll be left alone. Sleep is the great escape.

We agree that telling the truth about being angry, annoyed, or frustrated would likely lead to confrontation and then you'd really not get the sleep you want. Maybe sharing the truth at the moment that he turns toward you for physical intimacy is not great timing. But sharing the truth *at some time* is important—for both of you. We'll discuss how to do this in part 3.

If being tired won't hold up as the reason for not having sex, some women offer another explanation, in their effort to avoid admitting that the Mother Syndrome is the real culprit. And that is to say they don't feel attractive enough anymore. They don't look the way they did in their twenties, and they say that makes them feel inhibited and non-sexual.

While it's true that age and body image can affect libido, we're going to stick with our main principle: The number one reason most women lose their sexual zing with their husbands is not because of their diminished positive feelings toward their bodies. It's about a loss of positive feelings toward the one who should be the object of desire: it's about losing your esteem for your husband. When he is so lacking in merit that you are forced to act as his mother, you aren't going to respond to him like you used to. There may be plenty of sexual sap running through your branches, which could make you get flirty and provocative and cuddly and passionate, but it isn't going to be directed at him. The slacker, the incompetent, the cop-out who doesn't come through as a partner and needs to be supervised like a kid—that isn't the person who is going to light your fire.

Now what about special problems that some women have, problems that can lead to real sexual difficulties? Are we pooh-poohing them? Absolutely not. We acknowledge that there are legitimate reasons why a woman (or a man) may have lowered libido or other sexual issues. Some are physiological or hormonal, some psychological. They may require specialized help and treatment. But this chapter isn't about them; in this chapter we are talking to the woman who is basically sexually functional (for her age).

But *she has become her husband's mother* and

- puts up excuses why that situation can't change
- doesn't admit the effect that it has on her intimacy with her spouse
- blames their diminished sex life on factors that aren't the most significant reasons

And we are saying, take another look and see if the reasons you're offering really go to the truth.

A Short but Sweet Fantasy

Another way of seeing that all could be well is to indulge in a little fantasizing. See how well tiredness, lowered body image, any other excuse, or just the general claim that you aren't interested in sex anymore hold up against a little trip down Hypothetical Lane. Imagine that you met an interesting, attractive man who came on to you, and you snuck away for a booty call; do you really believe the excuses we've looked at so far would stop you from feeling desire or engaging in sex?

Place this story on a trip to Italy, if you must: suppose you and a woman friend have some vacation time, so you make a little trip to Florence and stay in a villa. And one day you head out on your own and you're looking at a wonderful Renaissance chapel and you see a guy who looks like Javier Bardem, and the two of you strike up a conversation and go have some lunch at a bistro he knows. And it turns out he is visiting from Spain, and the conversation flows, and at one point he takes your hand . . . If you aren't into the swarthy Latin lover, by all means substitute a guy who looks like George Clooney, Denzel Washington, or whoever spells *hot* in your language.

Are you really saying that you could not rise to this occasion?

Or if this scenario is too risqué for you, imagine that you are exactly as you are now, only you are divorced. Free, unencumbered. And you meet a hot guy who is obviously interested in you, at the local library or at the bar where you go after work with a couple of friends. Or back in Italy, with the scent of almond in the air. Would there really be no chance?

What we're trying to say is this: Maybe it isn't that you can't see yourself as beautiful in a man's eyes. You can. And it's not that you're just chronically so overtired that cuddling and stroking and arousal are simply no fun anymore. No, it's more likely that the attractive man who used to turn you on has been replaced by a guy who doesn't, a guy for whom you play the role of mother instead of partner. And the things you want to be feeling are being blocked by a different set of emotions, born out of anger and resentment and alienation.

"My Husband Isn't Interested in Sex Anymore"

"Okay," we hear some readers saying, "I might admit that I am capable of sex and it would be a darn nice thing, but forget everything I said before. Here's the real problem: my *husband* isn't interested in sex anymore." If that's really true, Houston has a problem. But is it true?

You say the guy just isn't horny.

Oh, really. Then let's interview him briefly.

Jake, are you still horny?

Yes, I'm still horny.

Are you sure?

Pretty sure.

So, how do you know *you're still horny?*

Well, there are several clues. For one thing, I often look at porn online. I look at women when I'm out and about. I masturbate sometimes. I have sexy dreams and fantasies, sometimes about . . . my wife.

The simple fact is that most guys are still horny on their deathbeds, absent any medical problem, and even men who can't get it up feel horny and will take drugs to bridge the gap. If he isn't coming on to you, there are probably other reasons. Here are four of the most likely ones:

- He fears that you'll reject him.
- You aren't sending any inviting signals. Or you're sending anti-erotic ones.
- He's riddled with guilt.
- He feels like less than an adult in your eyes.

Let's look at them one by one.

Being Rejected Ain't No Fun

The first reason a guy may seem uninterested in you sexually is that *he fears that you'll reject him.* Nobody likes rejection, but in the sexual arena it packs a special punch. Neil describes his interactions with his wife, Janelle.

Neil's story

Even when she said no, Janelle used to say it with a twinkle in her eye. I knew she still basically wanted me, but this wasn't the right moment. So I didn't feel rejected; I didn't feel defective in her eyes. Sometimes it just egged me on and made me want it more, when the time came.

But nowadays it's different. When she turns me down, I feel as if I'm, like, *distasteful* in her eyes. Like I'm a bad flavor. I have the wrong hair or the wrong eyes, or the shape of my mouth annoys her. Now, I know I'm still an attractive guy; I can tell that because sometimes women smile at me—no kidding! So I think what's going on is that when I make a move and she looks at me or feels my touch, *I remind her of the wrong things.* There's so much she's mad at me for, and as a result I take a lot of flak from her. I didn't do this; I messed up that; I forgot to pay this bill; I let the kids have ice cream when it was almost dinnertime. But you know, when you've already taken flak from someone, it isn't any fun to be rejected by them sexually. It stings. So most of the time, I don't even try.

What is really awful is sometimes Janelle looks so good to me. She doesn't even know it, I'll bet you. Like yesterday, she was wearing a green dress that she had chosen for a lunch outing with her girlfriends. And she came home and was sitting

> beside me on the couch. I love that dress. Her skin looks amazing next to it. It brings out her coloring, her hair and her eyes. And it fits her real nice. I was practically drooling over her, but I didn't make a move, because I didn't want to feel like a sexual loser. I felt like a guy who scored a date with the most popular girl in school but doesn't know how to get his arm around her in the movie theater. And he knows she isn't really into him, she's pining for that football star, and if he makes a move, she'll laugh at him. So he does nothing, because the fantasy is way more fun.
>
> Late that night, after she went to sleep, I masturbated real quietly in the bed beside her, to the image of what might have happened on the couch. How pathetic.

Does this sound like a guy who feels no desire for his wife? Or no interest in sex? Yet those are the reasons Janelle floated to us for the cooling off of their fires. What's going on here is a sad disconnect. She thinks she is no longer desirable in his eyes, and he's hanging back because he doesn't want to risk another rejection. What's needed here is to dig deeper into the causes of those past rejections.

You might wonder, in defense of Janelle, why Neil didn't tell her how good she looked in that dress. Why didn't he say, "You look really beautiful today." That's just what a guy should do when he is feeling something like that. But when there's a pattern of rejection that feels like humiliation, compliments are hard to give, because they carry a kind of vulnerability. Saying "You look lovely right now" says "You move me, you are getting to me," and that involves an opening of the soul by the complimenter to the complimentee. If you looked at the history of couples like Neil and Janelle, you'd find that compliments have become scarce in their lives. That's because compliments are a way of giving points to the other person, and when things get bitter enough, each side is reluctant to concede any points.

Compliments are in fact an interesting study in themselves. How often they're given, and especially how they're received, is a revealing index of the state of hostilities in a couple. Saying something nice about the other person is an advance, and if it's not received in a gracious, positive way, that's a kind of rejection. When one spouse tells the other they're good-looking or smart or brave or suave or hilarious, and this is greeted with a denial ("No I'm not, I'm fat/dumb/chicken/gauche/unfunny") or dismissed with a grimace and a scornful laugh, the message is either "I have a low opinion of myself, don't argue with it" or worse still, "You aren't the one I want compliments from; you aren't the one whose judgment I respect or whose praise I want to win."

A final point about rejection: It's usually mutual, even though one person in the couple may feel as if he or she is the one chronically being rejected. Sexual rejection is often a way of retaliating for another kind of rejection. When a woman approaches her husband as an equal and is continually made to feel she is a nagging mother, that feels like rejection. And it may well exact its revenge later, when a man makes himself vulnerable by making a play.

Lack of an Invitation

A man may also be deterred from making a move if *he isn't picking up any positive cues.* The lack of any encouraging or inviting vibes can drain a soul of the optimism on which sexual advances depend. Or a preponderance of negative signs—that'll work too. Bart told us about a trick his wife Nicole does.

Bart's story

> She has this way of taking her bra off at the end of the day. She already has her old T-shirt on that goes down to her thighs and has no shape. But we've just watched a movie we like and things aren't too cloudy between us. The time could be ripe. So she stands there and makes this Houdini move, where, without taking the T-shirt off, she is able to get the bra off. She pulls each bra strap out from under the T-shirt and down around her arm and sends it back into the sleeve, then reaches behind her and unhooks the bra and presto, it comes out from hiding and gets tossed over a chair. Thing is, I like looking at her in the bra. But she is all business, and it never occurs to her. She is in that practical "mom" mode and this is just another thing to get out of the way. You know what? I would really like it if sometimes she would take the damn T-shirt off and spend some time in the bra, maybe mix a drink and sit beside me and talk to me in the bra. I would like that.
>
> I know wearing a bra all the time can be uncomfortable, and sometimes she just can't wait to get out of harness. But do I always have to be reminded of it? It's like I'm in the sex-free zone. No Victoria's Secret here. Just Houdini's secret.

As we said in chapter 3, there are a hundred everyday ways a woman can send anti-erotic signals, not all of them conscious. Now remember, our purpose here isn't to give wives a hard time; it's to say that they are often mistaken if they think their husband has lost interest in them sexually. As these two examples indicate, and as we knew all along, men are visual. After the frenetic desires of youth or the thrills of a new relationship have cooled a bit, it may take a little showing of the bait to make a man rise to action.

Or a little wearing of the "lover" persona. If you are continually wearing an identity that conflicts with lover (say, by wearing five hats that add up to mother), it's very understandable that the primitive part of a man's brain stem that mandates sex may have trouble identifying you as "irresistible siren."

Why Guilt Is Not a Turn-on

As we've seen in previous chapters, lots of men are capable of awareness. They are not very happy about their wife having become their mother. They feel bad that they've retreated out of the domestic enterprise, be it cleaning, cooking, managing, or child rearing. They feel bad that their wife is overworked and that they are failing to step up as a partner and face the challenges with her.

So a man feels guilty. He knows he should be doing more, but he has lost the way back into the dance, is unsure of the steps to take to regain a sense of being a competent contributor, and when he tries sometimes to lend a hand, he often gets rebuffed or scolded for bad timing, bad planning, or bad execution. He gets rejected—there's that word again.

But guilt is not a pleasant thing to consciously feel. In fact, it's an awful thing. So he tries to avoid the situations that make him feel guilty, situations where he looks at her and sees her as the one who is exploited by him, or situations *where he may possibly fail her and take more than he gives*—because, after all, that is what her being his mom is all about.

For instance, sex.

So here she is in the bed, showing that tired aura, not giving off any "lover" vibe, and he wants her. He wants some.

And maybe he could get it: maybe if he rolls over against her and makes some cuddling moves, maybe she'll find it in her heart to reciprocate and he'll get his itch scratched. But if that happens, will he fail her? Will he get more than he gives? Will she not want to climb the mountain of her orgasm, or will he be worried that he might try to take her there and, after a slip on some slope, prove only to have been a fifteen-minute nuisance?

You may not believe that a guy could have this much of a conscience, but when guilt becomes the medicine you take every day, more guilt is not what you want. So maybe he leaves her alone. And anyway, the odds of rejection were pretty high.

Feeling like a Child

Let's recall what excuse it is that we're responding to. We are speaking to the reader who says, "Hey, our lack of a sex life is not caused by my having become his mother. It's caused by *x*." We looked at tiredness as the *x* factor, and then erosion of body image. We looked at waning desire. And now we're looking at the excuse that puts it on the hubby, saying he just isn't interested in sex anymore, or not with you. And our answer is, you're reading him wrong. He still does desire you, but he isn't acting on it, because he is afraid of rejection or isn't getting the right signals from you or is too full of guilt to go there.

There's a fourth reason that may partake of all the others, and it brings us right up against the ultimate cause of his lack of coming on. The deepest reason he may not be seeking sex with you—the ingredient that really louses up the chemical reaction—is that *he feels like less than an adult in your eyes.* Why? Because you're his mother. Let's face it, being treated like a child may not be the best way to inspire the male sexual apparatus. As one guy put it, "How can I get big if you make me feel small?"

Men suffer from performance anxiety, you may have heard. That's because the erectness-or-not of their crotchal member is very plain and obvious to see. Once performance anxiety sets in, it can be hard to dissipate. What makes it go away? What brings back the phallic fun? Well, confidence and desire don't do too badly. Things that make a guy feel like a big deal make him big. Or just sheer lust, if it's intense enough, can make a dude forget that his trusty staff may have let him down on some occasion.

So there are two ways that feeling like a child is counterproductive. One is that it saps a guy's confidence. In spite of many sitcoms and modern movie comedies, most men want to be looked at as an adult by a woman. They want to be admired, respected, looked to for support and a witty riposte. So when your own wife seems to have given up on the idea that you're a grown-up, has effectively dismissed you from the circle of her equals, that squelches the lothario in you pretty well.

The second way that feeling like a child hurts the fun is that it is bad for desire. That's because most men don't want to feel like they're sleeping with their parent, or their supervisor, or their boss. When he sees you as his mom, that quenches the jets a bit. A man may fantasize about sleeping with his real supervisor at his day job, but even in those fantasies he is likely to turn the tables and not feel like less than an equal. (There are, of course, power fantasies that can be lots of fun between consenting adults, but we'll leave them for another book.)

* * *

We are looking here at a relationship that is out of balance, and we are saying you shouldn't assume too easily that your husband "don't want you no more"; it's more likely that his very real desires are being stifled, just as yours are, by the topsy-turvy mommyfication that we're exploring in this book.

Chapter 11

"I Can't Rely on Him with the Children"

We've all heard women jokingly include their husbands as they count the number of children they have to parent. If you're one of those women, you know there's often truth behind the humorous remark.

Sure, you sometimes feel like you want to pull your hair out or run away because your children don't listen or don't follow through on their promises to keep their rooms clean or wake up on time. But it's okay: you accept reminding, nagging, cajoling, and supervising as part of your parenting responsibilities. It's different when your *husband* leaves his clothes lying on the bedroom floor or the bed unmade. That evokes a whole other level of anger, exasperation, and frustration. Why? Because you *expect* that your kids' priorities are not the same as yours. And you expect that your husband's are.

That's one way that having kids raises the stakes on the issues we've been talking about in this book. Before you have kids, it may be a little easier to ignore or deny the mother role you are playing with your husband. But raising children throws a harsh spotlight on the one who is supposed to be a grown-up: you see him side by side with them, and it's all too clear that you're having to treat him the same way.

Another thing that makes you see him as a kid is the feeling that you can't share the parenting with him, that you are not working together as a team and behaving like the kind of adults you hope your children will grow into. If he isn't equipped to help you with the kids, that makes him one of them.

After all, parenting is the ultimate test of adulthood.

And that's why it's so pivotal for this book. If, in your eyes, your husband fails the ultimate test of adulthood, there is going to be a giant obstacle in the way of him becoming your equal partner again, and you ceasing to be his mother.

So we need to take a hard look at the ways in which women argue that their husbands fail to be "parent" material. What qualities do these men lack? In what ways do they screw up? We'll hear what the wives have to say and how the husbands respond. Then we'll weigh the charges and see if there's any light at the end of this parenting tunnel.

An Outing with Dad—Too Dangerous?

Many mothers say that, unlike dads, they've learned all through life how to be responsible and care for others. It starts with bathing, dressing, feeding, and taking care of lifelike dolls in their toy strollers, and it ends with nurturing real babies as they grow, and raising them into adults. Among the capacities they bring to the table:

- always being available to meet their children's physical and emotional needs (ready to supply a high-energy breakfast before their kid's crucial stickball game or a reassuring chat if it doesn't turn out as hoped)
- being eternally vigilant to their safety and health (noticing when a child is favoring her right knee or seems overheated)
- being able to plan and orchestrate complicated timetables and handle fluid situations (like having to adjust to the domino effect that one change of schedule has on all other aspects of their own lives and the lives of others)

But unfortunately, the story goes, men are insensitive to kids' needs and careless about their safety.

And they are logistically challenged. As one mother told us, "A man is not able to multitask the way a woman does, and is not a forward thinker like she is. My husband doesn't even remember to transfer the car seat into the other car before he takes off for the day." According to this view, a woman's ability to organize and orchestrate is partly learned from generations before her but is also part of her innate being—unlike that of a man.

We can add these new charges to the ones from the two previous chapters, where men were accused of being lazy and messy, not detail-oriented, and incompetent at cleaning and cooking. With this added ammo, there seems to be reason for disqualifying men across the domestic board.

But is there really? It's time for some evidence. Here's what Lorna had to say about a common logistical problem: getting ready for an outing.

Lorna's story

> It's impossible for me to be spontaneous since I have become a mother. When we were childless, it was much easier to pick up and be out of the house within a half hour. Now I have to consider my entire family's needs while we are out. Do we have enough supplies for the day? Food and water are essentials. A snack bag has become my second purse. An extra sweater for each of us if the weather turns cold, and a hat for everyone in case the sun breaks through the clouds. An extra pair of underwear for my daughter who is almost toilet-trained, and disinfectant napkins in case the kids are suddenly starving and can't wait until we get to a washroom to wash their hands before they have a snack. Did I mention tissues, Band-Aids, and an umbrella?
>
> It's absolutely amazing, however, that Stuart has not lost his spontaneity. He has no problem with leaving the house almost immediately. He just goes to the car and then demands to know why I've taken so long to get out the door. That's easy for him to say, because he's never prepared!

This all sounds pretty convincing, until you hear Stuart's response.

Stuart's story

> Lorna drives me crazy whenever we have to go anywhere with the kids. Even a trip to the mall is an ordeal. It usually takes longer for us to leave the house than it does to drive to the mall and run our errands. She's like a girl scout. Always prepared. But to a fault. It isn't as if we're going to a desert island where there are

no stores. Even if we're not in the mall, there's always somewhere to stop to buy something. For God's sake, the kids aren't going to starve or dehydrate in the time it takes to buy provisions.

Problem is that she's spoiled them. She's made them unable to delay their needs, because she works so hard at anticipating every one. She hounds them about whether they need something to drink. She feeds them before they're hungry. What, is she afraid their blood sugar levels will drop and they'll become faint? Kids let you know when they're hungry or thirsty, and they don't collapse if they have to wait a little while. Of *course* she's stressed whenever we go out. I would be too, if I had to think of a million things to pack.

If it were up to me, I'd teach the kids that nothing catastrophic is going to happen if you don't get everything as soon as you want it. I'd prefer that they learn how to problem-solve, to find creative ways to work through tricky situations. I don't want to spoon-feed them. I want them to grow up as resourceful and independent human beings. I also, for once, would like to leave the house on time!

So, who's right?

Well, both points of view have truth.

What she sees, he sees differently. Lorna believes that her job as a mother is to care for and protect her children. She believes that this is her role as a responsible, loving parent. Stuart believes that his role is to raise kids who are capable of fending for themselves. Lorna may say that this is just Stuart's way of copping out, of not taking on any form of responsibility. He just wants to live his life the way he did before the kids were born, and since he knows that she will do such a competent job of filling his gaps, why not take advantage? In fact, she may believe that he hasn't fully embraced his role as a parent. How could he, she may wonder, when he was so used to being taken care of by *his* mother?

Lorna is reminded of a time when she and her mother-in-law, Joan, were discussing the brash, edgy way in which Stuart had talked to Joan on the phone.

Her mother-in-law asked Lorna, "What's the matter with Stuart? He's awfully jumpy these days. Perhaps he's not sleeping enough or eating well." Lorna felt that she was being personally attacked for not taking good enough care of Joan's poor baby boy. She wondered if Joan was insinuating that if only Lorna provided home-cooked meals every day (with the recommended daily allowance of nutrients) and didn't force Stuart out of bed so early in the morning to drive one of the kids to school, maybe then he'd be more patient with his mother. Ironically, Lorna is often reminded by her mother-in-law, "I'm the only mother he's got."

Then why, Lorna asks herself, *does she make me feel that I should be a perfect substitute for her?* Nevertheless, Lorna grits her teeth and remains respectful. "Yes, perhaps he is a little tired lately, Mom. This weekend I'll make sure he gets to sleep in. I'm sure he didn't mean to upset you. You know how much he adores you."

"I know he does," Joan says, "and it's nice to know I can count on you to make sure my baby is well taken care of."

At this point, a couple of uncomfortable thoughts may dawn on Lorna. Maybe her own style of parenting is rather similar to what Joan's was. And if Joan raised a son who didn't grow up to be fully adult, maybe that's what Lorna is in danger of doing with her own children. That would mean, ironically, that when Stuart rebels against Lorna's overmothering of the kids, he may be right. He is trying to save them from his own fate, trying to make them grow into more complete people than he is! That's why he thinks they'll benefit from sometimes thinking for themselves. Maybe it's good to have to decide what you need on your way out the door, and learn independently that if you forget your sweater, you may be cold. Maybe if that happened, you'd learn to bring one next time. After all, Lorna would hate it if, some day in the future, her own daughter-in-law were to blame her for raising a man-child!

But what *about* safety? There are lots of real dangers to worry about. A lamp with an empty socket, waiting for a curious finger; a pile of leaves with a sharp stump under it; thin ice on a river, veiled by snow. A mom could be forgiven for wondering whether her husband is vigilant enough about them.

Laura told us about a "damned if you do, damned if you don't" dilemma.

Laura's story

> Saturday evening was especially exhausting. I had a million things to catch up on around the house while Phil and the kids watched television. I finally fell into bed around 2:00 a.m., looking forward to a lazy Sunday around the house. I thought that maybe we'd have a BBQ, but I guess he'd had enough of being cooped up and wanted to go on a family outing.
>
> "Let's go to the zoo," he suggested to the kids early that morning. They were thrilled at the idea. I was teed off that he hadn't discussed it with me before mentioning it to them.
>
> "Well . . ." I started.
>
> "Oh, come on, Mom," my daughter pleaded, "we haven't gone in a long time."
>
> "You don't have to come with," Phil said. "I'm quite capable of managing the kids on my own."
>
> Sure. Except his idea of managing the kids is quite different

> from mine. Like when they wandered off in the mall and he had to get security to help find them. I knew that going to the zoo, despite how tired I was feeling, was the lesser of two evils. The worse evil was pacing at home, worrying about the kids wandering off on their own and falling into the bear pit while their father stood mesmerized in front of the baboons.

When we asked other mothers why they worried so much about their husbands' taking the kids out, the same concern emerged loud and clear—the fathers' lack of attention to their children's whereabouts. They said their husbands would often be distracted by an activity instead of holding their child's hand, or would send the kid to the washroom alone.

There was even a note of humor in one mom's concern about when her husband and son went bike riding together. Annette said, "It freaks me out when I see my husband and our boy go down the street on their bikes. Colin is usually *ahead of Luke*. How would he know if Luke was lagging too far behind or strayed into the path of a speeding car? Even when we're with the kids and going for a walk, he'll often walk ahead of us. The kids and I sometimes play a game. We stand still for a little while, maybe duck into a doorway, and watch how long it takes before Colin realizes that we're not behind him. Sometimes he's a block ahead of us before he realizes it. We laugh about him being in his own little world, but I worry."

But again, men have a response. A man may believe he is portraying the fearless leader when he forges on ahead of the family pack. And Colin, when pressed as to his lead position, had this to say: "Annette is just paranoid. I always know where the kids are. If it were up her, they'd be handcuffed to me until they were sixteen, at least. She doesn't give the kids or me enough credit.

They have their eyes on me too and they know where we're going. Geez, I don't need to have eagle eyes on them every second that we're together."

When Fathers Fight with Kids

Letting the kids go on an excursion with your husband may worry you, but it isn't the only scenario that raises concerns. There's also leaving them at home with him, absent your supervision. We have another story, and it's one of the more distressing ones we've heard. In it, Meg relates an incident between her husband and her thirteen-year-old daughter.

Meg's story

> My daughter's screams can be heard halfway across the house. Then I hear my husband's voice, louder and deeper.
>
> "You're a little bitch," I hear Kevin yell, and then a door slams. Amy has run to her room, crying.
>
> I feel my blood boil, wondering why their conflicts always have to end badly. I leave what I was doing and find him in the living room, remote in his hand, watching football. "What's going on?" I ask, trying to remain calm.
>
> "She always gets to watch what she wants on TV," Kevin shouts. "It's not fair. The one time that I want to watch the game, she insists that her program is more important."
>
> I ask how the situation got resolved, knowing full well that the outcome wasn't good, but trying to sound like I want to hear his side of the story.
>
> "Well, she stormed away after I told her she was a little bitch."

"How many times have I asked you not to call her names? Can't I count on you to act more like a parent should? Can you please go apologize?"

"No," he says with defiance. "I'm sick of apologizing. This is her fault. She has to realize that she can't always get what she wants. And she started it. She called me an idiot."

Now it's my turn to storm off and knock at my daughter's bedroom door. "Go away," she says, thinking that it's her father. When she hears my voice, she tells me to come in. She's face-down on her pillow. I sit at the edge of her bed and stroke her back. "I hate it when Dad calls me names," she says. "Can't he be more mature?"

After talking to her about not using inappropriate language or name calling, even when angry, I try to validate what she's saying: "I'm sure Dad didn't mean to hurt your feelings, honey. I guess you both wanted to watch different shows and you're angry because he's watching what he wants and you're not."

"That too," she says, "but I'm especially mad that he called me a bitch. That's not great role modeling. Can't you speak to him and make him stop?"

When we ask her about this incident, Meg tells us it isn't unusual: she has often found herself in the role of buffer between her husband and daughter. The two, she says, have similar fiery temperaments. It's not a role she relishes playing, but given their personalities, it's one she is resigned to. Fights are bound to break out between them. We pointed out to her that she sounds more like she's mediating a dispute between two kids than dealing with a father and daughter. She laughs ruefully and says, "That's exactly right, because Kevin puts himself on the same level as Amy. Which leaves me as the sole parent."

When we talked to Kevin, he had a dramatically different take. "I am trying to teach her that she can't always have her way. Meg spoils her, pampers her, by always wanting her to be happy. It doesn't work that way. So I'm left without a leg to stand on. When I explode at Amy, I guess half my anger is really at Meg. If Meg would listen to some of my ideas and not always side against me, maybe I could act more like a dad. I know I shouldn't speak to my daughter that way, and I feel lousy after I do it."

Kevin admits he's in the wrong, but he is also feeling an adult kind of anger. So what is he so mad about? He's been preempted as a father. He finds himself in a household where he doesn't have much influence on the parenting philosophy, where his own instincts aren't validated or supported. He's out of the adult loop, and that "demotes" him to the level of child, where of course he promptly misbehaves.

What Men Can Contribute to Child Raising

There seem to be two sides to each of these stories. The women are right that the men's actual performance as parents is less than stellar, but the men claim they're getting a bad rap, and they *could do better* if they had a chance. That suggests a deeper question: Do men even have the basic *talents* needed for parenting?

Take planning and logistics. Can a man's brain go there? In particular, take multitasking. Well, a wise person once said there is no such thing. Humans can't do two things at once. Have you ever watched someone pour boiling water into a coffee filter that was sitting on the kitchen counter, while talking on the phone? Have you ever had a collision with a texting driver? If you haven't, you're lucky.

What we call multitasking is really having several projects on the go at once and shifting adroitly between them. In order to do this, you have to start more than one project at once, and we have seen that men are reluctant to do this (but they can and do overcome the inhibition).

What about all the other logistics? Can men handle the challenges of child rearing? Well, if you look at househusbands, divorced men with custody, widowers, or men who have otherwise ended up in sole charge of their children, you find that yes, they can adapt. Their "mothering" techniques become almost indistinguishable from those of women. Once again, it seems more a question of desire than ability—desire being partly a matter of attitude and partly a matter of one's parenting *goals*.

Can men plan and administrate and orchestrate, while keeping things spic and span and serving meals on time and meeting impossible goals? Can they outfit the team for an excursion? Consider this. What may be the greatest achievement in planning and logistics known to history was originally created and staffed by men. It's known as the army. Or consider men who manage construction sites, men who direct movies, men with jobs in management.

Okay, what about that vigilance that monitors children's needs, safety, and health? Are men capable of that? Again, men who shoulder the job of parenting alone do all right. Certainly a man is capable of carrying out *his* sense of what the priorities are. What has emerged in our spousal dialog so far is that many men don't necessarily have the same parenting philosophy as many women. In answer to the general charge that women can't trust them with the kids, men may answer, "Can *women* be trusted not to coddle, pamper, overprotect, and otherwise spoil their children into having unrealistic expectations of how they're going to be treated in the real world?"

Turns out that many men have their own ideas about childhood and what it should be like. As one guy said, "When it comes to kids—boy, what happened to freedom and spontaneity? Why does everything have to be scheduled? Why can't kids have more independence? Why can't they be more respectful when they're with adults? We are the grown-ups, not them. Women want a perfectly safe world where everything is predictable, but that's impossible, and trying to create it is not always the best way for children to learn how to work their way out of tricky situations."

What about just sheer nurturing ability—what we called in chapter 1 the infinite, often invisible caring that goes into answering children's questions, listening to their stories, entertaining them, giving praise, providing discipline and boundaries, and suggesting activities? It may be true that women have more talent for this, but it's also true that men have big hearts, and when they turn them in the direction of their children, good things happen. What sometimes gets in the way of this is when there isn't room for the man: another parent—the woman—is already taking up most of the nurturing space. That degree of involvement may have developed naturally, and with only good intentions; but in any case, the exact shares of involvement aren't written in stone. They can change.

And some men want them to. Men have a lot more capabilities in the parenting area than they're often given credit for, and as we've seen, they have some valid ideas of their own. Many men want to be more involved than they are, but for this to happen, women need to let go of some control, be open to men's point of view, and treat men as responsible beings rather than inept flunkies. (As men need to take more responsibility and not pooh-pooh their wives' concerns.)

Parenting researchers resoundingly proclaim the huge benefits of a father's greater engagement in his children's lives. Children with more involved fathers do better in a host of areas, including mental health, physical health, education (one notable example: teenage boys apply themselves more in school), handling stress, and relating to others. They have fewer problems with crime, drugs, and acting out. They even have more successful marriages.[1] So if you help this to happen, you'll not only be lightening your own parenting load but doing serious good for your children. Not to mention improving your marriage and theirs!

And it must be said: there are many ways in which a woman can sabotage a man's attempts at fathering. Research on gatekeeping often features parenting, because that's the area where wives have the most trouble letting go of their influence—the sweet prestige of being the one with the answers and the skills, the one the kids turn to instinctively. And men are extra vulnerable here, because the stakes are so high. It's one thing to fail at bathroom cleaning; it's another to fail in your attempt to engage with your own children.

It isn't hard for a mother to sabotage her spouse's attempts at fathering. There are so many weapons in her arsenal, so many ways of outshining her husband with the kids or making him feel inept. One is to undermine him in front of the kids. Of *course* your child won't respect your husband if he's made perfect peanut-butter sandwiches and you roll your eyes and say, "Your father will never remember to cut off the crusts." And it may be hard for him to discipline the kids when you're around, if they know they can run to you for comfort and protection—that all it takes is a few tears to pull at your heartstrings and then, without even knowing what's transpired, you'll be all too quick to shoot him down, to turn him into the bad guy. Then there's out-and-out competition. You may have to step out of the way in order to give him a real chance to gain ground. It's hard for a guy to encourage independence in his kids if his wife is around and the kids are more inclined to have her make their lunch, cut the crusts off their sandwiches, and pour them their favorite juice—or even serve them on a tray while they watch their favorite TV show.

And as we've seen before, most men no longer walk into the house with the special merit badge of being the sole breadwinner, nor do they have the questionable advantage that used to come, before the women's movement, just from being male. So as they try to find their footing in the parenting dance, they don't begin with the same presumption of respect that once buoyed them up.

It's a delicate dance, a tricky exchange. To make your husband more of a father involves giving up power, and even giving up some of the affection and contact that you drink from the fountain of your kids. It's just as fraught on the male side, because he may easily be in danger of seeming like an interloper or a second-best. Once parenting habits, tactics, and territories are staked out, they aren't easy to redistrict.

But it can be done, and it has to be done if your relationship with your husband is to be restored to an equal, adult one. You can't stop being his mother if instead of being your co-parent, he remains one of the kids. In part 3, we'll dig deeper into this untapped potential, and what women need to do in order to avail themselves of it. If your husband truly wants to be more involved than he is, how can you foster this? Sociologists have shown, not surprisingly, that when a woman encourages her husband as a father and expresses appreciation for his parenting talents, he achieves greater involvement. The lesson here is that you have a huge amount of power in shaping your husband's fate as a father. You have power for good or ill. It's your choice.[2]

After all, wouldn't it take some of the load off your shoulders if your man was an equal partner in the parenting arena? Equal doesn't mean that he will think things through exactly as you do or even take care of things in the way that you would, but perhaps you can let go of some of your control, be open to his point of view, encourage him when he does show competence, and not roll your eyes when he says something that you deem unintelligent—especially when the kids are around.

Most important, what better gift to give to children than to know that their mother believes in their father's ability to take care of their needs—even if his ways are different from hers?

That completes our tour of the flawed beliefs and attitudes that keep the Mother Syndrome ticking. Now that we've deconstructed them, we're ready for the final stage: explaining our plan for how you and your husband can get to a better place.

Part Three

Getting Your Partner Back

We hope part 2 has shown you that you don't really have to stay in a place where you're being a mother to your husband. The beliefs that keep you both in that predicament don't hold up under scrutiny. You can let them go.

That means there is a way out. In the next seven chapters we will show you how to dismantle the Mother Syndrome, envision a better lifestyle, and get your husband on board. We'll map the process out for you step by step, so you can find your way back to a healthy partnership with your mate.

Chapter 12

Clearing the Air Emotionally

Couples have all too many excuses for staying right where they are: with her being his mother. We've seen the details in part 2, and they aren't pretty. Some spouses persist in this self-defeating behavior because their parents did, some out of fear and insecurity. And many go this route based on the dubious joys of putting down the other person. While there are a few germs of truth scattered among the rationalizations, none of them really stands up under sane scrutiny.

The bottom line is, men are capable of a lot more than they are doing, and women do too much. Both are enabling a situation in which they are basically unhappy because they have lost what they valued most in each other. When we drilled down to the truth, what we uncovered was anger, hurt, and a sense of abandonment on both sides. One surprise for women is that men are actually wounded by the demotion they suffer on the domestic front, which is, after all, where couples spend most of their time together. Sure, there's conflict between women and their mothered men, but we found that there's an even deeper conflict *within* each gender—between what they are putting up with and what they really want. Making a home together shouldn't mean losing your good relationship. Neither should raising kids. It's sad when two people who once shared a great love are reduced to a wary disconnect.

Believe it or not, having the upper hand at home is not an irreversible condition. It may seem, once you have become his mother, that you can't go back, that he can never be restored to a full adult in your eyes (or his). But he can. The guy who now seems like a child, who seems inept or irresponsible, even ineffectual, can make a comeback and be someone worthy of your respect again. We aren't talking about forgiveness, though forgiveness is needed too; we are talking about recovery and rebirth, about a granting of new territory and new chances on both sides.

It *can* be done: you can walk each other back from the brink. It requires shaking off the assumptions and accusations that we deconstructed in part 2, and we hope you're ready to bid them a hearty "Good riddance." And it requires looking at each other with new eyes, letting each other shake off the chrysalis and be butterflies. You're not in the home-free world where you fell in love: you're in a domestic pressure cooker where things got out of kilter. You need to get to a place you *haven't* been yet, one that is domestic but also has the equality and joy that you experienced when you were starting out. Getting there will take a willingness to experiment, to try new roles and wear new hats, to be flexible. To be open. To see the humor in the plight of the overstressed adult, to meet as innocents, the way children do.

Spouses need to be equals who value and respect each other, and work (and play) together as partners. But *how* do you get there? We'll offer a step-by-step pathway out of the impasse, which only requires that you and your spouse really want it (we'll show you how to get him on board). What we'll recommend is a combination of blunt honesty (starting with yourself), benevolent manipulation, and, above all, open-minded negotiation. Throw in some list making and a dash of outrageous provocation, and you'll have a recipe for moving your man and yourself to a better place.

Negotiation lies just around the bend. There's much to talk about with your husband, including the myriad tasks of running a home and raising children. We saw in chapter 1 how an unequal division of these tasks can plant you in the role of his mother. That mothering role is hard to budge when you take it all at once, hard to extricate yourself from. But it turns out that when you break it down into individual tasks, there's plenty of room for give and take—and for change. But before we get to that meeting of minds, it's a good idea to work on the emotional atmosphere between the two of you.

If we thaw the hearts out, the minds will be ready to follow.

We looked in chapter 2 at how the dynamics between you got tarnished by the mother-child way of relating, and in part 2 we saw lots of examples of how blame shifts back and forth like a toxic flame, so that respect and affection are lost. If you begin to improve those embittered behaviors, the clouds will lift and you'll find that when it's time to carry out the game plan for recovery, you'll have the benefit of a nicer atmosphere. So in this chapter we'll present some things you can do to reduce the irritation and resentment that have infested your day-to-day interaction with your spouse. Claws and fangs, your hour is ending!

In a short while you are going to bring your husband to the negotiating table and the two of you will talk things over like adults. But even before you take that step, you can start to change his behavior by changing the signals that you send. You have so much power.

We've heard women reply, "I don't want to manipulate him into doing more, because that would just mean I am being his mother again."

But we say pish. The first step in shedding the unwanted role of his mother is to lose the obnoxious behaviors that are part of that role. Adjust your own attitudes that have gone sour. That will give him a chance to raise his head, sniff the air, and realize it might be possible to act differently.

Let's look at what you can do.

Controlling Anger Reactions

Anger is a *choice,* though it may not feel like it most of the time. Anger feeds on itself: one person gets mad, that makes the other person madder, and escalation ensues. Stop the cycle of anger and you make room for something else to happen.

Take Cyndi. She had just arrived home from shopping for groceries to find Mitch on the phone. By his numb tone and brief responses, she could tell he was talking to his mother. She also knew this was bad news, because his mother had a way of jerking his chain, subtly disparaging his marriage, and guilt-tripping him about neglecting her, all at once. She definitely had talent in the area of giving him flak.

When Mitch hung up, Cyndi asked, "How are your mom and dad?"

"Same old."

After a pause, Mitch asked, "How was shopping?" in an echoing tone, as he opened a container of pomegranate yogurt.

"Same old," she responded.

Every time Mitch was on the phone with his mother, Cyndi waited for the ax to fall. After forcing himself to behave on the phone, he became the petulant son in his own home. It didn't take long for his tirade to begin.

"What's this?" he said as he held up the yogurt container. "Nonfat? Why is it that we all have to suffer when you're on a diet? This has no taste. I might as well be eating milk of magnesia."

Cyndi bit her tongue—hard. What she really wanted to say was, "If you don't like it, try shopping some time." Or more expansively, "There you go again. Taking your mother out on me. That's *really* the same old. Maybe you should grow up." Either of these responses probably would have been justified. Mitch had a habit of complaining when his grocery needs weren't being met and generally picking on how Cyndi did various tasks, instead of pitching in and helping with them. And he also, as we've said, had a habit of turning his unresolved issues with his own mom on Cyndi, who often acted like a mother to him. But we're not talking justification here, or retaliation. We're talking a unilateral, unannounced truce.

Cyndi had recently had a look at the ideas in this book, and she thought to herself, *Don't feed the anger cycle.* So she said nothing. She just continued unpacking the groceries.

Mitch left the room and she saw him lie down on the couch with his newspaper. She felt her hackles rise but again did nothing. She could tell by his vibe that he was expecting her to pursue him into the living room and rain some shrapnel on him. She wanted to do exactly that, to order him back into the kitchen to help her unpack the groceries, but she knew that being in the room together at that moment would do neither of them any good. Space to cool down was what Mitch needed. And oddly enough, she found it wasn't that hard to conquer her own knee-jerk reactions, now that she was looking at them from one level higher, as a pattern she could choose or not choose to buy into. *I have a purpose here,* she reminded herself. *I am going to change the dynamic between us, and he is going to change too, because before very long we are going to remove the* causes *of all this anger and hostility.*

Half an hour later Mitch came back into the kitchen. He looked at her in a wondering way, trying to read the reason for his reprieve. She was starting to empty the dishwasher, and he touched her arm and said, "Let me do that." He began to put the clean dishes away and then turned and looked at her again.

"I'm sorry I yelled at you," he said. "It's my mom; she drives me bananas."

"I should have gotten you some creamier yogurt," she said.

"That's you, always so selfish." He was kidding, and his grimace said, *You aren't the selfish one.*

We aren't suggesting that a dialing down of anger will always achieve miraculous results. But when a spouse is *expecting* hostile behavior (because it's so pervasive in the marriage), the lack of it can make a pretty dramatic impression. And most people don't want hostility. They are sick to death of it.

And sometimes anger is the total opposite of the reaction the other person is trying for, and there's a very different emotion that would make pretty good sense, if anger could just get out of the way long enough for that other feeling to have a chance. So we encourage you to give this a chance. Don't throw out the idea without trying it.

Here's a story about that.

Blair and Richard had just moved into a new house. Actually

it was an old house, not very large, and they had been forced to move because Blair had lost her job and they couldn't afford their swank apartment anymore. They couldn't really afford the smaller place either, but they could just scrape by if they curtailed their eating out and other indulgences. They were in the throes of unpacking and trying to fit ten rooms of stuff into a six-room place, and to make matters worse, some of the prime pieces they owned just didn't fit in the cottage they now called home. So they needed some new things, but they had to think carefully about which ones to buy and how much to pay. One thing they definitely needed was a shower curtain: instead of the smart stall they'd left behind, the new place had a tub with a moldy old shroud hanging around it, featuring a grinning, once-green froggy.

So Richard came home from work to find Blair hefting a box of books. "I have a surprise," he said.

"You do?" she said warily.

"Something you're going to like." He held out a bag from Bed Bath & Beyond and led her into the second room featured in that snappy name.

Blair gave a flinch of a smile, black smoke already rising in her. She had ruled their former home and now she was trying to hold the reins in their reduced circumstances. What had he bought without consulting her?

She had not yet realized that a sea change was taking place in her psyche: her job had stressed her cruelly; nasty employers had made her a bear to get along with. She had more time now and her income from unemployment meant she didn't have to rush into another bad position. She was free, and she was on her way to a comeback as a companion one could enjoy. Her husband already sensed it. But she didn't, not yet.

Richard pulled the object out of the bag. It was a shower curtain. Beaming at her, he unfolded it and let it hang down. The maroon color suited the bathroom's odd, periwinkle shade. The seersucker material was okay too. But she hadn't chosen it, it was a little more ornate than she'd had in mind for the bathroom, and it had cost money.

"What did you pay for this?" she said in a scalding tone.

His face fell. "Twenty-five dollars."

"That's too much. And it's too busy for the room."

"I—I thought you'd like it."

"You *didn't* think. This is the kind of decision we're supposed to make together."

As soon as she said this, Blair knew it was absurd. This had cost twenty-five dollars. She was focusing all the alarm and trepidation of recent events on a trifle.

Richard let the purchase fall to the floor. He would normally have gotten defensive, but he too was changing. The struggle to make the move had melded him to her, and he was grateful for several things: the amazing speed with which she had found the little cottage, the lifting of her job stress off her shoulders, and a few little moments when they had laughed in the midst of adversity and even acted a bit sweet toward each other. Wanting to avoid conflict, he retreated as far as he could in their cramped new quarters. He ended up in the chair in the corner.

She followed him, feeling lost, and he tried to tell her about how he'd found a buyer for their California king, which didn't fit in the new bedroom. But he was obviously deflated.

She crumpled onto the floor in front of him, in a sort of yoga pose.

"Honey, I'm sorry I didn't like the shower curtain," she said. She was full of remorse. He had gone out of his comfort zone to buy the kind of thing she typically liked, and she had jumped all over him. He had done well.

"It's okay," he said. "I *was* being kind of impulsive."

"I like it. It's good."

Blair hadn't heard the ideas in this chapter, but she knew that chronic anger had blocked her from giving her husband kudos for stepping up and scoring one for the team. She resolved to give her mate a chance and to try to rein in the bitterness that had become a habit.

It also occurred to her that she didn't have to manage every tiny detail of their life. We'll return to that idea shortly.

Meanwhile, you probably have a steady supply of fairly trivial misdemeanors committed by your spouse that vex you enough to bring out an angry response. We're saying, walk away. He comes home from work and dumps his briefcase by the door, when he promised you he would put it by his desk. This was *discussed,* dammit! You speculate that he just said that to placate you. What a grand opportunity to get mad. So don't. (And maybe he'll surprise you and move it, after he races to the bathroom to have unscheduled diarrhea and finishes a phone call from his boss.)

Controlling Control

Our friend Blair decided maybe she didn't have to micromanage every design detail in the small home she and Richard had just moved to. Maybe he could select a shower curtain without her supervision. Maybe he could do even more, like choose a painting to hang above the couch.

That illustrates our next point: as part of your purposeful strategy for creating a less toxic atmosphere, *take control over your impulse to control everything*—just for a week or three.

For instance, don't redo tasks that he has made a good-faith effort to do. A classic example of this issue is the making of the communal bed. We touched on it in chapter 2, when the wife insisted on pointedly remaking the bed after her husband had tried his best to do it. Many, many women like the bed to look a certain way when it isn't being slept in, and they are continually irritated by their spouse's either failing to make it or doing it wrong. But some guys attempt the feat. If your guy does, then during the "period of amnesty" we're recommending, leave it be.

And consider this: there are deeper issues lurking here, ones you may not have considered. A guy who tries to make the bed the way you like it may be overcoming deep inner resistance, for your sake. Therefore, he deserves credit.

What kind of resistance? Well, to be frank, and J.M. is speaking purely as devil's advocate here, decorative pillows suck. Why? Because you don't *use* them, and they get in the way of the things you *want* to do with a bed, like lie on it. And they have no place to go when they aren't blocking access to the sweet comfort of the "real" pillows that lie beneath them. How many men have dragged their aching limbs up the stairs, desperately needing a nap, and found these monstrosities piled like some mocking obstacle? What are they for, and why are there so many of them, and why do they have to be arranged in a certain configuration, just so? He wants them out of the way, so he can dig down to the actual pillow he likes under his head. But where to put them? There is never a place. You have to throw them on the floor. There should be some elegant netting that hangs from the ceiling into which a dude could toss them, and maybe leave them there for a month or two. But no. So he throws them on the floor, where they gather dirt and dust and trip him in the dark before they make their daily migration back onto the pristine bed. Nice.

The problem is even more graphic when you go to a fancy B&B while attending the wedding of a relative. You walk in and survey the room where you're going to live for three days, and there are no surfaces available: no desk, no shelves, just a ledge by the window and one uncomfortable brocade chair. And the bed is literally full of pillows. So in order to lie down after your long drive, you have to wreck the room.

So think about it: when you install fifteen decorative pillows, you have quite possibly made the bedroom into a room he doesn't like.

Okay, 'nuff said about pillows. The point is that many decorative touches are downright impractical, and a guy who puts up with them or even tries to support them may deserve a break. The more general point is, many of the things (decorative or not) that you are accustomed to controlling might very well be done some other way, and might be better for it.

When you give up control for a while, you will discover that male humans have their own ways of doing things, and sometimes even have reasons for them. Maybe there's a reason why he likes to soak the dirty silverware in a plastic glass of water that you think becomes yucky: it makes it easier to wash. Maybe there's a reason he hangs his wet bath towel over the shower rod instead of using the hook on the back of the door where it would rub shoulders with other towels: he wants it to get the air so it can dry in a sanitary way and be reused. (Maybe it's his fear of laundry and the moral black hole it entails: if he can make towels last longer, he'll stave off the moment when a wash must be done.) Come to think of it, many of the things men do are designed to postpone laundry. When he carefully drapes his shirt over the back of a chair (on which there are already several shirts), it's because that way it won't get all wrinkled and he can wear it again, since it wasn't next to his skin (a T-shirt was), and it would take too long to find a hanger and put it in the closet, and besides, the shirts in the closet are the ones that haven't yet been worn since they were laundered, and he wants to keep the "slightly used" ones separate.

The joy of control is a boon, and it should be shared. Let him get his rocks off for a few days by being able to do things the way he likes to do them. When he says, "Honey, want me to pick up a hoagie for supper on the way back from the hardware store?" don't say, "That sounds good, but can you go to the store later because that way the sandwich will be fresher?" Just say, "Great idea!"

We're not saying stop doing the things you normally do that need doing. We're saying step back from micromanaging things he is doing, when you can.

An End to Nagging

We talked about this before. Nagging is not simply asking someone to do something. Nagging is bringing in the past and invoking the perp's sheet of past offenses, deplorable cases of dereliction or inattention. It's also an admission of powerlessness: *I have to repeat this because I don't have your respect, which would make you do the needed task after* one *request.*

So stop nagging. In fact, as far as you can, try to stop asking or telling him to do things that imply that you know his business better than he does. Just let him do the things he seems to think need doing. Of course, there are some matters it is hard to shut up about, even for a week or two, because they impact you too. If the electric bill is lying there unpaid, better remind him to pay it. If he has blood in his stool, you have to urge him to go to the doctor or you could lose a husband.

But if he's the one who will be impacted by not doing whatever it is, and the blow won't be too serious, try to hold your tongue. For example, if you would usually remind him to take a warmer jacket to the night game, don't. Let him feel a little chilly and complain that you didn't alert him to this danger. Tell him you didn't want to nag or remind.

What we're suggesting here is the discreet use of a clever technique that adults sometimes use to avoid overparenting or bad parenting: *using consequences* to teach a child lessons he needs to learn. Instead of yelling at him or ordering him around, instead of always trying to warn him away from harm before he can learn his own lessons, give him autonomy and let him make a few mistakes. Without nagging or getting angry, you'll still get to see your wisdom validated. There's still a consequence for his negligence, but you aren't the bad guy anymore. It's perfect. It's really a restraint-of-parenting technique, and it will help you along the road to not being your husband's mother.

Take Naomi. She was married to Brit, who happened to be an alcoholic. But that is not what concerns us here. Brit also was charming, handsome, creative, irresponsible, and lazy, and he needed parenting, which Naomi provided. In particular, Brit didn't take care of his car. He didn't change the oil when he should, and worse still, he would not bother to get the gas tank filled up when it was running low. What he *would* do is take Naomi's car if his had a problem. (Hers was always in tip-top shape.) That forced her to take his, and one time she did and ended up broken down in the wrong part of the city at night and narrowly avoided being mugged by some enterprising young men.

So Naomi decided to put a stop to his strategy for eluding responsibility. She removed her extra car keys from his chain and started hiding them in a place he wouldn't access (his toolbox). Then one night his car ran out of gas about a hundred yards from home, when he was in a hurry to meet his buddy at the basketball game. Her car was sitting there but she was out, and he turned the house over trying to find the keys. No luck. He didn't make it to the game. He had a long time to think about how easy it would have been to get gas that afternoon.

Carmen used consequences to teach her husband to change lightbulbs. Josh was not an alcoholic but a workaholic. He was truly dedicated to his insurance job, but that meant no time for much else. She used to nag him about a lot of things, and one of them was to change the spotlights that shone at night on the parking area behind their house. Guests would typically park their cars, ascend the wooden steps that led to their deck, and come in through the back door.

One of the spotlights was out, then both were. Changing them involved climbing an extension ladder and having a long reach. The ladder was partially buried in the garage. Josh procrastinated. Carmen decided to stop nagging. It was a slightly dangerous decision, but she had had enough of being his mom.

One night Ben, a close friend of Josh's, came over to play guitar with him, accompanied by his slender and beautiful new wife, Tabatha. In the darkness Tabatha couldn't see the gap between the parking asphalt and the slab at the foot of the steps, and she slipped. She was a dancer by trade. She caught herself, but just barely, and twisted her ankle. It wasn't sprained, but she was livid when she walked into the dining room, and Josh took too facetious a tone with her, which led to a serious fight. Ben had to side with his wife, and the quarrel led to Ben's feeling disrespected. Being a man of great dignity, he never came near Josh again. It was a tough lesson, but Carmen told herself it was all part of Josh's growing up, and anyway she had never really liked the slightly pompous Ben.

Use consequences. It's fun, it's entertaining, it works. And you don't have to play the nagging shrew. You may, perhaps, want to choose areas less perilous than Carmen did, but if you play your cards right, your mate will become more responsible and you'll find it easier to refrain from hostilities.

Appealing to the Best in Him

When a man feels demoted to a child, when you have made a point over time of finding ways to solve problems without calling on him, he may easily sink into a feeling of uselessness. There is no better antidote to this—no better way to perk a guy up and make him feel honored and valued—than to ask him for help with something important. What we're talking about is pulling him into your sphere, treating him as a co-pilot who is worthy to take the wheel in some area that you often reserve for yourself because it is so critical.

So go ahead: ask your husband, on occasion, to do something that means you trust him with responsibility. For example, ask him to talk to your daughter about the sad thing that happened at school, and don't tell him *how* to do it.

Nothing is more flattering than a co-parent who has confidence in you.

Brent often felt intimidated by Cheryl's general knowledge. Whenever the kids had a project that required them to research places around the world or peculiar names of plants, Cheryl seemed able to extract helpful starting points from some part of her memory bank that Brent felt he couldn't match. Over time, Brent didn't even offer to help with homework. Cheryl was doing such a good job, and the kids seemed aware of it too.

Not that Brent was happy with this situation. He wasn't. He felt marginalized and insulted, and sometimes he made sarcastic comments about how Cheryl should have been a fricking professor, since she knew it all. Cheryl enjoyed being needed by her kids and using her knowledge, but she also had trouble finding the time to do this, and she knew it contributed to the tipping of the marital ship. So she was looking for a way to let Brent back in.

One day, their oldest son, Andrew, came home with a homework project on saving energy. Cheryl remembered all the hard work Brent had put into charting the times of day and days of the week that allowed them to save money on their hydro usage. So she suggested to Andrew that he talk to his father about his project. Andrew seemed surprised but agreed. Brent too was surprised, but he felt honored when Andrew approached him. Brent pulled out the notes that he had filed away and went over them with Andrew, who listened intently. As Cheryl watched them together, she was glad she'd given up a little chunk of territory. It took the load off her shoulders and allowed Andrew to see his father as knowledgeable and capable too.

This one action began a thaw in the relations between husband and wife, because child rearing was one of the most important areas in which they had lost their balance. As Cheryl thought about it, she realized there were several subjects where Brent could offer the kids guidance as good as hers, or maybe better. She resolved not to hog the educator role anymore.

A man who feels honored is much more likely to come cheerfully to the negotiating table, and if you find valid ways to appeal to the best of him, you may find that there is less to negotiate.

Brenda shared the following story.

"I had planned on getting to work at around nine, after I'd dropped the kids off at school. When I woke up and noticed the dog limping, I thought, *Oh shit, I'm going to have to find a way of getting her to the vet this morning.* I thought about calling the neighbor to ask if she could help with the kids or calling work to say I'd be late. I didn't even consider that I might ask Mark for his help, even though he had some flexibility in his day. I was so used to handling everything on my own that he didn't even figure as a possible option. I guess I typically don't ask him because I worry that he won't ask all the right questions about Mitzi, our dog, or that he won't come home with the proper instructions about what to do for her."

As a result of Brenda's automatic assumption of Mark's incompetence, she had not only taken on the primary responsibility with regard to parenting but had also become the primary caregiver for their animals. And he was hurt by this, because he had a real bond with them too.

But Brenda was an early adapter of the advice in this book, and she was looking for a way to invest more faith in Mark than he (or she) was used to. So that morning she decided to let go of some of her reservations and ask Mark for his help. He rose to the occasion. He not only got the pooch to the clinic, but he engaged in a searching conversation with the vet, found out that there was a better flea preventer they could be using, and came home with a complete mastery of how to wrap the supportive bandage around Mitzi's leg, even showing Brenda how it was done.

When Brenda replayed that last vignette, she saw two grown adults working as a team.

* * *

You have to be a little careful in choosing tasks here. Some things he might just say no to. Only *you* know which functions are likely to make this tactic succeed. One key is to try to choose an area where *you know he has felt left out and hasn't been happy about it.* An area where he wants to take more responsibility because his feelings are engaged, and his sense of his own competence is at stake. If you give this a try and he begs off, don't conclude that you've failed. You may have to try more than once. He may need time to realize that he's missing chances to be a go-to guy. But if, underneath, he's unhappy with the way things are, he'll come through and show you. We'll talk more in chapter 14 about how you determine if he is really ready—with your active leadership—to shake off the straitjacket of the Mother Syndrome and make changes.

Asking for Advice

If you have become the manager of the house, and of your husband, and that has led to bitterness and nasty behaviors, there is no better way to counteract them than to ask him for advice on a significant decision. He may not believe what he is hearing at first, but he will want to.

Pick an area where you really are tired of going it alone or the choice to be made is actually hard for you. For instance, ask him whether you should incur another big repair bill on your car, or would it make more sense to stop throwing good money after bad and put those funds into replacing it? Let's say you're leaning toward replacement. It doesn't matter whether his input confirms your impulse or leads you to make a different decision; maybe the two of you will chicken out and decide to get the damn radiator replaced because you don't want the trouble of searching for a used car and vetting it. He will still get the benefit of having his thoughts valued and playing a role in decision making, and you will get a feeling of greater security because you're in it together, and because two people are more likely to think of all the factors that matter.

Patricia took this advice when she was thinking about an upcoming holiday weekend. One of her best college friends was coming to visit: she hadn't seen Lynn, who lived across the country, for six years, but they kept in touch on Facebook and sent each other outrageous greeting cards. Then she had a fabulous stroke of inspiration: she could also invite the other two friends, now married, who had been part of their circle back then. (The other link in that old chain was Joel, Patricia's husband, who now, after ten years of marriage, was deep in mothered territory.)

Fran and Clarence lived about three hours away, and they saw them a couple of times a year. This would be amazing—a lovefest! Lynn could sleep on the couch in the guest room, and Fran and Clarence could use the pullout bed in the TV room.

Normally Patricia would have set the whole thing up, planned every event in their itinerary, and told Joel about it after the fact, expecting him to grumble for a while and then passively go along. Patricia was about to call Fran when she thought, *Okay, this is one of those chances to ask Joel what he thinks.* She went into the bedroom where he was reading. She told him the plan and hardly believed her own voice when she said, "Do you think this is a good idea?"

Joel also looked a bit shocked. He put down his book and sat up straight, scratching his head.

"You already asked Lynn, right?"

"Yes, she's flying in on the Friday night."

"So you want to make it even better and ask the Malicks."

"Right! We can get crazed and forget we're grown up!"

"Okay, I get that." He smiled at her, then frowned. "I do see one problem."

Joel explained that he saw a bad scenario developing. Couples always trump single people, and Lynn was still unattached, right? Patricia said that was right. Well then, Lynn was going to end up being the fifth wheel. Even more important was the next point he made.

"You and Lynn are kind of a one-on-one thing, no?"

"Yeah, we like to get into those *deep* conversations."

"You won't get any alone time with her. It'll be bedlam and the couples will drive every decision. She won't be able to talk about the miseries of being lonely, and you won't be able to talk about the miseries of being married."

"Oh God, you're right. Shit, this could have been a disaster."

"There's another thing too. Even though it's a holiday weekend, I am going to be up to my eyeballs in this deadline for the Bristol account. I'll have to be downstairs at my desk a lot."

Patricia got more than she bargained for. A token attempt to "involve" her husband in the loop turned out to save an important weekend, during which she got to truly bond with one of the souls on earth whom she loved best.

A final for-instance: Maybe you're about to send an incendiary email, to a co-worker or a friend who did you wrong, or the mother of a kid who has been bullying your kid in the schoolyard. Before you hit send, you remember the person who shares these walls with you and knows you better than most anyone else, and you have him look it over. And he points out that emails are easy to share these days and the offended party could go viral with it, or that it lacks nuance and could be easily misinterpreted, where a phone call or an in-person chat might be scarier but would be a whole lot safer. . . . You know the drill.

The opportunity can come in any number of ways. What you're doing is turning to your partner in a way that indicates that he is intelligent, has relevant experience, and can be relied on as a team member. What a powerful way to cut right through the habits that have made him feel like he doesn't exist.

A Spoonful of Sugar

Two final tips for dispelling the toxic dynamics that have beset you and your mate.

Remember that thing called encouragement, that thing you do with people to *draw* them in a certain direction instead of prodding them? Give him some of that, to help pull him out of the hole he's in.

Mix some sugar with the medicine. Find things to compliment him for. They don't have to be big things. Be like the wife who told her indecipherably scribbling husband that his *O*s were very nicely formed. Notice what he's doing right, or when he's looking good, or when he says something funny, and give him applause. On the one day that he pulls out that nice shirt to wear to your friends' place, say, "You look hunky." When he's about to make an egg, ask him to make one for you too, because nobody gets them just firm enough like he does.

Even better, talk about him in a positive way to other people, in his presence. Or report to him how you quoted him to your best friend because what he said was so on the money.

Let him think that once in a while, he is the star of your own movie. Because he is.

Our second tip: Be on the alert for opportunities to enjoy

each other. In the brighter atmosphere that you've tried to create, there will be chances to laugh together, to share feelings, and generally to bond. Make sure you nurture them and let them flourish. Among them would be chances for *rich, mutually satisfying communication.* So if he shows signs of trusting you with some personal feelings, take the time to listen. And don't forget the old reliable advice that when the other person vents, the first step is to *validate* that person, not to problem-solve or correct.

Of course, it doesn't have to be about soul baring or mutual therapy, though those things are often good. It could just be a bit of silliness, a funny story being shared, or a quiet time together. The point is, look for the kind of moments that tend to reaffirm and rebuild a positive bond between you.

It takes a secure person to concede ground to someone else. The nerve of you, unilaterally putting down the boxing gloves, disarming, changing your husband's world so it is less full of opposition and attack. For a while he may keep ducking, not quite realizing that the sniping has stopped. Or rather, that he's the only one doing it now. So he doesn't need to. So he stops ducking and stands up straight.

It takes a secure person to bury the hatchet. But the thing about security is, it grows when it is bestowed on someone else. It spreads. Your strength will leak into him and he'll get stronger too, so *you* will have more to lean on.

When you carry out the plan described in this chapter, you will create a whole new ball game in which the idea of sitting down and negotiating a new world order with your man will not seem so remote. So you had best start figuring out exactly what you want that world order to look like. That's what we'll tackle next.

Chapter 13

Getting Your Wish List Straight

The first rule of negotiation is, *Before you can* get *what you want, you need to* know *what you want.* Starting in the next chapter, we'll talk about how to reach a new agreement with your husband in which he will take on more jobs and responsibilities so he can lift them off your shoulders, free you from the role of mothering him, and restore his status as an equal partner and a lover. But before you can be ready to forge a new deal, you need to take stock of what exactly you want to ask for. You need to get your own goals straight.

So, supposing for the moment that you could get him to agree to everything you want. . . . What would that "everything" be? That deceptively simple question is what you'll answer as you work through this chapter. You won't be *presenting* your ideas to him yet. That will come later; this stage is you deciding what your ideas *are.*

The way to do that is to formulate a detailed wish list, and we'll help you put one together. You'll get better results if you boil your objectives down to specifics. That way you won't forget to ask for things you really need, and you won't overreach by demanding things that might in fact make you unhappy. Because if you're not careful, you could get your husband to take on things that would leave you feeling stranded, disconnected, or frustrated. So a little self-knowledge is called for here, a moment of musing, some careful sifting of scenarios. All of which we'll get into.

We are about to present the Questionnaire That Will Set You Free, in which we itemize household tasks and invite you to decide which ones you'd ideally like to assign to him. But before we do, a couple of words to the wise. When you first look upon the questionnaire, you may tend to break into a sweat, have tremors, and vent, "OMG, this is too big, too detailed. This is like the SATs!" To which we say the following:

- You don't have to fill out the whole questionnaire. You can just fill out the parts that matter to you.
- When you download the questionnaire from our website, www.howcanibeyourloverq.com, if you don't like your first run at it, you can do it again.
- You can create your own version from our template, in which you include any components you like of ours and add your own.

In other words, you can tailor this resource to your own needs.

But yes, it is detailed. We *had* to go into detail and bring it down to individual tasks, because they are what people do and they are what people understand (especially men). We are talking about you *transferring jobs* to your darling husband. It won't do to be vague. You can't transfer the cleaning to him, because people don't clean, they clean *something*. If he agrees to do "more cleaning," that won't do any good because neither of you will know what he just signed on for. But if he agrees to clean the toilet, now you're getting somewhere. That is a task, not a category. We need to transfer *tasks*.

So the questionnaire does not suffer from too much detail. In fact, it may not go far enough in that direction. You can't get anywhere arguing about who's working harder or who isn't. Or about flaws of character: who's too lazy and who's too controlling. We've been there in part 2; we've done that. It's much more productive (and actually more fun, as you'll see) to parley about who's gonna roll up their sleeves and do what.

Now it's true some tasks could possibly be *bundled*. For example, all the tasks that go into doing the laundry could be bundled together, with some imaginative label like "doing the laundry," and one person could sign on to do them all. We get that, but we don't want to assume in advance *which* things you want to bundle together. We want to talk about it with you, in this chapter, before you talk about it with your hubby. Because it all depends on how you do things and how you like them done, and who's capable of what.

Plus, you can't approach this recipe with too blunt a knife. It isn't just about what you will keep doing and what he will start doing. (That's why you'll find more than two columns in this questionnaire.) There are tasks you'll want to *share*. There are tasks you would like him to do, but only if he learns to do them up to your standards. And—believe it or not—there are tasks that you'll be willing to pass off to him, even if he does them his way and his way is different from your way. We should have put an exclamation point after that sentence, because it is surprising. But we *want* you to surprise yourself—and him. We need you to.

That's right, we need you to give up some control, or this lovely chapter might not change anything. You started experimenting with less control in the last chapter, and that needs to continue. Because being in charge of him and his home, being his mama and the boss of him, is just what we are trying to get you away from. So we're going to chat more about that too, by looking at some tasks you may think you need to control, but you may be wrong about.

We're not only going to present the right questions, which will give you a foolproof way to bring change to your marriage; we're going to talk over the tricky issues that lurk in the answers, so you can see what is at stake.

And now, without further ado (drum roll), ladies, the Questionnaire. Take a quick gander at it (don't fill it out yet) and then join us on the other side.

		Who do you *want* to do it?					
	1	2	3	4	5	6	7
Task	How often should it be done?	Who does it now?	You want to do it yourself	You want to share it with him	You want him to do it, *your* way	You want him to do it, *his* way	His response
CLEANING **cleaning up after meals**							
clearing the table							
washing some items by hand							
loading the dishwasher							
wiping the kitchen counters and sinks, taps							
unloading the dishwasher and putting things away							

	1	2	3	4	5	6	7
Task	How often should it be done?	Who does it now?	You want to do it yourself	You want to share it with him	You want him to do it, *your* way	You want him to do it, *his* way	His response
sweeping/ mopping the floor							
cleaning the living room							
neatening up the living room							
vacuuming the living room							
cleaning the bedrooms							
neatening up the bedrooms							
making the beds							
vacuuming the bedrooms							
changing the bedsheets							
cleaning the bathrooms: toilets, sinks, tubs							
scrubbing the toilets and the toilet bowls							
cleaning the sinks							
cleaning the tubs/showers							
cleaning the mirrors							
sweeping/ mopping the floors							
trash/garbage							
collecting the trash from all over the house							
taking the trash to the curb							
organizing the recycling and taking it to curb							

	1	2	3	4	5	6	7
Task	How often should it be done?	Who does it now?	You want to do it yourself	You want to share it with him	You want him to do it, *your* way	You want him to do it, *his* way	His response
			deep cleaning				
dusting/wiping surfaces, ornaments, shelves							
organizing and cleaning cupboards							
cleaning the fridge							
cleaning the oven							
deep-cleaning the bathroom							
cleaning mirrored and glass doors							
cleaning windows							
			LAUNDRY washing				
sorting the dirty clothes							
putting various loads into the washer							
washing delicates by hand							
			drying				
sorting the washed clothes							
using the dryer for various loads							
hanging some clothes on hangers							
laying some clothes flat to dry							

	1	2	3	4	5	6	7
Task	How often should it be done?	Who does it now?	You want to do it yourself	You want to share it with him	You want him to do it, *your* way	You want him to do it, *his* way	His response
ironing							
splitting up the washables							
the his and hers method (see chapter 13)							
the three hamper method (see chapter 17)							
MEALS							
planning meals							
reading cookbooks and other recipes							
watching cooking shows							
shopping for meals, food staples, and other supermarket staples							
putting groceries away							
making breakfast for the kids							
making lunch for the kids							
making dinner							
ingredient prep: washing, chopping, etc.							
cooking (frying, baking, assembly)							
serving							

	1	2	3	4	5	6	7
Task	How often should it be done?	Who does it now?	You want to do it yourself	You want to share it with him	You want him to do it, *your* way	You want him to do it, *his* way	His response
			MANAGING/SCHEDULING				
sorting the mail							
managing/paying bills online or by mail							
scheduling social engagements with friends							
scheduling medical appointments							
making reservations at restaurants							
making long-term financial decisions, such as							
- investments							
- how and when to pay off debt							
- major purchases							
doing the taxes							
planning travel, day trips and longer							
planning vacations							
interfacing with his family (we assume you want to do your own)							
waking the children up in the morning							

	1	2	3	4	5	6	7
Task	How often should it be done?	Who does it now?	You want to do it yourself	You want to share it with him	You want him to do it, *your* way	You want him to do it, *his* way	His response
CHILD REARING							
making school lunches							
doing homework with the children							
getting the children to and from school							
getting the children to and from extracurricular activities							
vigilant, preventive monitoring of the children							
getting the children into bed at night							
entertaining the children							
having fun with the children							
conversing with the children							
going on outings with the children							
listening to the children							
teaching the children							
disciplining the children							

	1	2	3	4	5	6	7
Task	How often should it be done?	Who does it now?	You want to do it yourself	You want to share it with him	You want him to do it, *your* way	You want him to do it, *his* way	His response
formulating rules and boundaries							
organizing the children's medical appointments							
organizing the children's play dates							
scheduling the babysitter when you go out as a couple							
shopping for children's clothes and supplies							
YARD WORK							
cutting the grass and other lawn care							
tree care							
snow shoveling							
gardening							
planting							
weeding							
pruning and clipping							
other gardening							
MAINTENANCE AND REPAIRS							
your vehicle							
his vehicle							
house exterior							
house interior							
HVAC/appliances							
plumbing							

	1	2	3	4	5	6	7
Task	How often should it be done?	Who does it now?	You want to do it yourself	You want to share it with him	You want him to do it, *your* way	You want him to do it, *his* way	His response
utilities (cable, phones, etc)							
SHOPPING OTHER THAN FOOD							
liquor							
pharmacy stuff							
hardware and related stuff							
office supplies							
clothing							
home furnishings							
electronics/ entertainment							
games							
computers							
PETS							
feeding							
grooming							
cleaning/ maintenance							
cats: changing litter, sweeping around litter tray							
dogs: walking							
scheduling vet appointments							
taking the animal to the vet							

Okay, we're glad to see you on the other side of midnight. Or dawn, because a new day is coming.

First, print a copy from the website www.howcanibeyourloverq.com for easy consulting. Next, some observations.

As you will have noticed, the questionnaire takes you through the mothering roles/jobs that we discussed in chapter 1, those famous "hats," broken down into component tasks so you can really get to the individual moving pieces. It will help you think about what parts of cleaning, cooking, adminisrating, and child care you would ideally like your husband to take on. We didn't devote space to hat number four, appearance and etiquette coach, because we think that the changes you're going to make in the other four hats will go a long way toward fixing this one. That's because a husband who becomes a full partner is much more likely to put on his big boy pants and go shopping for a big boy jacket, as well as to raise the level of his social behavior, because he is now a person of influence, a mover and a shaker whose words are listened to and deeds appreciated, a dude of consequence on the home front and elsewhere.

Speaking of your husband, soon (in chapter 17) you are going to share this list with him, not as a honey-do list but as a proposal to be discussed. So, your decisions don't need to be final at this point: they aren't cast in stone. They are a first try at figuring out what you want. They may well change when you get more input from your husband and eventually the two of you figure out what works best for both of you. *You can leave some areas unresolved.* If you aren't sure about a given task, make your best guess, jot down a question mark, and plan to talk it over with your spouse. Maybe you'd be happy to have him take over any three of a certain five tasks, but you don't care which ones. That's fine: record that fact and work it out with him when the time comes.

Some of you may think at this point, "You're just asking me to go into higher gear on being his mom! This questionnaire is just an elaborate way of me telling him what to do, ordering him around—being a mother to him." So let us emphasize: This is you deciding what household work you would choose for him (and you) to do if you could wave a magic wand and things would be that way. You are not going to order him to do (or share) tasks exactly as you have checked them off here. No, you're going to present this to him as your side of the story—what you would vote for—and then you are going to ask for his side. And then negotiate something you can both be comfortable with.

If you're still thinking that it's motherlike for you to be doing the groundwork and prep here and leading him through this process, we can grant your point, but look at the potential upside! If things go well, you will find yourself in a world where he shoulders his share of tasks and responsibility and you feel a hell of a lot *less* like his mother. If you have to be the leader now, because you are the one who has read this book and become conversant with the problem, surely that is not too high a price to pay.

Another thought may also nag at some of you. You may be thinking that this whole exercise won't work if he doesn't change his overall MO. He has bad habits that apply to *whatever* jobs he takes on, like promising what he doesn't deliver, starting what he doesn't finish, and not putting things away after he works on a project. These are serious problems, no doubt about it, though not all mothered men exhibit them, and lots of wives have them. We will talk about them in chapter 17; for now, try to set them aside and focus on how you would *like* things to be.

For each task or role, our questionnaire asks you a couple of questions:

1. How often should the task be done?
2. Who does it now?

Then it offers you several choices: you'll need to pick *one* of them and mark it with a yes. These choices are

3. You want to do the task yourself.
4. You want to share it with him, so both of you contribute.
5. You want him to do it, but he needs to learn to do it up to your standards.
6. You want him to do it, and it's okay if he does it his way.

There is one further column, left blank, for him to fill out when you sit down together to discuss this. That's the column where he gives his initial response to the choices you indicated, by agreeing or disagreeing with each one. We think his response may be a little more complex than that, but we put column 7 in as a reminder that he *will* get to give his response and nothing is decided until he does. We actually think a great idea will be to have him fill out his own *full questionnaire,* the husband version, because you will both learn so much from comparing the two. (Or have him mark up the same one you did, in a different color; that way it's easy to compare responses.) For now, let's just say he will respond. But that moment is not here yet (it will arrive in chapter 17), so don't let him see you filling this out. This is your chance to hatch your nefarious plan at your own sweet pace, under no pressure other than our suggestion not to cackle too loud.

Bending the First Three Columns to Your New Vision

Okay, get out a sharp pencil, in a color you like. And let's take a closer look at the choices to be made.

In column 1 you decide how often, in your opinion, the task should be done. Some tasks pretty much cry out to be performed when their moment comes—like making dinner every night for hungry stomachs. Others hang back in the shadows, politely waiting their turn, like the dusting of the knickknacks. But even urgent, frequent tasks can get neglected or short-shrifted when there isn't enough help. So instead of making dinner, you order a pizza, because the grocery shopping didn't get done or you're just too tired to cook.

But we don't want you to be blinded by the adverse circumstance you're in now. When asking yourself how often the bathroom should be cleaned, you may ruefully think

> Well, let's see. First there's the *ideal* frequency, how often it would be cleaned in the perfect home of my dreams or the one I'm forced to witness on TV commercials, where housewives have so much time that they deliberately spill cherry juice on the floor to compare the absorbent power of dishrags and plush paper towels. Number two, there's the cruel bite of reality: how often someone in my house (me) *actually* cleans the bathroom. And three, there's how often my *husband* thinks it should be done (yearly, or when his mother is visiting). I might as well choose two, because at least it's realistic.

But the idea here is to start fresh and ask yourself, "If my husband were making a manful effort to do his share of all the delightful activities of domesticity, what might be achievable? In *that* world, how often would I want this task to be done?" It's true, as we saw in chapter 8, that his threshold of when a room is so disturbing that it needs attention may well be harder to reach than yours. But for now, stick with what *you* want. And remember that some things that are not being done as often as you wish are going to be done more often, when we summon the cavalry. Things can and will improve.

Column 2 asks, "Who does the task now?" In the extreme

case, you go down the list and for every single task, you answer "me" (or "W" for wife). If things aren't quite that bad, maybe you answer "him" to some of them. But it's inescapable: in all likelihood there aren't enough cases where you can say he currently does it. After all, this book is for women who are doing too much and have thereby become their husbands' mothers. And the direction we're trying to go in is to move a fair share of tasks off your plate and onto your husband's.

Will any tasks be moved in the reverse direction? Well, maybe. There may be some things he's already doing that you want to take over, but we assume that would only be true if they are outweighed by other things that you want him to take over from you.

So column 2, once you fill it in, is basically a graphic witness to the fact that you are doing too much of the heavy lifting.

You check column 3 ("You want to do it yourself") if, in the future, *you* want to be the one who does a given task. Obviously the goal here is not to have column 3 match column 2 ("Who does it now?"). Column 3, if used too much, traps you in the status quo. We want lots of blanks in column 3, indicating that you're electing *not* to do such-and-such anymore; we want tasks moving to 4, 5, or 6:

4. You want to share it with him.
5. You want him to do it, *your* way.
6. You want him to do it, *his* way.

Above all, we don't want you choosing column 3 out of some pessimistic belief that columns 4, 5, and 6 are a hopeless mirage. Especially column 5 (he does it your way). For quite a few tasks, you may think the choice comes down to you doing it or him doing it up to your standards. If you doubt that you can ever get him to improve in that way, you may retreat into saying *you'll* do it. But don't. This is about what you *want,* not what is happening right now. This is your wish list, and you deserve to formulate it for yourself, because everyone has a right to know how they want the world to be. And it's for him too, because before couples resign themselves to hell, they have a right to know what they're really disagreeing about.

So we would suggest this: If you are not able to tackle column 3 in an optimistic and aggressive way (i.e., if you are tending to say yes to too many items), then for the time being, leave it alone and go on to columns 4, 5, and 6, where you will rev up your mojo of hope and change.

So let's talk about those three options.

The Joys—and Pitfalls—of Sharing

A checkmark in column 4 means you want to *share the task* with your husband. That could mean you do it together. In the grand old world before dishwashers, it was more efficient to do the dishes together, one person washing and the other drying and putting away. This was a good time to chat about the day's events and maybe dance to a tune on the radio. Then machines cut in on the action and destroyed a moment of domestic solidarity. [That's what technology often does—so we end up with as many (or more) phones as there are family members, and the same for computers and even TVs. More and more activity takes place in a private fragment of space-time.]

But some tasks can still be shared. Vacuuming, for example: it's a lot of fun to have two people hold the handle and try to walk around the room. Oops, maybe not. Technology scores again.

Well, two people can clean a bathroom. One can work on the

toilet while the other scrubs the sink or the tub. Meanwhile, they can chat about the dangers of abrasive chemicals. Two people can clean a fridge, one washing the drawers that were taken out and the other wiping the cool metal cavities with a cloth. Two people can make a meal: it's been done. Easier if you have lots of counter space. Child rearing can be shared, some of it.

So let your imagination run wild and try to think of tasks that you can do with your husband, both at the same time.

Failing that, there's another kind of sharing, where you *take turns* doing a certain job, or you do some of it and he does some of it, at different times. It's called rotating the work. Like maybe you'd like him to clean the bathroom every second week, and you do the weeks in between. Maybe he cooks some meals and you cook others. And the person who cooks doesn't have to clean up after dinner that evening. This is a very sensible arrangement, because both people get a reward for doing their half.

For some couples, the person who gets home first starts dinner, but that doesn't work very well if it's always the same person. What also doesn't work is when one person deliberately cops out on a task so the other will tackle it: many a wife has shared her frustration about arriving home from work to find her husband on the computer or taking a nap, secure in the belief that she'll handle dinner if he just shirks it long enough. Of course, she has less to complain about if she regularly gives in to this ruse.

Rotating the work requires either two willing people or a system—or both. Some couples power-cook on weekends so there are plenty of entrees to take out of the freezer; others have a regular seven-day menu with, for example, him serving pasta on Fridays and her tacos on Tuesdays, substitutions allowed, of course, when the cook feels spontaneous. If you're doing all the cooking now and don't want to, maybe the reason is inertia—you tend to dive in and do it and he tends to hang back—and maybe this can be easily changed by *getting him to sign on for definite days.*

Another area where many women would welcome the rotation approach is in minding the kids. As one mother put it, "I am tired of always steering the ship. What if I want to be working on my computer all evening but I have to stop to figure out when the kids last bathed or washed their hair, while my husband relaxes in front of the tube? How come he gets to go to sleep whenever he's tired, but I don't get to do the same until my twelve-year-old daughter and her friend are in bed? I'd really like it if we could take turns at steering the ship. We can do alternate nights or alternate weeks or just alternate weekends. Just so I don't have to feel like I'm always the one on the hot spot."

Steering the ship is a good metaphor. The captain, the one in the pilothouse, is the one who can't pass the buck. The one who must remain vigilant, must make sure the vessel stays on course, and who can't rest until the ship is in the harbor.

Rotating the work is a very, very good idea and we can't recommend it enough. If you see where you'd like that to happen, check column 4.

And this brings up a crucial recording point. In order to get this questionnaire to fit onto one page, we had to cut corners. (In one version we had twenty-seven columns.) So you're going to have to make some side notes on areas that can't be handled with just a checkmark. The "sharing tasks" column may inspire you—likely will—to come up with some very specific and creative scenarios that you'll want to discuss with your husband. In many cases you'll need his input to resolve the details of a sharing arrangement. So start a side-note pad. We recommend using 8½ x 11-inch lined tea-green paper pre-drilled with three holes for easy binding—just kidding, use whatever you want. Write a heading like "sharing meal making," and under it, make good clear notes on how you want to rotate the cooking and the cleanup, along with any details that still need to be figured out. Then put an asterisk next to your checkmark in column 4, to remind you to refer to the side notes. Do this whenever useful complexities occur to you regarding a task or bundle of tasks.

Now consider the laundry. According to research, it's the job most avoided by men (we saw some of the reasons in chapter 9). It's huge and never-ending. Therefore it will make a big difference if you can get him to do some of it.

But it's hard to split up. Suppose you assign one person to do the washing and the other does the drying. Take a look at our breakdown of laundry jobs. It's all so clear: the drying person sorts the washed clothes and does various things with them (like hanging some on hangers, putting some in the dryer, laying some flat—you know the drill). Unfortunately, most of this is better done fairly soon after the washer buzzes its happy message of completion. Also, sadly, you can't load a new wash until the old one is removed. So if you're the "washing" person, you end up stymied if the drying person isn't on hand to move the goods down the line.

Even harder is to share *either half* of this task—like the washing. One wife complained that her husband could never intuit what stage she was at with the dirty clothes. Maybe she had gathered them but hadn't sorted them yet. So he throws them willy-nilly in the washer and they don't get the right cycles. Or worse than that, there was the time she had already put a load into the washer but wasn't going to turn it on until that evening, when she could be there to greet the clothes on the other side of SPIN. Her husband thought he'd pitch in, saw clothes in the washer, assumed they were clean, and put them in the dryer. God help us.

There is another way. Actually, two. One is, you divide the whole wash into two parts: his and hers. He washes and dries his own clothes and, let's say, the towels, and she washes (and dries) . . . everything else. (Nobody can screw up towels, and oddly enough, he knows how to clean his own clothes.) This idea has merit, so don't reject it out of hand. Instead of thinking, "He is selfishly doing only his own stuff," think, "I don't have to do his stuff anymore—or the towels!" (We added two lines to the questionnaire to make this option easy to choose, under "splitting up the laundry.")

The other approach: If you have an apt child or two, teach them to do the laundry. That has the merit of not asking you to teach an old dog a new trick. New dogs are amazing. You may want to create additional columns for the kids and pencil in what they could contribute. In chapter 17, when you sit down with hubby to go over the questionnaire, we'll talk more about this nifty idea.

Getting back to laundry, there's even a third approach, which painlessly allows your husband to do most of *your* laundry too. We'll unveil it in chapter 17 so it'll be really fresh in your mind when you talk with him.

Managerial tasks may be harder to share, because they require continuity of purpose and execution. Paying bills, for instance. The juggling of deadlines and online payments and snail mail and the bank account balance is usually best handled by a single brain. But some can and should be shared, and maybe they aren't being shared now: like deciding on long-term investments and on how and when to pay off debt, choosing which major purchases deserve your hard-earned bucks, and planning vacations.

The biggest area that often needs more sharing—meaning both parents involved at the same time—is the raising of children. Too often in today's overscheduled travesty of childhood, everything involving children is reduced to a matter of logistics—getting them to the right place at the right time, where some further adult then drags them through some activity or other. Then add in the tyrannical ideal of efficiency, no doubt instilled by the spread of MBA logic into all crannies of life: "Let's throw the least resources possible, including person power, at the problem. If one parent can do it, why should two?" To some extent we have no choice, people's time and energy being limited, and some things (like tutoring) are best done one-on-one. But let's not forget an astounding fact: you can have both parents in a room or in a car at the same time with kids, and they can all interact!

You'll see an entry under "Child Rearing" in the questionnaire, called "entertaining the kids." At first it was meant to stand in for a whole category, but we realized it wasn't enough. So we added some more items, like having fun with the kids, conversing with the kids, going on outings with the kids, and listening to the kids. We did this with column 4 especially in mind, to give you a chance to think about how much of this is currently being shared—done together—and how much you would like to be shared in future. We'd also like to throw in a plug right here for *unstructured time,* an endangered species in our world. Not all activity has to be goal-oriented, and not all play has to be in the form of a game with rules and winners. One way of inculcating the love of the spontaneous in your children is to spend fun time with them that has no earthly purpose. When this is shared with both parents, it's even better. So let this topic have a moment of your time as you consider what gets a checkmark in column 4.

Three final notes about sharing. In column 2 ("Who does the task now?"), you may have said "both of us" because he presently does some part of the task, but you may *also* want to *change* the way in which he shares it with you (so he does more, or does it better). So even though it's shared now and you want it to remain shared in the future, change is in the wind. If so, put an asterisk in column 4 and write a side note about the new arrangement you want.

Sometimes you want to share a task or an area with him, but only if he improves his quality and gets it up to your standards. If so, check off both columns 3 and 5 and write a side note on what you'd like him to improve.

Finally, when your plan is to share an area by rotating the work, it may seem as if some of the details in the questionnaire are unnecessary. For example, maybe you've decided to propose that you and he take turns cleaning the bathroom on alternate weekends. A great plan. But then why do we need the breakdown of all the *components* of cleaning a bathroom? One person will do them all this weekend, the other next weekend. Since the whole set of tasks goes together, why can't you just put a checkmark in column 4 next to "cleaning the bathroom"—and be done? Our answer is simple. This questionnaire is a very painless way of acquainting your co-negotiator with the wonderfully detailed nature of reality. It will be good for him to see the little jobs that go together into cleaning a bathroom.

Your Way or the Highway?

Okay, on to columns 5 and 6. Let's discuss them together. By checking 5, you say you want him to do the task but he needs to (learn to) do it *your* way, up to your standards. If, however, you check 6, you are willing to let him to do the task his way, even if his way is different from yours—just so he does it.

The choice between 5 and 6 is likely to be the most contentious one you'll make—contentious within your own head and contentious when you talk it over with him. The conflict in your own head is over whether to give up control. So there's a kind of toppling of the dominoes here that can take you all the way from column 6 back to the cold comfort of column 3. For instance, you're doing the questionnaire and you come to laundry. You mull it over and think, "I choose 6. Yeah! I want him to do it for a change, and I'll relax and let him figure it out for himself." After a brief moment of euphoria, you think, "No, that won't do, because he'll shrink my sweaters and scorch my fine blouses." So you switch to 5: he still does it, but he has to do it up to your standards. That sounds good until you face the question, "How am I going to get him to do it up to my standards?" So, reluctantly and with a big sigh, you erase the checkmark in column 5 and put one in column 3: you'll just keep doing it yourself.

This is not what we want. For one thing, you skipped column 4 (sharing it), always a good refuge when discouragement rains. As we saw earlier, there's an easy way you can share the laundry: split up the actual washables into two piles, his and yours.

Or he may be more teachable than you think, even with your clothes and dainties. We aren't saying you should give up control, though. At least not when it means valuable garments will likely be ruined. In some areas, yes. For Pete's sake, let him fold things his own way. But you can still get all the way to him doing the job, even a sensitive job, and you can retain control, *if you can teach him to do it right.* That's the "if" you really have to wrestle with.

As we saw in part 2, too many women take the attitude that men should already know what they (the women) know, or that by not knowing these things, men mark themselves as stupid. Both these attitudes are typical of a certain obnoxious group in our society: bad teachers. In order to teach someone (especially an adult) something difficult, you have to be respectful and patient, and you have to have the even rarer ability to see the topic from the student's point of view, not your own. You have to be willing to listen to how he sees things, even if mistaken, so that you can fill in the missing pieces of the puzzle and help him grasp its solution. You think teaching is easy? It isn't, but most people can do it if they hunker down and take a Zen attitude, with a smidgen of humility and maybe even a little humor. The reason many talented children (and adults) get turned off on some art or science that they could have mastered is that they were mistreated by a teacher. Being abused for an honest mistake will do it; being castigated for not knowing something is effective too. Maybe he already tried to pitch in with some of the domestic work and met with these reactions? Maybe they were part of the gatekeeping that you now wish to refrain from?

Then become a better teacher, and the task will still be done the way you want. Because in some areas you can't give up your standards, and that includes laundering your own precious clothes and those of your children.

But there are other areas where you may want to seriously consider unclenching your hands and giving up your sense that only you know the way it should be done. Always remember what we said in chapter 9: the noble defense of higher standards is often a mask for something more base, the desire to defend one's territory—or more plainly, to *get one's own way*. Just because it's the way you habitually do it doesn't mean it's the only way to do it. Take cooking, for example. It may pain you to see the way he chops vegetables on the board you've reserved for making sandwiches or refuses to use the microwave to heat up a hoagie, but bug off. As long as he doesn't mishandle raw meat, let him do it his own way, because then you don't have to do it! (If he doesn't know how to deal with raw chicken, educate him.) Most people have their own way of doing the dishes. Let him alone. We already discussed the making of the bed. Honor his unique humanity by not imposing convoluted pillow rules.

In other words, try to lighten up on your version of perfection so that more jobs can be moved to column 6 (he does it, his way), because column 6 is the win-win column, where you get to rest and he gets to express himself. That applies in spades to child rearing too. If you simply can't decide between 5 and 6, draw an arrow across both and plan to present it to him as a dilemma you face. (Presenting it that way is much more likely to get him to make a generous move and understand that this is really a problem. Possibly he may react this way: "You shouldn't have to choose an option where it isn't done the way you want it to be done. I'll learn to do it your way.")

We'll talk more about the touchy choice between your way and his way in chapter 17, when you and he sit down and negotiate. We will also talk about what his first sighting of this questionnaire is likely to do to his psyche, and how you can enjoy that moment. And we'll offer some crucial tips on how to resolve disagreements about who should do which tasks.

For now, go through the questionnaire, ponder it in your heart, fill it out in whatever level of detail suits you, and use it to stimulate a detailed vision of how you would like things to be done in your home *if* you were able to get a willing and able partner on board—one who turned out to be none other than your husband. Make side notes galore when your thoughts overflow the grid, and add your own tasks or bundles of tasks whenever the notion suits you.

Figure out what you want. Next, we'll show you how to get it.

Chapter 14

How to Know When You're Ready to Negotiate

By working through the previous two chapters, you've accomplished a lot. Using the guidelines in chapter 12, you've started to clear the emotional atmosphere between you and your spouse, and hopefully you've begun to feel the difference—and he has too. There should be less animosity between you, a lifting of clouds and a return of sunny moments. It's true you've paid a price for this, and it's been unilateral. But it has already shown that you have the power to change his days, and that when he encounters less flak, he becomes more cheerful, more gracious, and darn it, more glad to see you.

Working through chapter 13, you have turned a generic wish for change into a specific road map to a better world where you and he would be equal partners again: you now have an itemized draft of what tasks would be shared (and how) and what tasks he would take over.

So we're on the threshold. But before we step over, we want

to ask: Do you and your husband have what it takes to negotiate together?

What is it that motivates two people, or two nations, to sit down and try to work out a deal? Fundamentally, it is that they share one conviction: *the way things are now isn't okay.* In the classic peace negotiation, two warring sides hunker down and admit to each other that there has to be a better way than to go on fighting and killing each other. Too much damage is being done; it could go on and on. Lives are being wasted. It has to be preferable to strike a compromise. It's worth accepting less territory than one originally wanted in order at least to be able to enjoy that territory. The desires to avoid bloodshed and to have a viable life are very strong motivations that can lead arch-enemy nations to make nice and parley.

An end to death and destruction—that's a pretty strong motivation. And even though your situation is more personal, in a way the stakes are the same: an end to the death and destruction of the relationship that once was, and still should be. The root conviction is also the same: we can do better than we're doing now.

As the instigator of this negotiation, you already have the goal in mind: a world in which you and your spouse will both be happier, because instead of your being his mom, the two of you will be loving partners again. You've already envisioned that world, and you've got details you want to present about how to get there. He doesn't yet have the same picture you do: that will require bringing him up to speed.

We'll discuss how to do that in the next chapter. Right now we want to raise a more fundamental point. You're already motivated to go through this process, because you've understood the problem and the prize. The question is, does *he* have the incentives in place to carry him to where you are? Can you get him to sit down and talk with you? Once begun, can the negotiation move to a favorable outcome?

There are no guarantees, but we are ready to wager that your odds are pretty good. Just to confirm that fact, we're going to run some statements by you. They are a measure of how your husband feels about you, *as seen by you*. If, as we expect, you can respond to them with a *yes,* it'll be a strong indication that the right factors are present to make for a good negotiation. (Just to confirm your readiness, we'll look at the reverse image too: whether you feel these ways about him.)

The Seven Motivations You Both Need

As we lead you through our seven statements, we'll ask you first to consider whether each one is true of your husband. We'll go over each in depth, giving examples of how the answer may reveal itself in daily life. We'll also talk about how these factors set the stage for a successful negotiation.

Here they are:

1. He loves you and cares about you.
2. He wants you to be happy.
3. When you're not happy, he wants to find out why and help solve the problem.
4. He is unhappy with the way things are.
5. He wants to be partners again.
6. He is willing to talk with you about this kind of thing.
7. He is willing to compromise and make changes so things can be better between you.

Before you respond, you may have a question for us. Why didn't we talk about this at the beginning of the book? If a successful change depends on these issues, why not save time and make sure from the get-go that this was worth pursuing? Our answer, very simply, is that it was too soon. People who are caught up in a hostile, dysfunctional pattern are often not able to see their true feelings for each other. Their vision is clouded by resentment, anger, frustration. They tend to identify the way someone *acts* with who that person *is,* the behavior with the person. They tend to forget how they would feel if the behaviors changed.

We didn't want to ask you to consider such important issues until you could give a best-case response. We wanted you to go through parts 1 and 2 of this book so that you could see exactly what circumstance has befallen yourself and your husband, what is behind the bad dynamic that currently exists between you. When you look at "being his mom" as a syndrome, an identifiable condition that has ensnared you, you start to be able to separate that condition from the two people who are in the grip of it. Part 1 did that. In part 2 we went further and exposed the buttresses that hold the Mother Syndrome in place and sustain it, and we deconstructed them. That perspective helped to pry you loose from the belief that being his mom is somehow inevitable and reflects the way it has to be—who he really is and who you are. Finally, the undeclared truce of chapter 12 has, we hope, shown you actual proof that things can be different, that the man you're dealing with can be a sunnier fellow, someone whose presence you welcome again.

Okay, let's get to the seven statements. If you want, think of these as affirmations before an important powwow.

1. He loves you and cares about you.

Does this matter? Oh yes. If not this, then what does?

But it may be a little hard to quantify sometimes. When things aren't going so smoothly between you, he may not always show that he cares. We've seen how egos can get in the way and people can be afraid to show vulnerability or softness. But still, but still . . . a man who loves you and cares about you isn't going to be able to hide it *all* the time! In little ways, it's going to peek over the scenery.

That may happen when things are atypically upbeat—at moments when you both give your problems the slip and laugh together, and you forget to be estranged and grab each other for a real hug. Or when a favorable wind blows. Maybe he has a good day at work (gets some good news?), and on the way home he vows to cast off this negativity and turn over a new leaf with you. He doesn't know exactly what's been wrong but he comes up with a random act of affection, shows up with flowers or a dinner reservation, hope in his eyes.

Simple love also shows itself when something threatens you. There are a million ways. He holds his umbrella over your head to keep you from getting wet. He worries if you aren't breathing well at night and brings you a decongestant. He asks you to call him to let him know when you make it to work okay, because you're driving through a blizzard. He doesn't like it when you're sick.

When you're getting an important medical test back, he offers to drive you to your appointment and sits patiently in the waiting room. When the test comes back negative, he is visibly relieved. Even elated. (And not just because he can now feel free to fight with you again.)

These little signs are indications that the feelings that drew you to each other in the first place are still there, lurking just under the surface.

2. He wants you to be happy:

Your being happy, your having moments of joy and enjoyment, matters to him.

That's why, sometimes, he lets you choose the movie even though you know that he's been dying to see a different one. (Turns out he likes it more than you do.)

Or he spends his last dollar on a coffee to share, even though he really wanted tea, or he takes you to buy a dress for your birthday because he's concerned about picking the wrong color.

In spite of everything that has gone on between you, he is a fan of times when you show the world your best stuff. He wants you to get the job you tried for, and he wants it to live up to your expectations. He listens raptly to your reports on how it's been going and how your new boss is treating you, and when the reports are good, he nods like a man whose team has won.

He sometimes tells you that when you're happy, he is too.

He reminds you that you have a beautiful smile.

These moments may not happen as often as you would like, but they still happen.

We're offering these examples to tweak your own storehouse of positive clues. Take a few moments and see what you can come up with, and by all means, write them down for future support. Each of the affirmations you're now making will not only give you confidence for the negotiation you're about to have but will help guide you to the best way of conducting it.

3. When you're not happy, he wants to find out why and help solve the problem.

The thing about love is, it's often hard to know we're feeling it. When we aren't getting along, we ignore or devalue things about the other person that we should really be celebrating. We may even resent them when they have a good laugh or a good time. If your husband feels that you are his critic, his resentful mom, he may seem at times to cheer against you, because he wants you to be punished for punishing him.

But let something adverse happen to you, and even his sleeping heart awakens. So take stock of this: when you suffer a blow from life, when you are struggling or sad or scared, that isn't okay with him. He notices that you are off-key and your affect is blunted; he can even hear it over a bad cell phone link. When you are really down, he gets you to talk about it. He knows you well enough to know when you just need to vent, and if it goes beyond that, he wants to help you figure out how the situation can be fixed.

Again, think of some examples of when this has actually happened. Add them to your stock: you may even bring some of them up during the coming meeting to show him why you appreciate him.

And why you count on him to be there for you now. "In the past you've come through for me when I was unhappy. Well, that's how I am now." Yes, this point directly aids the negotiation you're about to embark on, and will be mentioned during it. It means you have leverage, based simply on the truth. When you make it clear to your husband that you feel like you've become his mother and you don't want to live that way because it is making you miserable and harming your relationship with him, he will see that as a reason for action: he will want to do something about it. It won't be a long walk to enlist him in your common cause.

Points 1, 2, and 3 are probably things you can feel pretty certain of before you start the negotiation. The remaining points will need to emerge through his feedback, but we want you to think about how you see them right now. In order to get properly revved up for this confab, it will help you to preview what you think he'll say.

4. He is unhappy with the way things are.

We expect that having read parts 1 and 2 of this book and knowing him as you do, you probably have a pretty clear sense that he is not overjoyed at the current state of the union. We've already detailed the bad dynamics that crop up when a wife becomes her spouse's mother, and they include lots of behaviors that a happy spouse wouldn't display—like loss of confidence in handling things he used to be able to do; guilty skulking when you're slaving at demanding chores; bitter, even cruel remarks that seem designed to get revenge on you; and a backing off in the sexual arena. We've explored the hurt feelings that men suffer when they lose their equality on the home front, which is, after all, the place where committed couples (as opposed to courting couples) log most of their together time. We explained the sense of demotion a man suffers, the wounded pride that doesn't know its own name.

Does he look at you sometimes with a sort of desperation, a plea in his eyes, like a man who is lost and cut off from you?

"This isn't who you are," you want to say to him. "This isn't who we are." And if you say it in the right way, as an appeal to your better selves, you just know he is going to leap on board. With huge relief he is going to say, "You're so right, I've been miserable. I never wanted to be this way with you."

Of course, we're not saying that he already has this syndrome nailed and analyzed and knows that the reason he's unhappy is that you've become his mother. What we're saying is that he's unhappy. He doesn't like how the two of you interact or how he feels about himself in relation to you, and vice versa. The purpose of the negotiation will be to make the penny drop for him—to make him understand that the problem is you've become his mother. The fact that he already feels things aren't right will make this a lot easier to accomplish.

5. *He wants to be partners again.*

Again, he may not consciously realize that "being equal partners" is the thing that has been lost, the missing piece of the puzzle. But in all sorts of ways he signals to you that a lack of equality is eating away at him.

- At times he is bossy and rude, but that usually just ends up making him look bad; at times he is almost obsequious and you want him to act like a man.
- He tries to earn your praise, tells you he fed the dog or took out the garbage, and you wonder what he's going on about.
- When he attempts to contribute to a plan you're making and you overrule him because you have to pick up the rental car *before* work on Tuesday, he walks away like a dog that's been kicked.
- At a completely illogical moment he says, "We should go dancing," and you're sort of amused but it seems childish and you flick it away in the midst of your responsibilities.

Signs like this mean he hasn't given up on being partners, but he's not having much luck at making it happen.

In chapter 12 we suggested that as part of the unilateral amnesty, you ask your husband for advice about the car repair or the weekend you're planning with an old friend—or with anything else that is important enough to jar him out of the ash can of not being consulted. We hope you tried it, and we hope you saw unmistakable signs in him of how welcome this was—like a return of blood to an atrophying limb. That too can be a sign that he wants to be partners, that he needs it like oxygen.

6. He is willing to talk with you about this kind of thing.

Is he? You'll soon find out.

Hopefully there is a history, even if not recent, of times where you and he have occasionally hit a rough spell and been able to talk about it.

What we're hoping to hear from you, to give one example, is that there have been times when the two of you had a fight, and someone felt bad and apologized, and the other person then apologized too, and then there was a clumsy but slightly adorable contest to see who could accept more of the blame. Because you don't like being mad at each other, or even having a simmering chronic resentment, and both of you know it.

People say that men have to be dragged kicking and screaming to discuss a relationship, that "We need to talk" is like the knell of doom to a guy. People say it. Rom-coms say it. So it must be true, right? No. What is true is that men don't like to be indicted; neither do women. Being dragged in front of the court and having your crimes listed is not all that much fun. And therein lies a warning: If you approach this negotiation as a chance to list his sins and make him confess and reform, you are going to fail. If your stated goal is to teach him to be a better human being, to improve his character, it won't work. What will more likely happen is that he will end up flying the coop and being a "better person" with someone new. No man wants to make love to his improver.

If you accept no blame for what has gone wrong, you may not achieve liftoff. Having read part 2 of this book, it's better if you are ready to admit that

- You may have grabbed territory a bit unceremoniously.
- You may have sometimes taken control because control is fun.
- You may have enforced your own particular standards or ways of doing things when other ways could be valid too.

Even if you think it's entirely his fault that you became his mom, *saying* so is not the best move. That vibe is very unlikely to attract him into an honest and constructive dialog. But we hope that having come this far, you don't think any such thing. After all, it perpetuates the very thing that needs to be fixed—the sense of him being a child who needs you to reform him. The whole point here is that he isn't a child. He is an adult. You aren't his mother. You are another adult. Events have conspired to put you into the role of his mother, and him into the role of your child, but that ain't how it really is.

You will need to approach him as an equal, not as a failing student who is being given one last chance. In other words, make a quantum leap, in advance, into the attitude that is the ultimate objective. See him *as he will be if this works out*—your partner. Pull him into the right future by acting as if it's already here.

If he senses that from you, he will want to sit down and talk.

We want you to *ask* him for the changes you desire, and offer changes of your own—not to rake up the past in a condemning tone. Say, "I want to ask you to do *x*," not "I want to ask you to do *x*, which you would already be doing if you weren't an unworthy worm."

7. He is willing to compromise and make changes so things can be better between you.

This is another point that you can't fully know until he proves it. But if you've been able to give a *yes* to the first six affirmations, we think this will be lucky seven.

You're going to say, "This is what I think has gone wrong. I have ideas about how we could correct things. I want to tell you my ideas, I want to hear yours, and I want to figure out with you what will work."

And you're going to tell him that rewards are in the offing. Many rewards. Not just a chance to get along better and enjoy each other again. He is going to have more input, more control, more self-expression . . . and more laundry. He is going to get his woman back.

He is going to get a free pass out of the doghouse. Well, maybe not free, but free of condemnation.

"I have fallen short in various ways," you're going to explain. "I have been too controlling. I have failed to explain exactly how to do the things I can't compromise on that you want to contribute to. And I have failed to compromise, sometimes."

Because after all, you love him and care about him and want him to be happy, and when he isn't, you want to find out why and solve the problem; oh, and you too are unhappy and want to be partners, and you are willing to talk with him about this kind of thing, and yes, you are willing to compromise and make changes.

That's right, we've been making a wild assumption up to this point, that you feel all the things toward him that we've been affirming that he feels toward you. If he dares to believe that you feel them too, he isn't going to be wrong.

That's why this negotiation is going to work out. In fact, the points we've just gone over are not just harbingers of a successful negotiation, they also indicate why it's worth doing. The fact that you both still harbor these good feelings for each other means you have something that shouldn't be squandered. So you can also think of them as seven reasons in favor of reclaiming the marriage you lost.

Now you may be wondering, "Am I going to ask my husband these questions during the negotiation? Do I get him to confirm each one 'on the record'?"

Our answer, which may surprise you, is no. Mostly no.

Asking people to declare their emotions on your timetable (when the mood may not be right for them) is not often a good idea. It can make a person feel manipulated or cross-examined. More important, we think you won't *need* to ask him. If he does feel these things, you'll know it from his presence at the table, his general attitude, and his responses to the problem and solution you're going to present to him.

And you'll know it from his natural responses to the feelings *you* express. On several of these points you are likely going to hear from him loud and clear. If you follow the outline we give you in Chapter 16, you will be showing some powerful cards, such as that you appreciate that in the past he has tried to help when you were unhappy, that you are unhappy now, and that you want to be partners again. That will cause him to let you know how he feels, and if he doesn't make it clear, we'll encourage you to ask him what you need to know.

What we've been doing, then, is laying the groundwork for your coming discussion with him, by showing you that there's a strong wind at your back. If you were able to give a *yes* to most—or even better, all—of our seven points, you should be in a good position to work things out with your spouse and get to a better place together. You're ready to proceed.

The Shadow of a Doubt

But what if you're not so sure? What if, on careful consideration, you're hesitant to sign on to some of the seven key statements? Does that mean it's game over?

No, it doesn't. Here's why.

We assume that if you've come this far, the doubt isn't about your own attitudes. You bring enough oomph to your marriage to want to sit down and fix it. So the hitch is that you aren't sure your husband does. You're not confident that he has enough good will left in his heart to motivate him to make some changes. Because after all, that's what the seven statements are: an *inventory of good will.* Could he just be too far gone into hostility or indifference, too remote to be reached? What if he doesn't care if you're happy? What if he doesn't want to be partners again—not with you? What if he isn't willing to talk about this stuff or make changes?

Well, we'll concede this: if he really doesn't share the seven attitudes we've gone over, then your marriage could be in the grip of wider problems. We say this because the Mother Syndrome itself can often be reversed. But the prospects are worse if it is accompanied by other serious problems that have the power to make a marriage unsalvageable. If left to molder, the Mother Syndrome can and will destroy a marriage, so you have to try to fix it. If you find you can't succeed, something more may be in play.

So, if he *really* doesn't feel those positive things toward you, a negotiation may not lead to a cure, and the case may call for a more radical treatment. Some marriages do have issues that go beyond the scope of this book, and sometimes those relationships require professional counseling and may not even be salvageable that way. We have never claimed that the Mother Syndrome is the only problem that besets marriages. But we *are* saying that it is a huge problem, that a great many couples have it, and that it can be fixed.

And there's another crucial point. Even though the Mother Syndrome doesn't usually obliterate the good will that a couple needs, it sure as hell has the ability to make it *seem* as if that good will is gone. So even if it isn't crystal clear to you that he loves you and wants to fix what is making you unhappy, these may still be facts. They may just be hidden. The Mother Syndrome is a nasty thing, with a scary power to mask or suppress good feelings that still exist. We've tried to dispel that power, at least in your head, in parts 1 and 2 of this book. We hope our discussion has helped you see that the man you valued is still there. But he doesn't yet have the benefit of that perspective, and if he's been affected badly enough by this syndrome, to which he doesn't yet have the key, he could be unable to show you the love in his heart. Anger, resentment, and alienation may have cornered him, so that he *seems* like an unloving, uncommunicative spouse. That doesn't mean he is happy that way or that he won't consider trying something that might change things.

So it's better to assume that he can be brought around, and give it a try. The best-case scenario is that you agreed with our seven premises for negotiation; you were able to see in your husband the feelings that promise a good outcome. But even if you're in the not-as-good position where there's some doubt, you shouldn't give up on him. Because no matter how he's acting, he probably feels, deep down, the same way you do. So it's better, for the sake of your marriage, to put your qualms aside and give him a chance to prove that he is in your corner. Sure, it's a leap of faith, but sometimes all it takes to bring out the best in a person *is* a little faith.

And anyway, it would be crazy to just assume he's not on board, when you haven't *tried* him. It's way too soon to give up on negotiating when he hasn't had the benefit of the positive things you're going to say, and you haven't heard his response.

There's also this: what have you got to lose? Your marriage is already in serious trouble. Even if you don't feel totally confident that this negotiation will work, you might as well try it, because it *might* work. If it doesn't, you can live with things the way they are or decide to end the marriage or try counseling or some other course of action. But you'll at least have tested this approach. There's also the (remote) possibility that this attempt at negotiation might spook him so he walks. But you have to ask yourself, if he would rather end it than work toward a healthy partnership, do you really want to be with him?

Bear this in mind: the process that we're proposing in part 3 of this book is, in effect, a test of your marriage—and that's all to the good. By trying to clear the emotional air, by attempting a momentous negotiation and putting all your cards on the table, you're bravely showing that you're willing to find out what you and your husband have got as a couple. If the endeavor succeeds, loud cheers. But even if it doesn't, you will have learned something important. Maybe, in the worst-case scenario, it'll be that you don't want to stay with this man. That may not be happy news, but you'll still be better off knowing it.

We believe that most of you will find your husbands amenable to a chance to recover a healthy marriage, just as you are yourself. Most couples would gladly return to feeling like partners again, if they knew how.

A clue to this is what happens on those blessed occasions when the two of you make a clean getaway from the domestic fortress. Assuming you are lucky enough to take an occasional vacation together or even just a weekend spree or a day trip (preferably without the kids, if any), what happens? Many couples report that things suddenly get friendlier, and the old connection starts to resurface. You tell each other stories, you analyze strange things that have happened, you take little side trips just for the hell of it, you laugh about awful gaffes you've made, you find a little forgiveness wafting through the air. Fun rears its incorrigible head. That's understandable, because you're away from domesticity and back to the level playing field where you started once upon a time. It's particularly helpful if the role of taking care of things is lifted from your girlish shoulders: a vacation or a trip where you don't have a lot of chores is just the ticket. (A situation where the wife is only plunged into a different *sort* of domesticity—from camping to condo dwelling—may not be so fruitful.)

Okay, the preliminaries are over. We've had our pep talk, and we've fortified you with reasons for believing that a good negotiation can take place, which also helped you see how best to make your case.

So let's get to it.

Let your husband know that there is something really important that you want to talk about, and agree to a time and place.

Out of the house is often best, for obvious reasons. Choose a time and place where you won't be interrupted or distracted, like a quiet café on a weekend, or a park you drive to—whatever works for the two of you. Make it somewhere away from where your friends hang out, maybe a place you don't normally go. Away from your children. Away from any pets. Daytime (when you're less tired) is better if you can manage it.

How much time do you need for this get-together? We think a minimum of three hours; four is better. (The conversation will have two parts, and it's better to cover both at the same meeting, as you'll see shortly.) A whole afternoon on a weekend would be good. This kind of thing can't be discussed in the heat of daily activity (or battle): you and your husband need a time-out so that you can stand back from your troubles and talk calmly about them, with a readiness to see each other's point of view. (If you doubt that you and your husband can find that kind of time for this meeting, consider that divorce will take a lot longer than four hours.)

If he says he's too busy to work on this right now, consider that it may actually be true. Maybe he has a lot on his plate. If so, then respect this and ask him to commit to a future time slot, even if it is several weeks away. Ask if he's okay with your marking it on the calendar, and get a firm pledge. (He may also resist for other reasons; we'll discuss that eventuality in the next chapter.)

He's going to be curious and may even ask that you share some of what you want to talk about in advance. Ask him to wait. Allow the suspense to build, but reassure him that he will appreciate what you want to talk about.

Once he has committed to being there, you are already in a good position. You're going to get a chance to explain things calmly and clearly, and you're going to do it in a way that doesn't throw down red flags or make him wary but instead lets him know that a dark cloud is lifting. We'll get to the details of how you do that one chapter from now, but first a short interlude on what to do if, in spite of your conviction that his heart is in the right place, he balks at meeting.

Most readers are going to find that their husbands will agree to meet and talk. But a few of you may hit a hurdle. If your guy is resistant, even though you just know in your gut that he is good negotiation material, you may need to up the ante to catch his interest. The next chapter will very briefly explain how.

Chapter 15

Exit Mother, Enter Lover

What if your guy is reluctant to have a confab? What if he just flat out says no, because he is too chronically angry at you to want to talk, or he's afraid of what you might say or wary of more nagging?

Our first thought is that maybe you didn't give the chapter 12 amnesty enough of a try. Really it was more than an amnesty: it was a cessation of hostilities accompanied by a laying on of positive treatment. If that never took place, then he hasn't felt the kind of lift that would take away his wariness and replace it with more friendly feelings. Did you really carry out the plan, for several weeks? Did you put a lid on your anger reactions, get control of the urge to control, stop nagging, ask him to handle some important responsibilities, seek his advice on major stuff, give him applause and compliments, and capitalize on opportunities for enjoyable bonding? Sometimes people read things in a book and imagine them and it's all very lovely, but they don't actually *do* them. If so, we request that you reread chapter 12 and this time really carry it out, for at least two weeks. Then approach him again about wanting to talk.

If you *have* given that a sincere try and he still balks, then wheedle, plead, and cajole a bit. If still no success, take a time-out and ask yourself if he may be that "remote man" that we mentioned in the last chapter, the one who's too far gone to reel in.

If, however, you believe his heart is in the right place but he's being kind of evasive, you could try something more extreme.

Here's a gutsy strategy that is well worth a look. You'll find it interesting even if you aren't one of those who need it. The main idea is this: Your husband has this mother-drudge-scold figure in his life, and even though she and he are not happy, he is quite attached to her and to the way things function with her around. He needs something to shake him up and make him realize that ain't gonna fly no more, so he'll be open to some other solution. So get rid of her. Make her go away. And replace her with some serious competition. That's right, get rid of Mother and let another woman sashay onto the scene, one who is more enticing and reminds him of what he's been missing. In other words, be the "other woman" in your husband's life. It may sound a little schizoid, but it's all in good fun: be your own rival, be the femme fatale that lures your husband away from . . . the old you. Make the latter go away, and bring on a new woman to outshine her, one he'll want to win over.

As you can see, there are two prongs to this devilish strategy. Here is the first.

Send Mommy Packing

Your husband is attached to the status quo and needs to be broken free from it.

It stars a certain woman—the wife who has become his mom. Call her Mother.

Mother is in the way because, oddly enough, he is addicted to her, attached, used to her; he thinks she has to exist and he has to be with her.

That's why he is resisting the big talk.

So make her go bye-bye.

You already started this process in chapter 12 when you stopped nagging, controlling, and getting mad. But now it's time to really make Mama disappear. So he can't rely on her anymore.

How do you do that? Simple. *You stop doing the tasks that she does, that you no longer want to be doing. (They are on your list of things your* husband *should be doing.)* In fact, feel free to even stop doing some of the things you plan to keep doing under the new regime, that directly benefit the big lug.

Go for broke; don't pull your punches. Some possibilities:

- Stop doing his laundry. (Let him run out of skivvies.)
- Stop doing the dishes when you made the meal. (What a terrible habit!)
- Don't make a plan for dinner or do the necessary shopping for it. (Let him flail.)
- Stop making his doctor appointments. If he asks why, tell him, "I'm not responsible for you."

These are just examples. We're sure you can choose some potent sins of omission of your own—little and big. This requires careful judgment, because you don't want the things you're not doing to drive *you* crazy or to impact innocent bystanders such as your children. It's harder, admittedly, to find the right things to leave undone if you have kids, because the remorseless engine of family life must be served. Fool with any small gear and the whole apparatus may stall. But don't be discouraged: by clever dereliction, you can still bring off a dramatic effect!

Best to pick things he will notice, that you can live with for a while.

Okay, suppose he does notice. If he says, "Why didn't you tell me to do that?" you say, "I am not your boss" or that old reliable, "I didn't want to nag."

If he says, "Why didn't *you* do that?" you say, "My dance card was full," or some other sprightly metaphor. Or you could go even further and say, "I don't do that anymore." Or even, "That woman is gone."

The goal here is to wake him up and have him say, "Holy cow! Something has happened in my world. My housekeeper quit. The stuff that used to get done automatically isn't getting done. Maybe I need a plan B."

Or more simply, "The sky is falling! The sky is falling!"

Once he realizes the old order is gone, he might be ready to look for a new one.

The New Girl in Town

The other prong of the attack is where a new character appears on the stage and eclipses Mother, who is now MIA. This is where you get your husband motivated to cheat on Mother with someone who's a whole lot more fun. You.

What is the polar opposite of the mother-drudge? It would be a captivating, delicious siren he has the hots for, one who makes him pursue her—the lover, not the mother. We saw in chapter 3 how the Mother Syndrome can muffle the erotic antennae and make a couple see each other in distinctly unsexy ways. We also noted in chapter 10 that many men seem as if they've lost interest in sex but in fact they are still horny. What your guy may *really* have lost is a clear sense of you as the answer to the hunger he still has. It could be guilt, fear of rejection, feeling like a child—or lack of an invitation. They're all part of having Mother in his life.

But now she's fading, so bring on Ms. Delicious to rock his world. Give him a glimpse of the rewards that await He Who Negotiates.

Increase your goddess factor. If you know how to be especially appetizing in your husband's eyes, do it. Press his buttons, on purpose, by undoing yours. Make a point of looking sexy, when you have the time and opportunity. We're not talking about blatant display or cheapness here—well, not *necessarily*—but sometimes when the lover thing has gotten cold, women stop taking the trouble to look alluring, even (or especially) at bedtime. (Flip through chapter 10 again for details.) Start making him notice you in that way. When he does, and it creates a craving in him and he makes a move on you, be very nice but say with a mysterious smile, "Maybe another time," and if you feel like it, give him one brief, promissory kiss. (This *no* will become a *yes* shortly, but he hasn't earned that yet.)

Make his lover juice pool; make him unable to get you out of his mind.

Instead of a domestic drudge, be candy.

It's all about introducing him to the more appealing partner who waits on the other side of negotiation. Again, you went partway in this direction in chapter 12, when you showed him your nicer side, asked for advice, and gave him applause. And a friendly housemate is a nice thing. But we need more than platonic, and the spark that lights this tinder is sex. Because when a man lusts after a woman he respects, he falls in love (all over again).

Consider implementing this strategy (raising the goddess factor) even if your guy has agreed to come to the table. It will help him understand better what is to be gained, so he'll be more motivated to negotiate with an open mind.

So that's it. Make him realize he can't rely on Mother anymore. She's history, so he's going to have to look around and find someone new . . . And hey, check out who has recently appeared: someone he likes better than Mother (and always did)—his romantic partner.

In these ways, for the noble purpose of getting him to the negotiating table, gang up on him without a single overt act of hostility. Make him take heed of the sudden gap in domestic work, and of the woman he suddenly craves as a woman, not a parent. When these things get his attention, he will realize that the status quo is in upheaval—something is going on. The old world is crumbling, and the new one ain't lookin' so bad. So maybe he should find out what the hell is up for grabs, why the old formulas aren't working, what this interesting new creature (his wife) is trying to tell him.

So one evening he says, "What is going on?"

And you say, "That's exactly what I want to talk to you about."

Chapter 16

Cooler Heads Prevail: Making a New Deal

Okay, we're here at last. It's time to bust the chains and set your marriage free. Time to cast away the mother-child charade that has overtaken you. You are still the people you always were; you don't have to play those roles. You can team up again on a level playing field, and you can get there together by talking this through.

You've gotten him to sit down with you for a talk; he's aware that something serious is in the air. You've chosen a time and place where you will not be interrupted or distracted, and you've set aside three to four hours.

How do you approach this chat? Well, with finesse. Now that you've read up to this point, you may be all charged up and ready to conquer the world. But take a deep breath and move in carefully. If he feels as if you're bulldozing him into making changes, you're less likely to succeed. At this point you are vastly more aware of the issues and concerns. You've reflected on them, explored options, and gotten ready for change, while he may only be dimly aware of the problem. To bring him up to speed and engage him in the process will require patience and work. He is going to need careful guiding and clear communication just to get to the point of opening his eyes to what you now know about and want to work on. So you'll need to go step by step, make sure you've been understood, and then proceed. Don't just pour it all out at once.

Okay, so much for the cautionary note.

Now what do you say?

The Game Plan

The goal is to go through the following steps: admit that you're both unhappy, agree on the reason for that, agree that things have to change, and then, with the help of the questionnaire, talk about the specific changes you want. There are two main stages to the conversation: the first stage, which is all about *what the problem is,* and the second stage, where you negotiate *who is going to do what tasks,* by both of you using the questionnaire. The trick is to not get so bogged down in stage one that you don't get to the fun part—stage two. On the other hand, you don't want to just jump into the questionnaire without talking over what has gone wrong. In order to motivate real changes, you need a fairly intense baring of feelings that can lead to a heartfelt mutual resolve. He has to know how much is at stake in order to make real commitments to do more. This has to be serious stuff. So the way to make the questionnaire work is to first really talk about what has gone wrong and why. But it's best to spend no more than half your available time on the problem, then get on to the questionnaire.

Discussing the Problem

Okay, how do you talk to your husband about this? What do you say and in what order?

Well, you could just tell him what you're thinking, in your own words. In fact, we suspect that you're champing at the bit, wanting to share this stuff with him. You may have a good idea of what you want to say and how you want to organize it. If, having read this far, you pretty well know how you want to go about it, by all means dive in.

Some readers, though, may want more of a road map and some coaching. We can't give you an exact script; every marriage is different, every man and woman. You know him best and you know how to talk to him, what he's likely to "get " and what he isn't, what works with him and what doesn't. (And you know which parts of the Mother Syndrome are found in your marriage.) But we can give you an outline of high points you may want to hit. Kind of a checklist, so you can make sure you don't leave out anything you may want to include.

Rather than inundate you with things to say, we're going to approach this as follows. First, we'll give you the bare-bone points we imagine you may want to cover. Then we'll go back over them, providing backup material for when you need to go into more depth on a given topic, and tips for avoiding trouble, staying on track, and getting to where you want to go. (We'll be building on the coaching that was begun in chapter 14, as part of the seven affirmations.)

Please note that everything we're suggesting here is just a springboard for your own ideas.

Here's the bare outline:

I'm unhappy with the way things are going in our marriage.

In the past you've always cared if I was unhappy, and you tried to help the situation. I hope you will now.

I also suspect that you are unhappy too.

What is making me unhappy is that I feel like I've become your mother instead of your partner.

There are two parts to that:

1. **the jobs we do—with me doing too many of them**
2. **the bad ways we treat each other—with hostility, resentment, disrespect, anger, guilt, distrust**

I'm not here to put the blame on you or say it's all your fault. We both got ourselves into this, and if there's any blaming to do, I want to share it. I know some of the ways I've gone wrong and I want to correct them.

I want to be partners again. It isn't just about wanting you to shoulder more of the domestic load—though I do. It's also that I miss your input. I want us to be a team. I want to feel taken care of too. I want to feel less tired and more grateful.

My main goal is for you and me to be a whole lot happier and to enjoy each other again—in every way, including in bed.

I have ideas on how we could correct all this and get things back to where they once were. I've already started trying to treat you better, and I like how it feels. But things won't be right until we find a better way of dividing up—and sharing—the running of our home. I want to share my ideas with you, I want to hear yours, and then the two of us can figure out together what we think will work.

So, do you want to look at my ideas?

That's the basic outline. Before we get to the more in-depth stuff, an important note: we obviously haven't included your husband's responses. At various moments he may chime in with agreement or he may dispute something. Or he may remain silent, letting you finish and then giving his thoughts. You may sometimes want to ask for his response as you go along. In what follows, we'll give you our take on these possibilities.

Okay. Let's go back over the outline, taking it in bite-size chunks.

I'm unhappy with the way things are going in our marriage.

In the past you've always cared if I was unhappy, and you tried to help the situation. I hope you will now.

I also suspect that you are unhappy too.

This isn't a negative opening. Although you're saying you're unhappy, this is probably not news to him and it may even be a relief to both of you to have it on the table. This opening is also accompanied by a very positive note: that you appreciate his past concern and have faith in him.

Give a couple of examples, if you wish, of times when your husband helped you with things that were getting you down.

As far as your husband's response, you're in fine shape if he agrees that he doesn't want you to be unhappy, and that he's unhappy too. Beyond that, ask him to hold his thoughts till you can explain *what* is making you unhappy.

If he *doesn't* voice his agreement, let him be. It's early times. He doesn't even know yet what this is about. Do not say, "Do you solemnly agree that you will on this occasion do whatever you can to stop me from being unhappy?"

More generally, as the conversation unfolds, the last thing you want is a pattern where you're saying, "You have to agree to this point or I'm not going on to the next one!" More finesse is needed, less pressure. Let your confidence in what you're saying carry you along. If he doesn't sign off on every point, continue anyway. Especially don't ask him questions where you already know the answer (from his body language or other responses he's made). That can have a condescending, legalistic tone, as in "Do you admit that you're unhappy too?" However, if, after explaining your take on an important matter, you feel you can't continue without knowing how he feels, by all means ask him, but in an open-minded way. Really listen to what he says; it may be enlightening.

What if he says, when prompted (or without any prompting), "That's *your* problem. I'm fine with the way things are." Now *that* is a hitch. At this point you need to remember what we said two chapters ago: the very problem you're trying to deal with (the Mother Syndrome) may have sunk him into a state where he isn't in touch with his positive feelings for you. He may *think* he doesn't care, though he does, and if he misperceives that an attack is in the offing, that could be making him evasive.

There are several things you can do.

One is to simply move on. Tell him you understand that he feels that way, but will he please hear you out.

If you don't want to move ahead yet, you might say, "Really? So you don't think there's too much hostility between us? You don't wish things were friendlier—like maybe, a whole lot friendlier?" You might ask him if he remembers how you used to be with each other, how it was pretty darn nice. And you might remind him of times in the past when you were unhappy and he showed that he cared and tried to help you. (Nothing thaws a person more than reminding them of their past kindness.)

Another tack—more argumentative—is to humbly point out that if you have a problem with your relationship, that means he does too. Because a relationship isn't okay if one of the people in it is unhappy.

You could also reassure him that you are *not* out to get him. To see how this might run, flip ahead a few pages to the passage that begins, "I'm not here to put the blame on you or say it's all your fault." When you encounter resistance, this may be all he needs to hear in order for him to give you a chance.

If all else fails, there's the million-dollar question: Should you play the deal-breaker card? Let's ask it more generally. If at any point in trying to set up the meeting or in trying to go forward with the discussion, you find him simply refusing to continue, should you be ready to tell him, "This is a deal breaker for me. We talk about this or I want out of our marriage"? If that's the only way to get him to take this proposal seriously and give it a sincere try, and you've exhausted all other moves, then yes, say it. But only as a last resort. The threat of leaving, once on the table, can create a future inability to trust. It can also haunt any positive progress you may make with a shadow of abandonment. If it's already something regularly used in your marriage, this may be a good time to stop.

But hopefully things are unfolding better for you. We now continue with our outline.

What is making me unhappy is that I feel like I've become your mother instead of your partner.

There are two parts to that:

1. **the jobs we do—with me doing too many of them**
2. **the bad ways we treat each other—with hostility, resentment, disrespect, anger, guilt, distrust**

Okay, now the main mothering point is on the table. It probably bears expansion; it's the heart of the discussion.

So tell him that what's bugging you is that you're doing too much of the work around the house and are too much in charge of things. That isn't what you ever dreamed of; you wanted *him and you to be a team.*

Reiterate that it's more than that. "I also don't like the way I treat you. I nag you, I guilt-trip you, I correct you, I get cross with you, I push you away. I don't want to treat you that way. It sucks." If he doesn't chime in with his own confession of badness, go ahead and add, "And I don't like how you treat me. You act resentful, and guilty, and critical, and angry." (Use adjectives that apply. Describe the way it actually is.) Lead with your own misbehavior, as always.

You could sum it up thus: "Instead of behaving like loving and equal partners, we tend to act sometimes like I'm a mom and you're my kid. But we're grown-ups. So it gets weird. I become the bad mom and you become the bad child."

Make sure the "I'm unhappy" thing doesn't come off in an accusing way, but more as a plea for rescue. For example, tell him you feel bereft and lonely and isolated. That you aren't enjoying your home the way you should. Or him. That the joy has gone out of things. And it's all because you and he are out of sync. Say, "This isn't who we are."

Let's talk more about his response. There's a chance he may grasp the mother concept up front, before you even go into the details; he may recognize it as the perfect way of summing up what is wrong, and chime in with his agreement. If so, you are home free. Because he'll have an easy time seeing what kind of changes would cure the problem.

However, he may not see the problem that way—yet. Some men may be reluctant to admit at the start that their wife has become their mother; it hurts their pride. Yet they'll readily admit to being unhappy with the way the relationship is going. What you need to do is let him express this, listen to the details, and when possible, jump in and say, "That's one of the things that I meant by being your mother." Show him that the very problems he cites are what you've been talking about.

For example, he may say,

- I feel guilty.
- I feel inept.
- I feel like I'm not contributing.
- I feel like I'm using you.

It won't be hard to show him that these feelings are part of what you meant by being his mother.

Or he may make it more about you:

- You boss me around.
- You shut me out of decisions.
- You make me feel like a shirker.
- You make me feel incompetent.

Or even, hitting the bull's-eye of this book,

- You treat me like a child.

Don't get defensive about these statements. They are playing right into your hands. Rather than saying something like "I only treat you like a child because you behave like one," just say, "That's exactly right. That's me being your bad mom." He's admitting the main point, the one that supplies the motivation for the changes you both need. ***Do not slip into the blame game.*** This is good news, not bad. So by all means let him talk. That way you're building consensus and not having to convince him of things. Listen to him. Let him convince *you* how right you are.

At this point, it's quite likely that you'll need to shine more light on the metrics of being his mother.

"Here are some job areas where I do too much, to the point where it feels like I'm being a mother to you."

If it helps you, draw on the five "hats" a mother wears.

1. cleaning lady
2. cook
3. manager
4. appearance and etiquette coach
5. child rearer

Or choose your own specifics. The main thing is, concentrate on the fact that you are carrying too much of the load, and illustrate that point with the tasks or areas that bother you most. Stress the jobs that loom largest in your mind, but don't leave any out that apply to you and him, with one exception: at this point you may not want to make much of hat 4 (appearance and etiquette coach). It is pretty hard to talk about this without coming off as superior and insulting. It was important for us to discuss it earlier, because it's a real part of making you feel like his mom, but we also believe that it will automatically be defused if the general imbalance is cured. (When he is restored as your equal partner, his appearance/etiquette shortcomings will become less annoying and more an occasion for play, and anyway, he will tend to correct them on his own because that is what respected, confident adults do.)

It's possible that he may *accept* that you've become his mother but may try to say that it couldn't be any other way—defending the status quo in one of the ways we looked at in part 2. After all, those are the rationalizations that many wives and husbands offer! For example, he may claim that

- Housework is women's work; his mother did it this way, or your mother did (chapter 6).
- He needs you to take care of/cater to him (chapter 7).
- He is incompetent at domestic work (chapter 9).

So it's a good idea to look back over those chapters before you meet with him, and refresh your memory on why those excuses don't fly.

If you need reinforcement, have him read any chapters (or the parts you've highlighted) that will help him let go of these flimsy defenses.

That's right, don't be afraid to tell him about this book, but emphasize that you were feeling this way *before you read the book*. Let him read part 1 if he asks to. Or more. He is likely to get a few laughs out of part 2 if he looks at it, and he will appreciate that we stand up for husbands as well as wives. It could set the stage very well for the nuts and bolts of the upcoming discussion.

He may also say that you are the one who has kept him from participating as much as he wanted to. If so, he's onto the idea behind gatekeeping. It goes without saying that you shouldn't scoff at this; we hope you've already done some soul-searching and may have concluded that you're not innocent of this kind of territoriality. Admitting that this is true could be a huge step in showing him that you intend to be fair and honest, so that he will feel this isn't just a quest to score points and be in the right.

As you're giving examples of the jobs you do, he may pipe up and say, "So you want me to start doing that?" Ask him nicely to cool his jets for a moment. You'll *get* to those specifics. Right now your point is just that you're doing too much, and it's making you feel like his mother, and making you treat each other badly.

I'm not here to put the blame on you or say it's all your fault. We both got ourselves into this, and if there's any blaming to do, I want to share it. I know some of the ways I've gone wrong and I want to correct them.

Make this point as early as you need to, to help stave off conflict. Your whole approach to this conversation should exude this attitude. Remember, this isn't about who can score the most points in finding the other person at fault. A readiness to admit your own failings is much more likely to elicit the same in your spouse. And you do not want to come off as a governess bent on "improving" or reforming or correcting him. (If he senses any such thing, he will get his hackles up.)

I want to be partners again. It isn't just about wanting you to shoulder more of the domestic load—though I do. It's also that I miss your input. I want us to be a team. I want to feel taken care of too. I want to feel less tired and more grateful.

Husbands know something has been lost. They may not have put the "partner" name on it, but in all sorts of ways they struggle with the demotion they've suffered. The proof of this came in chapter 12, when you asked him for important advice and noticed what a lift it gave him.

That is why this is a fine negotiating point right now. When you say, "I want to be partners again"—when you extend this as the reward to be gained by making some changes—he will see it as solid gold. That is, once he understands it. You may need to say things like, "I want us to feel like a team again. I want to look at you the way I used to. I can't make it without you. I feel like I've taken over, and I don't want to take over. I hate that I order you around and nag you. I want to lean on you again." There are many ways to say it, but the message is clear. Equality, collaboration. The ticket back to you.

You deserve a response from him on this point. If he doesn't give you any clear signal, you can ask him, "Do you want to be partners again?" Most men will say they do. (A few men, maybe for reasons of ego, are going to underplay the idea that they aren't equals and say, "We already are partners." Then you remind him that you don't *feel* as if you are partners, and rephrase the question: "Will you help me feel that way again?")

To make sure he's on the same page as you, it may help to translate the prize into mother language. Ask him, does he want a world *in which you are not his mother*? He will very likely say yes. If he is basically on board but feeling playful, he may say something like, "Well, I do kinda like being lazy." That isn't a no; it's really a joking way of saying yes, he admits the problem and is willing to step up to the plate.

And keep in mind that the world without Mother will look even more appealing to him if he realizes that in it, he'll get you back as his romantic, sexual bedmate. Mother exits, Lover returns. Tell him that feeling like his mother makes you not feel sexual; explain it as clearly as you need to. "I don't want to be her, it's a drag. I want us to be fun, to be sexy again." (It'll be good if you have already started previewing what this means, as portrayed in chapter 15, or if you start bringing it to life in the near future.)

That's why the next point ends the way it does.

My main goal is for you and me to be a whole lot happier and to enjoy each other again—in every way, including in bed.

Then there's the final transition to the questionnaire.

I have ideas on how we could correct all this and get things back to where they once were. I've already started trying to treat you better, and I like how it feels. But things won't be right until we find a better way of dividing up—and sharing—the running of our home. I want to share my ideas with you, I want to hear yours, and then the two of us can figure out together what we think will work.

Inform him that you've already tried to stop acting like a mother, by tamping down various unfriendly behaviors. (Give some examples, or maybe he will guess a few.) If he expresses a wish to reciprocate, welcome it and say, "Let's each make a list, later, of the behaviors we're going to stop." We'll cover this in chapter 18, after the questionnaire. It's too soon now, because unless the domestic work gets leveled, the root cause of the hostility and resentment will remain, and the nice behaviors will peter out.

Explain that the only way you and he can really be free of the disagreeable dynamics is if you stop *doing the jobs* that make you his mother. So you've come up with a list that you want to run by him. It's a list of ideas, not orders. It's your conception of what might work. You want to present it to him and get his ideas, then go from there.

So, do you want to look at my ideas?

He'd be a fool to say no at this point.

You've now reached the halfway point in the meeting. The problem is on the table, and there's an intense, mutual desire to overcome it. In the next chapter we'll proceed with part two, the discussion of the questionnaire.

Chapter 17

Tackling the Questionnaire Together

Go ahead and show him the questionnaire you filled out in chapter 13.

When a man first lays eyes on this document, it may strike terror into the heart of him. Watch and enjoy. This crash course on the detailed nature of domestic reality can only do him good. If he feels a certain moral queasiness at the graphic depiction of how much work is being done in the home—work he isn't part of—that too is good medicine.

Make it absolutely clear that the filled-in questionnaire is not his new marching orders. It is not you telling him what to do. It is you sketching one route (that appeals to you) that could get the two of you to a place where he takes on more tasks and responsibilities. But you fully realize he may see different ways of getting there, and the two of you together may come up with the best plan of all. It is like when a couple tries to decide what itinerary to take on a vacation road trip. They both know they're going to end up in San Francisco, say, and maybe the wife has looked at the map and highlighted a series of roads that would get them there. But she wants her husband's input. Does he see a different way—one that may be easier, faster, or more scenic, or take them to other towns he thinks they'd enjoy? So they hunker down and talk it through. And they end up with a route that neither would have chosen alone. The fact that she presented her ideas first doesn't mean she was trying to dictate to him. The questionnaire is a series of suggestions, not a bunch of decisions you've already made.

Before he reads it in detail, give him a chance to look it over, and run through the seven columns with him up front—what each one says and, for columns 3 to 6, what each one means. That'll get him thinking. In the case of column 4, point out the two kinds of sharing: doing a task together versus alternating it, with each of you doing it some of the time. We're sure you'll also linger over the arresting difference between columns 5 and 6 (he does it your way versus he does it his way). Letting him know up front that there are two distinct alternatives here, and that it hasn't been an easy choice for you, will make him aware that his way of executing some tasks has stuck you with a nasty dilemma.

Then you get to the itemized tasks. There are a couple of ways to approach them. You can give him a *blank* questionnaire and ask him to fill out the same columns you did. Then compare his with yours. That will lead to a longer discussion, but it could also be very entertaining to see if there's any resemblance between the two pictures you paint. It's a little dangerous, though, unless you're confident he'll see eye to eye with you, because he may stake out a bunch of claims that you don't like and then you'll have them in your way. For example, maybe you've decided to off-load a good bit of the laundry onto him, using one of our methods. But he offers on his questionnaire to start shopping for food, something that you don't want to give up because you are planning to keep making most meals and you like to make menu decisions based on what you see in the store. So now you're in the position of having to shoot down his generous proposal and try to move him to a different one.

Another drawback of giving him his own blank questionnaire is that he may ask to fill it out later, when he has time, and then you could easily get into procrastination and lose the momentum that your chat so far has created. Also, it may be better for him to have the guidance of what you've said on the questionnaire to help steer his way.

For those reasons, we recommend one of the two following approaches. The simplest is to have him eyeball the questionnaire you filled out, and in column 7, answer yes or no to what you've said for each task or group of tasks and be prepared to explain his choice. The more revealing approach (and more labor-intensive for him, which is probably a good thing) is to have him fill out the whole thing—the same one that already has your choices on it—using a different-colored pencil. This method has the virtue of allowing him to really engage with what you said but also makes him go into detail on his choices.

You might think it would be a time-saver to have him only look at the jobs you've flagged for *him* to do (when you checked off columns 4, 5, or 6), but we think otherwise. Our reason has to do with a crucial question: *How can you maximize the odds that he will in fact accept the tasks you've earmarked for him?* We think the number one way is to make him aware of how much you are volunteering to *keep doing*. So you want him to read and digest every task that you've checked off in column 3. The more of these he sees, the more he'll start thinking, "I better step up to the plate on some of this stuff." In fact, he'll be *looking* for opportunities to level the teeter-totter and balance your workload with his. That means it's more likely that he'll say yes to jobs you've designated for him.

Just as you left some questions open for discussion with him, he may not want to give a definite answer on every task; he may want to talk it over with you. If so, have him mark it for further discussion (maybe put an arrow beside it) and encourage him to proceed onward and finish his first pass.

Once you've both declared your initial positions, it's time for the two of you to react to each other's choices and to try to reach agreement. Now comes a highly entertaining, intense, and sometimes surprising conversation, in which the two of you let it all hang out for each other, and in which you may both learn a lot that you didn't know. It may get heated at times, but don't let it get nasty. (Good-natured teasing is allowed, but not attacks on the other's character.)

Don't set the pressure too high for this first meeting by assuming every detail must get resolved. The conversation may spill over into further talks, and the plan will likely get revised as the two of you try things out. Some of your results will be experiments: let's try this and see how it works. Agree together that it's perfectly okay not to get every area resolved in the first discussion; some may be too complicated. Better to agree to continue talking next time than to exhaust yourselves or make a bad decision. It's a work in progress.

You may find more humor and fun than you expect in this process, because it brings to light some of the silly assumptions and misunderstandings that have underlain the rancor between you. Going in, you each may think you have solid knowledge of what the other person has been thinking about various tasks, but that won't last long. Keep in mind that the ultimate purpose is positive and that communication is oxygen and is to be encouraged. Surprises are especially welcome.

We now offer some tips on negotiating. Some are based on the experiences of couples who worked with the questionnaire after hearing the ideas in this book.

The Time Element

If and when he agrees on something you've asked him to take on, don't just pass it by and move ahead. Linger on the item long enough to consolidate it as a piece of progress. Express gratitude, elicit his thoughts on why he's for it, compare notes on how it'll work. Speaking of which, make sure the two of you address the time factor:

1. How often is he going to do the task?
2. How long does he think it will take?
3. When exactly is he going to do it?

If you don't nail down these factors, his agreement may come to nothing.

You really need a timetable, a schedule, of what he is agreeing to. If he says he's going to clean the bathroom, ask him how often. Make sure he gets to an answer you both like. Then ask him how long it will take. (This is a good time to refer to the breakdown in the questionnaire, which shows the subtasks that are part of the deal. Add more as you like. The components of *x* have to be clear to both parties, so *x* will be done *completely,* not partially.)

Once that is sorted out, ask him when exactly he is going to do the job. This is the *planning* element, often resisted by men because they need their "freedom," being desperados. But if he doesn't set aside a foreseeable time for the task, chances are that other demands will gang up to shut this one out. So you need a regular time slot that he actually has available and he is willing to "lose" to this chore. Is he going to do it on a weeknight, and if so, which one? (If you tend to have guests on the weekend, maybe Thursday evening is a good time.) If on the weekend, when on the weekend? Make it *before* watching the game(s) or doing other activities that might put a fella in the wrong mood for physical labor.

The Two Types of Jobs

When you're dividing up jobs or tasks, there's a useful distinction to keep in mind. There are two types of jobs:

1. jobs everyone in the house thinks are at best chores or at worst downright unpleasant
2. jobs that somebody might be crazy enough to actually enjoy

Jobs of type 2 are much easier to divvy up, as shown by the story of Walt and Nadine.

When Walt got ready to look at the "meals" area of the questionnaire, he was expecting his wife, Nadine, to make him do more of the cooking. And he feared this, because he was a klutz in the kitchen and didn't have the patience for recipe books. He thought she would forbid him to do the food shopping because he had screwed up a few times on ingredients, bringing home parsley instead of cilantro and rugulas (raspberry) instead of arugula. Or there was that time he'd shown up with cracked wheat instead of bulgur wheat for the tabbouleh salad, and she'd snapped at him to go back and get the bulgur because she really wanted to try out that new recipe for her guests.

But what Nadine had realized while filling out the questionnaire was that she actually liked food prep—she enjoyed the Zen precision of chopping, dicing, and blending—and she loved cooking, but she really didn't like food shopping (or cleaning up). Her impression was that Walt, on the other hand, liked food shopping (unless she jumped all over his errors) because it gave him a chance to walk around, palpate the fruit, and people-watch. She also appreciated that he had a head for prices—he would always take the time to look at the per-unit price—and he enjoyed nosing out a good bargain. She knew she had given him a hard time over tricky ingredients, but she also knew he could easily learn this stuff if she just bothered to explain it, and if he tried. He was already better than she was at choosing cheese, cleaning supplies, and toothpaste. In an optimistic mood, Nadine checked off food shopping for Walt.

Walt said, "You want me to grocery shop? You sure?"

Nadine: "Do you know Italian parsley from cilantro?"

"I do now. I have a clever method. I taste a leaf."

"You know, I actually liked that parsley in a taco. It doesn't stick to your teeth like cilantro."

"I still like cilantro," Walt said.

"Up to you, chief."

That's often the way it goes with jobs that someone actually likes to do.

If two people *both* enjoy a certain task, then you have the luxury of fighting over it. We should all be so lucky as negotiators.

Jobs of type 1 (at best a chore, at worst disagreeable) are the problem. Maybe no one in the house likes dusting (and several people don't know how). Vacuuming is not popular. Cleaning bathrooms can be a bit grim. Laundry is often thought to suck. Some people can afford to have an outside person come in and do these things, but many can't. So the thing to do is, try to divide them equitably, or rotate them, or both.

Alternating a chore is always a great way to go.

- You clean up (including dishes) when I cook, and I'll clean up when you cook.
- You scrub the bathroom one week, and I'll do it the next.

The great advantage of taking turns is that it's very easy to sell in terms of fairness. How can a guy say no to doing something half the time?

Trade-offs are hard to resist, and that also works for chores assigned to a single person. A lot of what you want can be achieved just by pointing out that if he does job *x*, you'll do job *y*.

That's how it went for Sondra and Rob when they had to divvy up the cleaning chores. Sondra was utterly sick of laundry. Her preemptive offer was to always be the one to clean the bathroom (including the tub) and to dust and vacuum the whole house. This made Rob ready to stick his neck out. "Okay, I'll do the laundry," he boldly said. Then he looked down at the questionnaire and saw the checkmark in the dreaded column 5. "Your way," he added.

And that brings up a theme we've talked about before: If you want him to learn something, be prepared to teach it properly.

Being a Good Instructor

In the past, Rob had not demonstrated a whole lot of mastery in the laundry area. So Sondra was not at all sure he knew what "your way" meant. But she didn't think she should have to put up with shrunken tops, ruined delicates, or pants that aged too fast (her navy flax linen pants couldn't seem to endure the dryer).

"I don't know how to say this," she said, "but you're going to have to raise the level of your game."

"I know, whites are hot and darks are cold."

"Um, yes, but there's quite a bit more."

"I'm not you. I don't know if I can do it in a way that will satisfy you." He quickly added, "But I want to."

She smiled. Something in his wording rang a bell. Then she laughed. "You want to satisfy me. Can I make an analogy?" she said.

"I love analogies."

"You'll love this one. You learned to make me orgasm. Remember that?"

"I do."

"You started off just assuming your natural male talent would get me there. But it didn't, not quite. So remember that time we were on vacation and we got a little tipsy and you asked me to teach you how?"

"That wasn't easy for me to ask."

"You scored major points. Hey, let's face it; the terrain is a bit foreign. You learned though."

"I listened to the expert."

"You did. You let me give you pointers, you applied yourself, you were patient, it worked, and then you actually invented some new stuff."

"I did?"

"It's been a while, but I'm pretty sure."

"Oh God, it has. I'm sorry."

"Not all your bad. And it's never too late. Anyway, back to the point . . ."

"Right—laundry. You could teach me."

"I can if you bring your big brain, the one you use on your own projects. That's all it would take."

"I can do that!"

But keep in mind that you have to give a little too. Not having the right information is not the same thing as being stupid. There are lots of things he knows that you don't know, so nobody needs to dishonor the other's intelligence. If your guy is ready to learn a new skill and park his ego at the door, then cut him some slack, be patient, and *explain things clearly*. Hopefully he'll do the same when you're the one who needs teaching. Don't rush through your instructions. Train him when you both are relaxed and have some free time. Use examples.

And help him see the logic, as Regina learned.

Regina's story

> For years I had been trying to get my husband to maintain order in the kitchen cupboards. He would agree to help me by doing so, and he would try for a while, but he never kept it up because it didn't make a difference in his life. Then he took over more of the meal making. And recently he shared with me (after organizing the cupboards himself) that he had had an epiphany. It struck him how much less time it took to make dinner when the spices had been placed back in the same spot and he didn't have to search for them. He even went out to purchase more plastic containers to store the rice, pasta, and other dry ingredients. Once he realized the benefits of organization, he was more motivated. Then I had my own epiphany. I had tried to force rules on him—that the spices go here and the staples go there—without giving any reasons! No wonder he couldn't get

> behind it. He thought these were arbitrary regulations, like I just wanted things my way because I liked control or because I couldn't stand not to see him busy!

Give reasons; explain the benefits of the way you want him to do a given task. If possible, arrange for him to experience those benefits. Don't make unmotivated demands on your man creature.

On the other hand, here's something to consider: sometimes a creative approach can *avoid* the need for any major training. To illustrate this point, we'll dip one more time into the subject of dirty clothes, before we drop it forever. Try this. Approach laundry the way the army would: make the process idiot-proof by organizing it in advance. Put three separate categories of dirty clothes into separate hampers. One (or more) for whites, that get a warm or hot wash and a regular dry. One for darks, that get a cold wash and a regular dry. A third hamper for delicates, hand-washables, or anything else that gets special treatment. Then let him handle the first two categories, and you handle the third. You'll be amazed at how much work is taken off your shoulders without increasing the need for worry. It takes a little more trouble to put the right things in the right hamper. And of course *you* don't really need to, because you know how to sort it on the fly. But that little bit of trouble makes it possible for you to off-load a whole bunch of work.

And bear in mind that in some areas of housework, your way is not the only right way. So don't let territoriality (maybe disguised as a "higher" standard) cause you to cling to a practice that could just as well be changed. His method, without any correction, is often perfectly valid. So learn to appreciate his way. Sometimes women do things out of habit or because their mothers did it that way. Sometimes another person's approach is more logical.

Teach Your Children

Another underused tactic for farming out the workload is to teach your kids to do some notable chores. Why should overworked adults be stuck with this labor? Many children miss a valuable part of their development by not being asked to contribute enough on the domestic front. It may help take them out of that "only my world and my friends count" mind-set, which afflicts too many adolescents.

To *really* make a difference in the future of human society, teach your son to do your laundry. Why not end the mothering-your-spouse cycle here and now, by raising children who are not trapped in the stereotypes of "women's work that males don't do"? Include your kids in the division of tasks, and *don't do it by gender*. If your boys learn to do laundry, vacuum, and contribute to meal making, it's much less likely their future wives will end up in the same place you are now. Kids have young brains and can learn anything, especially if it's presented in a fun way. Research supports this in another way: households in which kids do more housework also show fathers doing more. It's an embarrassment of riches!

A Few Thoughts on Specific Areas

Here are some ideas about specific jobs that we didn't have a chance to share yet.

Deep Cleaning

Some couples hire this out: someone comes in once a week (or less often) and does the really picky, strenuous stuff—fridge, oven, bathroom, et cetera. If you can afford it, it lessens the pressure on both spouses and especially means that they can share more time with one another rather than having their heads in the toilets. Deeper cleaning typically requires bigger chunks of time having to be put aside by either or both spouses, as opposed to keeping up with daily responsibilities, which is demanding enough.

Managing/Scheduling

Many women say that they don't like having to make so many decisions by themselves, especially decisions that affect the other person too. "Being the solo manager is lonely," says Elaine, "because it forces me to make a lot of decisions on my own, and half the time I worry that I'm not choosing the right thing. I *like* his ideas, I *respect* his judgment—and I lose the benefit of it."

Men say being left out of the loop frustrates them, but they feel as if the one who does most of the work should be in charge. "I mean, it wouldn't be fair if she makes all the meals but I get to direct things in the kitchen." So the retreat from tasks becomes a justification for also retreating from decision making; the pathology feeds on itself.

Some specific tasks are so critical that it makes sense if the same person does them all the time. But that doesn't mean planning and decision making should be solo activities. Take finances. Paying bills is fraught with dangers; even opening the damn things can be done sloppily and an invoice can slip through the cracks. So it may be wise to have one person dedicated to this function. But these days, when many households are on thin ice moneywise, it's better if the couple approaches crucial challenges as a team. Budgeting, for example, and paying off debt, and deciding when to borrow and for what, and when to spend and on what—not to mention how to save any green—are more likely to succeed if a couple agrees on a course of action and carries it out as a team.

It's partly a matter of taking down the wall that the Mother Syndrome has built, the bad habits that prevented a woman and man from seeing each other as collaborators. There are lots of decisions both *would like* to make together. Planning together is a fine form of bonding: it's how a shared dream gets realized, whether it's a vacation or the raising of a child.

Happily, there are two pieces of good news.

1. The more tasks a man takes on, the more he can naturally manage and be responsible for.
2. The more a couple come to see each other as equals again (instead of as mother-child), the more they will naturally join forces on planning and decision making.

If you've been doing most of the management stuff, your husband may have a tendency to hang back, because it's hard to jump into someone else's logistical stream. Things like paying bills are usually best handled by a single brain, or continuity and consistency can be lost, not to mention being on time while juggling deadlines, online payments, snail mail, and bank balances. But that doesn't mean you have to keep doing whatever you're doing, if there are areas you would really like him to take over and that you know he'd be good at. It's worth the effort and trouble of passing the torch. So talk about these things with him. Make sure the two of you scope out the "Managing/Scheduling" section of the questionnaire.

Not all of the negotiation in this chapter has to be like horse trading. Some of it can be you and him putting your heads together and mulling over what to do and how best to handle things. Talk with him about whether you are tackling enough decisions as a couple.

Child Rearing

If there are kids, and the husband wants to step up to the plate and be more involved, both spouses are going to have to be flexible and creative. Look through the components of child rearing as shown in the questionnaire and add any others that you think are relevant. Find out if the two of you can see any openings for involving your husband more. It's partly about reassigning tasks and lightening the wife's child care load, perhaps by taking turns being the one who is tasked with minding the kids. But it's also about attitude and inclusion—finding ways for him to spend higher-quality time with the kids and for the two of you to be with them together. Brainstorm about this in a non-competitive way and see what you can come up with.

And both sides should be prepared to make some concessions. As we saw in chapter 11, a man may have some valid ideas about what a kid's life should include that are not exactly the same as his wife's. A man may sometimes want to show the kids a more spontaneous, less planned side of life. A man may have his own way of teaching, and his own things he wants to teach. On the other hand, if your husband is a little too lax about safety issues, he needs to respect your concerns and, if he takes the kids on an outing, internalize some of your vigilance in return for your trust.

But let's not overstate the gender gap here. A lot of what a parent does is driven by the children's needs and wants, regardless of that parent's sex. The more involved a dad gets in everyday parenting, the more his responses are going to converge with his wife's. When little Sonny slips on the stairs and cuts his knee, Dad has to go for the same Band-Aid that Mom would. The bigger obstacle to overcome here may be your own resistance to giving up your paramount position. So bear in mind that if you ask your husband to take on more parenting, he needs to know that you think well of his skills and that he has your full support—that he won't find he's being undermined by someone who sees him as competition.

Both parents need to celebrate the variety that this type of sharing brings to the kids and respect each other's styles. They also need to truly collaborate on the areas where there must be agreement and consistency, like values, principles of character, and daily rules and boundaries. If this negotiation gives you a chance as parents to step back from the constant demands and compare notes on these areas, that's a big plus. (You may need a separate meeting just for this topic, if it goes beyond allocation of tasks.) If there's disagreement, try to resolve it, and if you can't, seek professional advice. There are many theories, and rational adults can have different opinions. Still, parenting is the most sacred partnership there is, and if you pull together, it can promote a very special closeness that translates into intimacy.

"But What about My Three Pet Peeves?"

We can hear some readers saying, "This is all very well, but unless we address his *general* MO, it won't matter what specific tasks he takes on." We have heard many wives complain that their husbands have certain bad habits that often spoil their attempts to contribute.

These wives wish there was some way to enforce the following three commandments:

1. Thou shalt not promise what thou dost not deliver. One wife told us she would rather her husband say he'll walk the dog *once* a week and actually do it than promise to walk the dog every night and then fail. She feels he makes rash commitments just to placate her, but the end result is to make him seem unreliable and dishonest.
2. Thou shalt not start something and not finish it. Another wife complained that her husband starts a task with a great positive spirit but doesn't persist. Her current list of his incomplete projects included

   - filling out his income tax forms
   - assembling her daughter's desk so she could do homework at it
   - organizing his filing cabinet
   - sorting through old photos and cataloging them

   "Anything that requires a protracted period of concentration," she said, "makes him give up prematurely and then find lots of excuses not to go back to it—especially if it requires monotonous, tedious work."
3. Thou shalt tidy up after thyself and put things back where they came from. This one needs no explanation.

Our response is this. First, a husband could have none of these habits and still fit right into this book. His wife has become his mother because he does too little, even though he makes no false promises, doesn't fail to complete what he starts, and is a tidy dude. So these three failings are not *essential* to the mothered husband. What's more, lots of *wives* violate these commandments too. Lots of women leave things half done and procrastinate on stuff. Men who are responsible for kitchen cleanup often report that their wives leave incredibly messy kitchens when they cook. The cook often lacks the cleanup person's awareness of how to do things so as to minimize mess. So these aren't necessarily gender issues.

If, on reflection, you see that you too are guilty of these infractions, then frame the discussion thusly: "You and I both have some things we do—or fail to do—that create annoyance between us and make it harder to delegate jobs, so let's both agree to work on them."

On the other hand, many mothered guys do have one or more of these tendencies. And they could easily threaten the new deal that we're trying to help you reach in this chapter. What good is it if he takes on a chore and then fails to start it, doesn't complete it, or creates a big mess for you to clean up?

So how do you deal with these sins? Well, one way is to tell him, maybe during the first part of the discussion, that these behaviors are a major reason why you feel like his mother. They are failings you would expect from a kid, and when you ask him (or nag him) to correct them, you feel like a disciplinarian instead of a partner. So can he please make a real effort to jettison these problems? It may help to tell him that you've been making a conscious effort (based on chapters 12 and 15) to make the unpleasant, nagging mother go away, and it would be really great if he would meet you halfway and make the unreliable child disappear. (The best time to make this appeal is after he has agreed that your being his mother is a bad thing. And that he would like to be equal partners again.)

We did emphasize earlier that if you come off too much as the reformer who is going to correct his character flaws, you will lose. But if you frame the issue skillfully, you may be able to work it in. "Please correct these things so I *won't* have to act like your mother" is a sound approach. It's important to make this discussion of the three commandments a sidebar to the main discussion—or leave it out for now, in favor of bigger goals.

Okay, deep breath. We realize you very possibly may not make it all the way through part two of the discussion. We asked you to arrange a long enough meeting to at least try, because we wanted you to get at least partway through the questionnaire while the motivation of your initial conversation was fresh and strong. You fired up the team, so it's important to hit the field and use that energy.

If you reserve the questionnaire for a separate meeting, things have a chance to slip: he may backslide or rebel, thinking it's gonna be worse than it is. But if you plunge in, he'll have fun with it and he'll see that in the end, it's a limited number of housework tasks that he'll be taking on, and some significant child care maybe (which many men will welcome), but it isn't some scary unknown mountain about to fall on him. It's important that he gets the feel of the questionnaire by actually interacting with it, or he won't know what the heck you two have been really talking about.

So it's very good if you got into the nuts and bolts of the questionnaire. But if you didn't finish allotting the chores, that's nothing to worry about. Schedule a continuation of the first meeting (the sooner the better) and agree to finish then.

And when you do make it through both parts of the discussion and a new deal is visible, how do you nail it down and turn it into achievable pieces? You need to consolidate your results, make a record of them that you both can go on. And a plan for the next steps and the longer term. That's what we'll cover in the next, final chapter.

Chapter 18

Making the New Deal Happen

Okay, the big meeting (whether in one or two sessions) is nearly finished. What else do you need to do before you wrap it up? We'll cover those steps in this chapter, and then we'll look at what to expect during the weeks and months that follow—how to consolidate your progress, adjust the plan, and complete the transition to a better marriage.

Before the initial meeting is over, it's a good idea to write down the results you've achieved.

What have you agreed on? Make a list of the changes that are going to happen:

- tasks he's agreed to take over or do in a new way (same for you)
- tasks you've agreed to alternate
- tasks you've agreed to do together

For each of these, summarize the details in point form. What are the components of the task; when will it be done (how often, during what time slot)? If it's being rotated, who does it on which days? If you're going to be doing it together, make sure you've found a time slot (or a choice of time slots) that you think is realistic. When does the new regime start? Make it within a week.

At the first meeting (or the second at the latest), we also recommend that you return to the discussion of bad dynamics and make a list of behaviors you are each going to try to put a lid on. Habits die hard, but they die easier if you are conscious of which button-pressers need to be avoided (and if work is being shared more fairly). It may be useful at this point to refer back to the list of toxic dynamics in chapter 2, and see if you can come up with a short list of maybe four or five items that you're each going to work on. (You yourself have already begun this process in chapter 12, but refresh it here and get him on board.)

Also make a list of unresolved questions (they aren't necessarily *issues*) about who will do what tasks. Record any *experiments* you've agreed on—"Let's try you doing this and me doing that, and see how it works." The idea, after all, is to have an amicable atmosphere where you feel free not to get the formula right the first time. Good faith will find the way.

Some things take a while to implement. If you've agreed to "train" your husband on a given task (or vice versa), *schedule the training*. If you're going to teach him to do the laundry or train him on food ingredients or bathroom cleaning, you'll need a proper chunk of time to do that in, and people can be busy, so it may not happen within a week.

Same with any changes in child rearing. These things don't happen overnight; you have to watch for opportunities and fold them into the recipe. But at least make a list of the directions you're hoping to go in. It will be especially important to check on these plans regularly and make sure they're happening.

Finally, during the first meeting it's desirable to schedule the next official meeting (again, make sure the circumstances are right), where you'll see how you're each doing, work on unresolved areas, and make adjustments to the plan. Give a little breathing room before this happens—maybe two weeks. You can't be reporting on how well it's going before you even have a chance to get the plan in place.

That pretty much completes the big meeting.

After the first meeting, we strongly encourage you and your husband to come together every couple of weeks over the next few months to talk about how you are doing and continue refining your goals. Don't get too corporate or efficiency-oriented here: keep it on a human level, not too heavy on the metrics.

Here are some questions to ask each other, to stimulate discussion:

- How has *x* job been going? Any surprises in how long it takes, how hard it is, et cetera?
- After a trial run, do we still think the new allocation of jobs is fair? Do we need to make any adjustments?
- How do you (the wife) feel now that your spouse is doing more?
- How do you (the husband) feel now that you are doing more?
- What positive feelings have made a comeback, for each of you? What still rankles? (We'll talk more in a moment about how to handle these kinds of expectations.)
- What else can we do to put the mothered husband behind us?

- How are we doing on staying on schedule? Where have we fallen off course? Let's think of ways that we can correct.
- As far as mother-child behaviors, did we finish formulating our list of ones to work on, and how are we doing on ceasing to act in those ways?
- What am I doing that's hurting our progress? Am I feeling some resistance to changes? Am I putting up any roadblocks and if so, why? (This can be asked by both of you.)
- In the child-rearing department, what other concrete changes can we make that will improve the balance of parenting? Let's not neglect this area just because it's complicated (and sensitive).

Also at each meeting, make sure you look at your notes from the previous one and go over any unfinished business: experiments you agreed to try and job/behavior areas where the plan still needed working out.

Ups and Downs

Bear in mind that this isn't a quick fix. This is a long-term process. At the beginning there will probably be a glow of euphoria, but that will pass and the proof of the plan will be in the doing.

Let's look at some of the things that may transpire. What ups and downs can you expect, as your husband tries to step up to the plate in various areas and take on new jobs? How do you deal with setbacks, and which scenarios may *look* like setbacks but actually be steps toward progress?

He doesn't meet the timetable. With optimism and bravery, you and your hubby have tried to shoehorn new activities (labor-intensive!) into his crowded routine. Suddenly, he is supposed to have chunks of time available for things he wasn't doing before. Guess what? This may not always work out. It may easily happen that an agreed-on hour passes, and you look around and the scheduled task didn't get done. Or even started.

Don't panic, don't immediately assume that all is lost. Several things may have happened:

- Unforeseen demands were made on him that closed off that time slot.
- The task schedule he agreed to doesn't make sense in practice and will have to be changed (at your next meeting).
- He forgot.
- He was too tired or wasn't feeling well.
- He didn't fully understand your instructions and is afraid of screwing up the job and thus failing.

So don't run him to ground and corner him with an accusation. He already knows that this is important—assuming the two of you had the kind of honest, open, serious meeting that we talked about. He knows, in fact, that it's do-or-die time in his marriage. So if he failed to clock in and do that task, he is probably madly trying to figure out when he *can* do it. Cut him a little slack. Don't make pointed remarks; don't get angry or sarcastic. Stay positive. Give him a little room to breathe and maneuver. If he doesn't do the task after a day or two, speak to him nicely about it. Don't moralize about keeping promises or harangue him on why the task is important: that's mommy talk. Just mention that such-and-such needs doing. If he explains why he hasn't gotten to it, let him say when he will, and accept that.

If he still doesn't get to it (if he seems to be acting like his old self), what do you do? We'll discuss that in a moment, under backsliding.

He does the work and finds out it's hard and time-consuming. It may seem like a setback when a husband finally does the laundry and realizes that it takes hours, or cleans the bathroom and notices that it's damn hard work. He may walk up to you with a sadder-but-wiser look on his face, shaking his head. He may complain that it's menial drudgery. He may curse and stamp his foot.

Stand easy and wait. He is not attacking you. He is attacking *work*: why does it exist and why do we have to do it?

But where does his nimble mind go next? He knows that you've been doing this labor up till now. So he only has two options:

1. He can think to himself, "Wow, there really *was* a problem. She was doing too much. This is *a lot of work*. No wonder she wasn't happy with the situation." So he redoubles his efforts and his dedication to change.
2. He can say, "This is just too hard. I want you to take it over again."

A worthy guy is going to go to option 1. The more unpleasant he finds his new tasks, the more he realizes the old regime was unfair and he wants to correct it, even if that isn't fun.

If he chooses 2, he is really saying that the marriage doesn't mean enough to him to make him accept his fair share of the work. *You* don't mean enough to him. He'd rather be lazy than have you. At that juncture you really have to ask yourself, *Do I want to be with this man?* If a guy, having personally experienced the unfairness of the old way, doesn't want to make it right, he has failed the test. Because as we said earlier, part 3 of this book is really posing a test of your marriage. You have come forward and expressed your concerns, and he's agreed to take on a greater load, but none of that proves anything unless he delivers.

We think that most husbands will desire an escape from the Mother Syndrome enough to choose option 1. The more he learns about how much you've really been doing, the more he will want to correct the imbalance.

Backsliding into old ways. Like we said, old habits die hard. When you've been acting a certain way for a long time, it isn't easy to snap out of it. That's just as true of you as of him. You run as great a risk of slipping back into the role of mother as he does into the role of child. As much as you don't want to be in that role, it is comfortable and familiar—or it was for a long time. Behaviors that signify disrespect and treat him as unworthy had become almost reflex after years of repeating them. That's why we launched you on a program to erase them and encouraged you *and* him to focus together on bad ways of acting that you're going to try to get rid of. But from time to time, especially on hectic and demanding days, these old dynamics are going to resurface. Best response: apologize immediately. Reset the compass.

Now what about when he fails to do some of the tasks he's agreed to or does only a token job? If you keep reminding him (even if your reminder gets results), you are still playing mother. You're back to nagging. You both need a way to separate the soldiers in the trenches from the generals on the hillside. Sometimes you're one; sometimes you're the other. Let's talk about that now.

Save your problems for the official meetings. If you try to *enforce* the new agreement in the heat of domestic activity, it can turn into a vendetta and get hostile real fast, which will just make him defensive and maybe cause you to lose all the ground you've gained. That is why we want to suggest a two-level approach to the new deal you're forging. We're not saying the following advice will be easy to follow: it won't! But it will be worth the effort, we promise.

There's everyday time, and there are official meetings where you get together to discuss the bigger picture. During everyday time, remain amicable; keep it cool, treat each other nice. Don't discuss moral issues like keeping promises and doing a job right (except when training or in answer to questions). Above all, don't act resentful. You have to be a bit of a stoic and a bit of a saint here, to avoid a disastrous relapse into hostility. If he hasn't gotten to something in a reasonable time, mention it calmly and let him tell you what he intends to do. Let that script play out. If some task of his becomes so urgent that you have to do it—but try your damnedest to resist any such impulse—go ahead and do it, but don't give off a martyr vibe or let black smoke rise from your head. That's what Bad Mommy does.

You may have to bite your tongue hard, walk away, distract yourself. It's still better to find a way not to allow your feelings to spill into the dynamics between you and him before the next meeting. Please accept heaps of praise from us for pulling off this feat of self-control. To motivate yourself, remember that diving back into nagging and hostility would be a huge step backward, possibly making him respond by saying, "I get it. Things are exactly the same. You said you wanted to change but you haven't." We understand that things will get very bleak if he keeps on saying he will do various tasks and *never* does. We know you will have a lot to say about that when next you have a progress meeting. A point could be reached when you realize this whole thing ain't gonna fly, and you'll have to assess what other options you have. But the goal here is to give your new agreement every possible chance to succeed, so you'll never have to say you didn't really try.

So wait till your next scheduled meeting and talk calmly about the problem in the context of all the questions we've suggested. This is when you and he sit down and look at the plan you've made and figure out how to make it succeed. You stand above the situation, on a hillside outlook where the view is broader and the breeze is cooler. You work it out. This is the time to assess progress and shortcomings, to share concerns and give pep talks. And when things have gone right, to give thanks and praise.

Don't press too hard for the hoped-for emotional results. Although it's fine to ask open-ended questions about how you're both feeling and reacting now that he's handling more jobs, it isn't so good to be obsessing on emotional metrics. Sure, we absolutely hope that your love for each other will bloom again and that your sex life will make a comeback. But getting out a clipboard and probing the day-to-day progress of this is not the way to go. If you follow the plan (he does his share of the work and you stop treating each other in toxic ways), you will start to feel like a team again, and your sense of partnership will recover. That will naturally leave you free to like each other more, and that may easily lead to a thaw in physical relations. The relief of being open to each other again, honestly admitting your feelings, and seeking a solution together can't help but thaw out your hearts a bit.

For some couples this will lead fairly quickly to a warmer time in bed. For others, the path won't be so pat. The very fact that you are getting along better and maybe are feeling hope again for your marriage can actually make intimacy scary, because you may be afraid you'll somehow shatter the magic spell. A guy who has been demoted into being less than a man may have a little trepidation: "What if, after all this progress, I blow it in bed?" A woman may feel the same thing. The only way to overcome any such fears is to take it slow and avoid big expectations that only intimidate. And be prepared, if necessary, to be as open and honest about this area as you have been about the things you've met about so far.

The good feelings you are aiming to recover may not always come when they are called. More likely they will bubble up when not expected. It's kind of like getting a cat to jump up on your lap; if you try to force it, the cat runs, but if you gently encourage it, the cat is suddenly curled up on you, and you are the lucky one who can't move for an hour.

Sometimes we have to have faith and live the new role before the attitudes that go with it start to be real. It will take a while before you see your husband toiling at something you used to do and think, "He cares." But if you stick with the program and encourage him, slowly the ship will turn toward the sun.

After a month has elapsed, we suggest you make a date to do something you both enjoy, like dinner and dancing, and dress up for it. Make it a celebration of your mutual effort to improve your marriage. Don't haggle or negotiate during the outing, but anecdotes are permitted and laughs are good. Take an evening to give yourselves credit for what you've done and to express gratitude and other positive feelings toward one another.

You and your husband are to be congratulated. You took on a big challenge here, one that called for bravery, honesty, and openness on both sides, and real effort, not just words. It isn't easy to look a bad situation in the eye and admit what it is. It's even harder to stare it down, overcome its momentum, and take up arms against it.

We have come a long way together, from unmasking a serious problem that afflicts many marriages to kicking away its underpinnings and forthrightly pursuing a solution. We can't promise that you'll always have blue skies, but if you and your husband continue on the path you've set, we think you'll notice a steady dying away of rancor and resentment, and a new flowering of joy and affection.

Afterword

People sometimes say that they're tired of the old chestnut that *a good relationship takes work.* Every now and then you'll hear someone—female or male—rebel against this hoary wisdom and say, "Hey, if you have to work at it, it ain't love. So why bother. Good relationships should just take care of themselves and flow along easy, like a river!"

Though it may seem surprising, we don't think this book is going against that current. We're totally in favor of less work, especially for those who are doing too much of it. And we don't want to make love itself any harder.

It all depends on what you're working *on.* We think that when a relationship is bogged down, entangled, and basically strangled by issues connected to one spouse doing too much housework and child rearing and mothering of the other one, the relationship can't breathe easy, can't flow. But when you take those obstructions out of the way, people can enjoy each other naturally, and the relationship itself takes *less* work.

If a woman doesn't have to do the work of being her man's mother, she will be freed up to enjoy him again.

And a man who pulls more weight in the domestic areas we've talked about will find it *easier* to connect with his wife.

Love takes less work if you get work out of its way.

Acknowledgments

Sara Dimerman

This project has been a labor of love for me, but I wouldn't have been able to grow it without the help of many other people.

First and foremost, this book wouldn't be what it is without my co-author, J.M. Kearns. In addition to his ability to balance things out, his voice and logic are unparalleled. His research brought a whole new dimension to this book, and his insight and wisdom, along with his exceptional writing skills, raised it to a whole new level. So, thanks, partner. Our relationship has evolved along with the book—not without bumps in the road or conflict along the way—but to a point where we are both very proud of our book.

J.M. and I both feel lucky to have had Linda Pruessen assigned to us as editor by Simon and Schuster. When Linda came on board, she fit right in. She understood our banter, she got our sarcasm, she really seemed to understand what we wanted to say, and so her voice entwined with ours in putting the final touches on the manuscript so that it reads as if it were written by one.

How could I ever begin to thank my mentor, Kevin Hanson, president of Simon and Schuster Canada? At the time that I approached him about this book, the moment was right for him to consider publishing it, and so he connected me with the right people. Thanks, Kevin, for always being such an ardent supporter of me and my writing and for never failing, despite everything else on your plate, to be there for me.

Thanks also to some very special people at Simon and Schuster, especially Alison Clarke, director of sales operations, who was our main liaison. And also to the many others at Simon and Schuster who have, and I know will continue to, promote and support us, including Felicia Quon, Anneliese Grosfeld, Vanessa Chan, Amy Cormier, Rita Silva, David Millar, and Sheila Haidon in the marketing, publicity, and sales departments.

Thanks also to the many clients I have been given the honor of helping over the years. I have always felt it to be a privilege to be invited into your lives and allowed to guide you through difficult times.

Friends and family mean everything to me, and my heartfelt thanks go to all of you too. You all saw me through 2011, which was a turning point for me. It was the year that we wrapped up the writing of this book, but it was also an incredibly difficult year. The same day that I celebrated my fiftieth birthday in September was also the day I said good-bye to my mother, my best friend, as she lay dying from cancer in a hospice. It was the last day that I would see her conscious and the last day that she ever uttered anything—"I love you too"—to me. She had read parts of this manuscript but was ultimately too weak to read as it took final shape. I always said that she should have been a published author. Her friends and family waited for her correspondence. They hung on her every word. She lived vicariously through my writing and would always be able to think of the right word when it wasn't coming to me. It was only because of the support of J.M. and my family and friends that I found the courage and the strength to complete the writing of this book once she was gone. I knew too that she wouldn't have wanted it any other way.

Even though the epiphany for this book came to me after many sessions of seeing the lover-mother theme emerge in my office, it was floating around in my head long before that. I had seen my mother in the role of mother to my father for their fifty years of marriage. I had seen the role grow stronger and more entrenched as they grew older together. I even found myself morphing into a similar role in my marriage and struggling to find a way out of it.

Aside from the crippling effects of the Mother Syndrome on my parents' marriage, I have now, since the loss of my mother, also seen the devastating effects that losing a wife/mother has on a man—my father—and how he must struggle to "grow up" now that she is gone.

I have saved the best for last. I would not be who I am without the incredible support of my husband, Joey. In 2011 we celebrated twenty-five years of marriage, and I feel truly blessed to have him as my partner, my lover, and my confidant. I'd be lying if I said that I didn't get several of the stories for this book from my own life, but that's okay. I now know, more than ever, how to continue to grow my partnership with Joey so we can always feel like equals.

My love and thanks also to my wonderful children, Talia and Chloe. A year away from graduating with a BDes in graphic design from OCAD University in Toronto, Talia, already a talented and dedicated designer, gave us valuable help in considering ideas for the cover. Chloe, the child we all yearned for, is a bright spark in our lives with her dancing, music, and joie de vivre. I continue to strive to be the best role model I can be because I know that my relationship with their dad will affect who they choose, how their relationships evolve, and perhaps even the ultimate success of those relationships.

A year away from graduating with a BDes in graphic design from OCAD University in Toronto, Talia, already a talented and dedicated designer, gave us valuable help in considering ideas for the cover. Chloe, the child we all yearned for, is a bright spark in our lives with her dancing, music, and joie de vivre.

J.M. Kearns

When Sara Dimerman first told me the idea for this book and invited me on board as her co-writer, it seemed like a slam-dunk kind of project. It turned out to be a bit more demanding than that. Not that the book hasn't been a lot of fun to work on, and not that we haven't had many good laughs and stunning perceptions along the way. I want to thank her for sticking with me through thick and thin, for her courage and her persistence. It's been a treat to partake of her imagination, her acuteness, and her knowledge of the facts on the ground in today's marriages. Co-writing is itself like a marriage, and I've been lucky in my partner.

I thank Kevin Hanson, president of Simon and Schuster Canada, for seeing the merits of this project and running with it, along with

Alison Clarke, director of sales operations, who has been a rock and a steady source of positive energy. Their enthusiasm relit the spark of this book. Thanks to everyone at Simon and Schuster, including all those good people mentioned by Sara, who shepherded the book all the way to the shelves and screens where it can now be found.

Our editor, Linda Pruessen, immediately captivated us with her humor and energy, and in the actual editing turned out to be serene, perceptive, and incredibly efficient. She made a complex process seem easy, and because of her the book is better in all sorts of ways.

The three years during which we worked on this book, off and on, have been very tumultuous ones for me, involving many life changes and uprootings. I'm not sure I would have made it through them without the steadying influence of this task: it was a refuge I could return to, regardless how my circumstances had changed. That folder of Word documents was waiting patiently, no matter what computer I was using and no matter where my desk had wandered to.

It's been more than interesting writing about marriage while being in one—and thinking back on the marriages I've known, starting with that of my parents and spreading out to my siblings' and many others that I've observed at close range. The matter of who does what work, and how a person's fate is bound up with the uneasy pairing of homemaking and career, has always been an issue to be reckoned with. Every marriage is a work in progress, and so is marriage the institution. It can easily slip off course, but people can steer it back if they see the way. That became poignantly evident as Sara and I thought through the themes of this book. I think, not so oddly, that I've learned something about being a better spouse from working on it.

Whether I have or not, I want to thank Debra Donahue for being there and for still being there. You are my inspiration. You keep showing me new things that can't be taken for granted. I like having your soul nearby. Your alarming beauty keeps me on my toes. I admit it: you are a ridiculously fertile source of thoughts, anecdotes, and other ammo that a writer can't do without. And yes, I like sorting your clothes before they go in the washer.

Notes

Chapter 3: The Sexual Fallout

1. The client in question, whom we haven't named, gave permission for these words to be quoted in this book.

Chapter 4: How Big a Problem Is the Mother Syndrome?

1. Arlie Hochschild, *The Second Shift* (New York: Avon Books, 1989).
2. Ruth D. Konigsberg, "Chore Wars," *Time*, Aug. 8, 2011: 44–49.
3. The U.S. Bureau of Labor Statistics (BLS) has been issuing American Time Use Survey (ATUS) reports since 2003. *Time*'s numbers that we cite are based on ATUS tables, as are some of ours, as noted.
4. In the authors' abstract of their article "Wives' and Husbands' Housework Reporting: Gender, Class and Social Desirability," J. E. Press and E. Townsley write, "It is concluded that changing and uneven social perceptions of the appropriate domestic roles of women and men have resulted in reporting biases that do not necessarily correspond to actual changes in housework behavior. These findings cast doubt on claims that contemporary husbands are doing more housework than their predecessors." The article appeared in *Gender & Society* 12.2 (1998): 188–218.
5. The Sept. 25, 2008, Pew survey is titled "Women Call the Shots at Home; Public Mixed on Gender Roles in Jobs." It is found

online on www.pewsocialtrends.org, at www.pewsocialtrends .org/2008/09/25/women-call-the-shots-at-home-public-mixed-on-gender-roles-in-jobs/.

6. For more on this measurement of secondary activities (work being done while the primary reported activity is leisure), see L. C. Sayer, P. England, M. Bittman, and S. M. Bianchi, "How Long Is the Second (Plus First) Shift? Gender Differences in Paid, Unpaid and Total Work Time in Australia and the United States," *Journal of Comparative Family Studies* 40 (2009): 523–45.
7. See Marybeth J. Mattingly and Liana C. Sayer, "Under Pressure: Gender Differences in the Relationship between Free Time and Feeling Rushed," *Journal of Marriage and Family* 68 (Feb. 2006): 205–21, and see Liana C. Sayer, "More Work for Mothers? Trends and Gender Differences in Multitasking," in *Time Competition: Disturbed Balances and New Options in Work and Care*, edited by Tanja van der Lippe and Pascale Peters (Cheltenham, UK: Edward Elgar, 2007).
8. The Feb. 28, 2006, Pew survey is titled "Who's Feeling Rushed?" It is found online on www.pewsocialtrends.org, at www.pewsocial trends.org/2006/02/28/whos-feeling-rushed/.
9. See page 538 of Sayer, England, et al.
10. The July 18, 2007, Pew survey is titled "Modern Marriage: I Like Hugs. I Like Kisses. But What I Really Love Is Help with the Dishes." It is found online at www.pewsocialtrends.org/2007/07/18/ modern-marriage/.
11. Paul R. Amato and Stacy J. Rogers, "A Longitudinal Study of Marital Problems and Subsequent Divorce," *Journal of Marriage and Family* 59 (1997): 612–24. The quote is from page 613.
12. Lynn Prince Cooke, "'Doing' Gender in Context: Household Bargaining and Risk of Divorce in Germany and the United States," *American Journal of Sociology* 112.2 (2006): 442–72. The quote is from page 449.

Chapter 6: "I'm Just Being a Good Wife"

1. This research, by sociologists Scott Coltrane and Michele Adams of the University of California, Riverside, and by Dr. John Gottman at the University of Washington, is reported in a 2003 article, "When Dads Clean House, It Pays Off Big Time," found online at http://newsroom.ucr.edu/news_item.html?action=page&id=611.

Chapter 9: "Even If He Does It, It Won't Be Done Right: Men Are Incompetent"

1. For more on this question, a good place to start is Sarah M. Allen and Alan J. Hawkins, "Maternal Gatekeeping: Mothers' Beliefs and Behaviors That Inhibit Greater Father Involvement in Family Work," *Journal of Marriage and Family* 61.1 (1999): 199–212.

Chapter 11: "I Can't Rely on Him with the Children"

1. For information on this topic, a good place to start is Sarah Allen and Kerry Daly, "The Effects of Father Involvement: An Updated Research Summary of the Evidence," University of Guelph, 2007, available online at www.fira.ca/cms/documents/29/Effects_of_Father_Involvement.pdf.
2. See page 14 of Allen and Daly.

About the Authors

Sara Dimerman

Sara Dimerman, C.Psych.Assoc., offers counselling to individuals, couples, and families out of the Parent Education Resource Centre, in Thornhill, Ontario, which she established in 1990. Sara is regularly quoted, has her articles published in magazines and newspapers, and appears on radio and television across North America. Sara produces podcasts that can be heard for free online at http://www.helpmesara.com/podcasts/ or by searching for "helpmesara" on iTunes.

A nationally recognized author, Sara's first book, *Am I a Normal Parent?: Expert Advice, Parenting Tips, and the Reassurance You've Been Looking For* was published in 2008. Her second, *Character Is the Key: How to Unlock the Best in Our Children and Ourselves* was published in 2009. Sara is married and mom to two daughters, aged thirteen and twenty. For more about Sara, please visit www.helpmesara.com, www.facebook.com/helpmesara, or twitter @helpmesara.

J.M. Kearns

J.M. Kearns, PhD, a writer of fiction and non-fiction, has at various times been a philosopher of perception, a crisis counsellor, and a music journalist. He brings to relationship books the unusual combination of a philosopher's analytical mind and a novelist's insight into emotions. His best-selling *Why Mr. Right Can't Find You: The Surprising Answers That Will Change Your Life—and His* (2007) was embraced by readers and the press on both sides of the Atlantic and has been featured on Oprah & Friends Radio and in *OK!*, *Glamour*, *Cosmopolitan* (UK), *Maclean's*, *The Toronto Star*, and many other publications. Since then, three more Kearns books have been published to critical praise: the novel *ex-Cottagers in Love* (2008), and the relationship books *Better Love Next Time: How the Relationship That Didn't Last Can Lead You to the One That Will* and *Shopping for Mr Right: How to Choose the Right Guy and Get the Most Out of Him* (2011). A witty, engaging speaker, J.M. Kearns grew up near Toronto, Canada, and now lives in Cape May, New Jersey, with his partner, Debra. For more on Kearns and his writings, please visit www.jmkearns.com.